The
Hispanization of the
Philippines

# NEW PERSPECTIVES IN
# SOUTHEAST ASIAN STUDIES

# NEW PERSPECTIVES IN
# SOUTHEAST ASIAN STUDIES

---

*From Rebellion to Riots: Collective Violence on Indonesian Borneo*
Jamie S. Davidson

*Amazons of the Huk Rebellion: Gender, Sex, and Revolution in
the Philippines*
Vina A. Lanzona

*An Anarchy of Families: State and Family in the Philippines*
Edited by Alfred W. McCoy

*Pretext for Mass Murder: The September 30th Movement and
Suharto's Coup d'État in Indonesia*
John Roosa

*Việt Nam: Borderless Histories*
Edited by Nhung Tuyet Tran and Anthony Reid

*Modern Noise, Fluid Genres: Popular Music in Indonesia, 1997–2001*
Jeremy Wallach

Illustration from Gaspar de San Agustín's *Conquistas de las islas Philipinas* (Madrid, 1698), depicting the complementary nature of the spiritual and the temporal conquest of the islands.

*From a copy in the Newberry Library.*

# The
# Hispanization of the
# Philippines

*Spanish Aims*
*and*
*Filipino Responses*
1565–1700

JOHN LEDDY PHELAN

*The*
*University of Wisconsin*
*Press*

*Madison, Milwaukee, and London, 1967*

The University of Wisconsin Press
1930 Monroe Street, 3rd Floor
Madison, Wisconsin 53711-2059
uwpress.wisc.edu

3 Henrietta Street
London WC2E 8LU, England
eurospanbookstore.com

Printed in the United States of America

A Cataloging-in-Publication record for this book is available
from the Library of Congress
LCCN: 59-8602
ISBN: 978-0-299-01814-6 (pbk.)

*For my parents*

# Preface

In the average Philippine community today three kinds of buildings are apt to capture the attention of a visitor. One is the Filipinos' homes, which are elevated on thick timbers and constructed with bamboo walls and nipa palm leaf roofs. This is the style in which Filipinos have been building their homes since time immemorial. Neither the advent of the Spaniards in the late sixteenth century nor the arrival of the Americans in the twentieth century has changed the style of Philippine folk architecture, which responds to the needs of that hot and humid climate. A second type of building also stands out. It is the Catholic church, frequently an ornate, baroque structure built under the direction of Spanish missionaries centuries ago. And the third building is the schoolhouse, constructed in the twentieth century under the auspices of the American regime. These buildings are visible expressions of the three movements that have shaped Philippine civilization over the course of the centuries—indigenous culture, Spanish culture, and more recently the influence of the United States. This book concerns itself with the meeting of indigenous society with Spanish culture.

The Spanish program in the Philippines envisaged a radical transformation of native Philippine society. Inspired by their previous experience in Mexico, the Spaniards launched a sweeping social reform in the islands, a reform which was religious, political, and economic in scope. To determine the nature of the Spanish program and to assess its permanent results are the basic aims of this book. In this ambitious design to reorganize Philippine society, Spanish successes were striking. So were some of their failures. The Filipinos were no mere passive recipients of the cultural stimulus created by the Spanish conquest. Circumstances gave them considerable freedom in selecting their responses to Hispanization. Their responses varied all the way from acceptance to indifference and rejection. The capacity of the Filipinos for creative social adjustment is attested by the manner in which they adapted many Hispanic features to their own indigenous culture. Preconquest society was not swept away by the advent of the Spanish regime. Rather, indigenous culture was transformed during the seventeenth century, in some cases profoundly so and in other cases only superficially. Significant though these changes were, a substantial degree of continuity between the preconquest and the Hispanic regimes was preserved. The principal aim of this study is to analyze how this result came about—in particular, to assess the role of the Spaniards as innovators and the complementary role of the Filipinos in adapting themselves to changes introduced by the Spaniards.

Since in this study I attempt to reconstruct the history of the Philippine people in the early Spanish period, Spanish historical materials constitute the principal sources. I have not, however, employed the historical method exclusively but rather have made an effort to combine sound historical practices with some anthropological techniques. Such an approach, already successfully applied by Ralph Roys, Charles Gibson, George Kubler, John Rowe, Howard Cline, and others, now has a designation of its own,

namely, "ethnohistory."* One of the major objectives of the
Philippine Studies Program directed by Professor Fred Eggan,
under whose auspices the research for this book was completed,
was to bring the disciplines of history and anthropology into closer
collaboration, and my study of Philippine society in the seventeenth
century is, therefore, oriented to a significant extent toward ethno-
history.

I have placed considerable attention on the religious aspect of
Hispanization. Events themselves suggest such a stress. The Spaniards put a heavy emphasis on Christianization as the most effective
means of incorporating the Filipinos into Spanish culture, and the
Filipinos themselves responded enthusiastically to the multiform
appeal of the new religion. Although it is abundantly clear that
Spain left its deepest imprint on the Philippines through the
agency of Catholicism, the economic, the political, and the social
aspects of Hispanization produced enduring consequences. Their
importance has not always been appreciated.

Spanish colonization in the Philippines cannot be viewed in a
vacuum. The islands constituted the Oriental outpost of a colonial
empire that stretched halfway around the globe. Spanish policy in
the Philippines was largely shaped in terms of previous experience
in North and in South America. Since this imperial perspective cannot be ignored, I have made a concerted effort in this book to draw
systematic comparisons between the intentions and the results of
Spanish policy in the Philippines, Mexico, and to a lesser extent
Peru.

The terminal date of 1700 was selected on the grounds that
the principal characteristics of Spanish influence had made themselves evident by the end of the Habsburg era. On the whole, this
working hypothesis has fitted the facts. In those cases, however,
where the terminal date has proved arbitrary or cumbersome, I
have not hesitated to carry the story into the eighteenth and nine-

---

* See Howard F. Cline, "Problems of Mexican Ethno-History: The
Ancient Chinantla," *Hispanic American Historical Review*, XXXVII (August,
1957), 273–95.

teenth centuries. The nature of the source material also suggested 1700 as a convenient terminal date. A substantial number of the seventeenth century sources in Seville at the *Archivo General de Indias* have already been published, and four months in Spain enabled me to examine many of the unpublished sources of that period. But for the eighteenth century the situation is quite the reverse. The printed sources represent only an infinitesimal fraction of the vast archival resources available to scholars, and until these sources are examined, it will not be possible to make any firm conclusions about the eighteenth century. It is to be hoped that this study dealing primarily with the seventeenth century will in time be followed by monographs of other scholars dealing with the later period.

This book was prepared under favorable circumstances. I spent two and one-half years in Chicago as a Fellow in Philippine Studies at the Newberry Library. This fellowship was a part of the Philippine Studies Program operated jointly by the Newberry, the Anthropology Department of the University of Chicago, and the Chicago Natural History Museum under a grant from the Carnegie Corporation of New York. To the Carnegie Corporation and to the trustees of the Newberry Library I should like to acknowledge an abiding debt of gratitude. Two committees are in charge of the program: a policy committee headed by Fred Eggan, of the University of Chicago, whose membership also includes Evett D. Hester, Sol Tax, Harvey Perloff, of the University of Chicago, Stanley Pargellis, Librarian of the Newberry, and Ruth Lapham Butler, Custodian of the Ayer Collection at the Newberry. An advisory committee presently consists of Fay-Cooper Cole, Felix Keesing, H. H. Bartlett, Paul Russell and Leopold Ruiz. I am deeply grateful to Mr. Eggan, Mr. Hester, Mr. Pargellis, and Mrs. Butler, all of whom have been unfailingly generous with their knowledge and their encouragement. The completion of this book was facilitated by a summer grant provided by the research committee of the Graduate School of the University of Wisconsin.

I am particularly grateful to Professor C. R. Boxer of the University of London and to the Newberry Library for their joint permission to reproduce some of the illustrations in his manuscript of an early Philippine codex, a photostat copy of which is in the Newberry Library. For a complete description of the document see: C. R. Boxer, "A Late Sixteenth Century Manila MS.," *Journal of the Royal Asiastic Society* (April, 1950), pp. 37–39.

I would also like to express my appreciation to the directors and to the staffs of the *Archivo General de Indias* in Seville, the Library of the *Palacio de Oriente* in Madrid, the Bancroft Library of the University of California, the Knights of Columbus Foundation for the Preservation of Historic Documents at the Vatican Library of St. Louis University, and the Library of Congress for many helpful and courteous services rendered. I would also like to extend my warmest appreciation to all my good friends on the staff of the Newberry, who have aided me in countless ways. In addition I wish to acknowledge my indebtedness to the following persons who have helped me in the preparation of this volume: Woodrow Borah, John Donoghue, Robert Fox, Charles Kaut, Benjamin Keen, Paul Lietz, Francis Lynch, S.J., Stella Paluskas McPherron, Melvin Mednick, John Parry, Randall D. Sale (cartographer) Willis Siebley, Lesley Bryd Simpson, George Smith, Lutie Mae Springer, and Doris Varner Welsh.

J.L.P.

*Milwaukee, Wisconsin*
*January, 1958*

# Contents

# Contents

# List of
# Illustrations

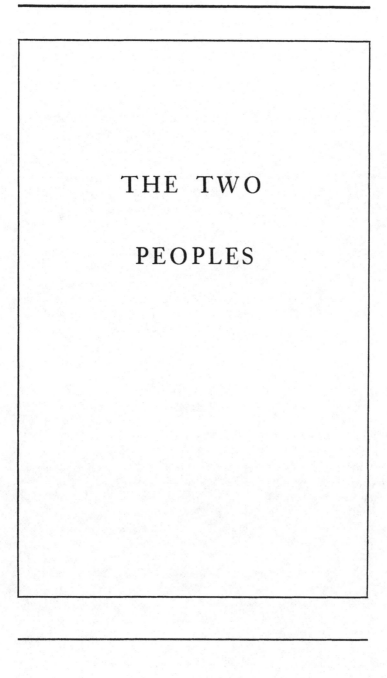

# THE TWO

# PEOPLES

# The Spaniards

F ew revolutions in history have enjoyed the good fortune of an immaculate conception, least of all, the Spanish conquest of America. In the conquest the whole range of human emotions found ample room in which to express themselves. Christian charity, humanitarian zeal, sadistic cruelty, and gross perfidy all had their personifications, and sometimes in the same man. There was more to the conquest than the sanguinary conquistador enshrined in the popular stereotype and the equally conventional image of the selfless missionary dedicated to saving the soul of the Indian. Conquistadores sought riches not only in the form of precious metals but also in the exploitation of native labor, for the latter was the traditional reward for those who had fought infidels in the Moorish wars in the peninsula. Many conquistadores were as desirous of fame as they were of riches. The heirs of medieval civilization, they were also men of the Renaissance who yearned for immortality in this world by having their deeds recorded for posterity.

Wanton destruction in abundance there was. The sanguinary character of the conquest cannot be minimized, but it should not obscure the more constructive aspect of Spanish colonization, which was partially an outgrowth of Spain's historical development prior to 1492. Spanish expansion overseas retained many of the characteristics of the centuries-long *reconquista* of Spain from the Moors. Both enterprises were essentially military in character, Christian proselytizing, and territorially acquisitive. The military subjugation of infidels—be they Moors, Indians, or Asiatics—and the imposition of Christianity form one continuous temporal and spatial sequence in Spanish history, stretching from the Cave of Covadonga in the eighth century to the conquest of the Philippines in the late sixteenth century, from the Pyrenees to the Pacific. In both America and the Orient the *reconquista* tradition of suppressing paganism was supplemented by a Christian humanist ideal of Renaissance inspiration. The Indians were to be Hispanized as well as Christianized. The natives were to be resettled in compact villages and taught to live and to work as European laborers. The more enlightened members of the Spanish regular clergy envisaged in positive terms a harmonious synthesis of some elements of primitive society with certain features of Spanish culture.

Spaniards of all classes during the sixteenth century were inspired by an almost limitless faith in their nation's power and prestige. The Spanish race appeared to them as God's new Chosen People, destined to execute the plans of Providence. Spain's mission was to forge the spiritual unity of all mankind by crushing the Protestants in the Old World, defending Christendom against the onslaughts of the Turks, and spreading the gospel among the infidels of America and Asia.

To those of mystical inclinations, Spain's task of uniting mankind under "one faith, one pastor, and one flock" seemed like the fulfillment of the prophecies of the Apocalypse. The millennial kingdom would be established under Spanish auspices before the second coming of Christ and the Last Judgment. Many of the early missionaries in the Philippines, for example, regarded the islands merely as a convenient doorway to the fabled lands of China and Japan, just as the Antilles had previously served as the base of operations for the conquest of the American mainland. With the conversion of the peoples of Asia all the races of mankind would be brought into the fold of Christianity, an event which some interpreted as foreshadowing the approaching end of the world. Not all the Spaniards were apocalyptical mystics. Most of them, however, were inspired by a truculent faith in themselves, and this exuberant self-confidence helps to explain how the Spaniards were able, during the course of the sixteenth century, to spread their culture halfway around the globe.[1]

Were the Spaniards colossal hypocrites? None of them proposed to undo the conquest, yet they argued endlessly about the moral and the legal basis of their authority over their overseas possessions. These wordy disputes, however, cannot be dismissed as elaborate rationalizations of a *fait accompli*. All Spaniards shared the belief that Castilian jurisdiction in the Indies depended upon the fulfillment of the commitment to convert the Indians to Christianity. This unshakable conviction explains why no Spaniard ever proposed to repudiate the fact of the conquest, much though many deplored some methods by which it had been implemented. To this extent the Spaniards were rationalizing what to them was an irrevocable fact.

The most influential minds of the age—jurists, theologians and bureaucrats—agreed that the evangelical enterprise provided their compatriots with no license to trample over the legitimate rights of the natives. In the forefront were the spokesmen of the regular clergy defending the cause of the Indians. The colonists, on the other hand, vigorously expressed their conviction that colonizing must be made profitable for them. That meant, of course, some form of exploitation of native labor. The dilemma facing the governments of Charles V and Philip II was how to work out a humane and realistic compromise which would take into account the legitimate economic interests of the colonists without abandoning the Indians to ruthless exploitation. It is to the credit of the Spanish Crown that it stubbornly refused to consider the possibility that the interests of colonists and Indians might be irreconcilable.[2]

A striking feature of Spanish imperialism was the inseparable union of the Church and the state. Although both retained a vigorous amount of autonomy, the two institutions were inextricably interdependent. In a series of concessions the Holy See granted to the Spanish monarchs sweeping powers over the administration of the Church's revenues and the deciding voice in the selection of ecclesiastical personnel. In return for the patronage of the Church of the Indies, the Crown undertook the task of supervising the conversion of the Indians to Christianity. The new colonial church, vigorously supported by the military and financial power of the state, responded enthusiastically to this unique missionary opportunity. The religious conquest in turn did much to consolidate the political control of the Spanish Crown over the conquered race. In dealing with the indigenous population, Church and state usually shared a common set of objectives. Conflict, however, could be acrimonious over the choice of methods.

Spanish imperialism was not only theocratic; it was also profoundly bureaucratic. Only at the top was the imperial bureaucracy highly centralized in the persons of the king and the royal Council of the Indies. The latter exercised by royal delegation supreme jurisdiction over all phases of colonial life. There were four administrative hierarchies in the colonies, namely, the viceroys and governors, the Audiencias, the ecclesiastical, and the fiscal authorities. In spite of the nominal centralization of power in the hands of the viceroys and governors, the three other hierarchies retained a substantial amount of autonomous power. Hence there was an endless series of clashes among the various magistrates. Motivating the Crown was an abiding distrust of its officers overseas. Fearful that colonial magistrates might prove disloyal or mendacious given the long distances and the slow communications with Spain, the Crown deliberately played one administrative hierarchy against the other. Several agencies exercised the same powers, and all of them were directly responsible to the Council of the Indies.

Since authority was in practice multiplex, there was some room for decentralized decision-making on the part of colonial magistrates. The celebrated "I obey but do not execute" formula, by which the enforcement of legislation could be postponed until fresh instructions arrived from Spain, was a standard administrative procedure. This device served to apprise the central authorities of local conditions about which they might be ignorant as well as to enable colonial bureaucrats to influence the formulation of policy directives emanating from Spain.[3]

The Spanish bureaucratic system did provide for some kind of balance between centrifugal authority and centripetal flexibility. The colonial bureaucracy was not fast-moving, nor was it outstandingly efficient in the short run. Yet it was effective in achieving some of the ultimate objectives of imperial policy. Spain did preserve her empire for three centuries without heavy dependence on military coercion. Strenuous and often successful efforts were made to protect the native population. Thirdly, colonizing was made profitable, if not for all the colonists, for at least a significant minority. None of these goals was fully realized, but substantial progress toward these ends was registered. In bringing about this result, the imperial bureaucracy made a decisive contribution, rivaled in magnitude only by that of the Church.

Such are some of the principal features of Spanish expansion overseas. In the Philippines—the remote, Oriental outpost of this far-flung empire—the shape and pattern of Spanish activity differed in some respects from that of the Spanish empire in America. The contrasts are striking. So are the parallels.

Three objectives encouraged the Spaniards to colonize the Philippines. One was to secure a share in the lucrative spice trade, which heretofore had been a Portuguese monopoly. Another was to establish direct contacts with China and Japan, which might pave the way for their conversion to Christianity. And the third goal was to Christianize the inhabitants of the archipelago. Of the three objectives only the third proved realizable. The intervention of the Dutch ultimately dashed to pieces Spanish dreams in the Spice Islands, and the "spiritual conquest" of Japan and China was to prove a chimera.

Perhaps the most significant fact about the Spanish occupation of the Philippines is its date. Permanent occupation of the islands began in 1565 with the arrival of the Legazpi expedition. By that date the influence of the Muslims over the central and northern Philippines was still superficial enough not to present an insurmountable obstacle to the Spaniards. In the southern Philippines, however, the Muslims were sufficiently well entrenched to repulse Spanish penetration for 250 years. If Mohammedization had been allowed to spread unchecked throughout the islands for a few more decades after 1565, Filipino resistance might have been of such a hostile character as to discourage Spanish colonization. Secondly, their arrival in 1565 allowed the Spaniards forty years in which to consolidate themselves in the islands before the Dutch intervened in the area. Even this period of preparation barely sufficed, as the Dutch nearly ousted the Spaniards from the Philippines during the first half of the seventeenth century. Thirdly, by 1565 the subjugation of the American mainland had been consummated for many decades. The Spaniards had a secure base of operations from which to launch expansion into the Orient, and they had already acquired a varied fund of experience in dealing with conquered peoples.

The government of Philip II regarded the Philippines as a challenging opportunity to avoid a repetition of the sanguinary conquests of Mexico and Peru. In his written instructions for the *Adelantado* Legazpi, who commanded the expedition, Philip II envisaged a bloodless pacification of the archipelago. This extraordinary document could have been lifted almost verbatim from the lectures of the Dominican theologian, Francisco de Vitoria, delivered at the University of Salamanca. The King instructed Legazpi to inform the natives that the Spaniards had come to do no harm to their persons or to their property. The Spaniards intended to live among them in peace and in friendship and "to explain to them the law of Jesus Christ by which they will be saved."[4] Although the Spanish expedition could defend themselves if attacked, the royal instructions admonished the commander to commit no aggressive act which might arouse native hostility. Philip II's project of a peaceful occupation of the Philippines was an outgrowth of that Dominican-led movement whose outstanding spokesmen were Vitoria and Las Casas. The Dominicans sought to outlaw bellicose methods. In this task they found in the philosophy of Thomas Aquinas a veritable arsenal of arguments. Both Vitoria and Las Casas stressed Aquinas' conviction that pagan peoples do not, as St. Augustine had seemed to imply, lose their social, political, and economic rights merely by coming in contact with a Christian people. The rights which all peoples enjoy by virtue of natural law and the law of nations must be taken into account by a Christian nation seeking to spread the gospel among the infidels.[5]

The adoption by the Spanish court of the Dominican-inspired ideal of pacification coincided with the founding of the Philippine colony. In fact, the Oriental archipelago became a testing ground for the new policy. In Legazpi, Philip II had a lieutenant with the patience and the skill necessary to execute such an arduous commission. Legazpi had to contend with firebrands in his own expedition, like Andrés de Mirandaola, who favored a conquest by fire and sword. The latter assailed the Filipinos as a "very vicious and treacherous race who are full of evil manners."[6] Nor did Legazpi's conciliatory aims always evoke the desired response from the Filipinos. They were often suspicious if not positively hostile to the initial overtures of the Spaniards. In a number of localities the Spaniards met some armed resistance, but this was the exception rather than the rule. In a boldly executed and relatively bloodless campaign Legazpi's youthful and dexterous grandson, Juan de Salcedo, pacified a substantial portion of the maritime provinces of Luzon.

Legazpi's task was facilitated by the geographical particularism and political decentralization of Philippine society. Small kinship units known as barangays were independent of, if not hostile to, each other. Hence armed resistance to the Spaniards on anything but a local scale was impossible. After testing the striking power and the determination of the invaders, the prevailing Filipino reaction was a prudent attitude of outwardly accepting the fact of Spanish hegemony.

The initial phase of the conquest under the leadership of Legazpi, who died on August 20, 1572, was not executed without some bloodshed. Neither can it be called sanguinary. Legazpi's achievement may not be as spectacular as Cortés' or Pizarro's, but it was a remarkable accomplishment. To the conqueror of the Philippines must be given the credit in large measure for realizing substantially but not completely Philip II's ideal of a pacific occupation.

Although the completion of the military conquest was swift and relatively bloodless, subsequent economic dislocations were more prolonged. An acute rice shortage in the 1570's and the early 1580's threatened the precarious existence of the new colony. Philippine agriculture was of the subsistence variety. The sudden descent of two groups of nonproductive consumers—the Spaniards and in much larger numbers the Chinese—created a severe food shortage.

The intensity of the economic crisis aggravated a virulent conflict between the clergy and the colonists over the exploitation of native labor. Following the Spanish custom in America most of the Filipino population was distributed among the colonists under the encomienda system. In return for the payment of an annual tribute, the encomendero was obligated to protect his wards and to indoctrinate them in the rudiments of the Christian doctrine. That the encomenderos abused their trust in a wide variety of illegal exactions is evident. The clergy, ably led from 1579 onward by the aged but energetic Bishop Salazar, caustically exposed these abuses to the authorities in Spain. From the pulpits zealous friars hurled threats of excommunication at those encomenderos who would not heed their strictures. Thus the encomenderos were confronted with a grim choice between the threat of external damnation in the next world and starvation in this world.[7]

### Chapter 11

# The Filipinos

Although the Spaniards were the conquerors and the Filipinos were the conquered, the meeting of these two cultures was not a one-sided process in which the Spaniards remade Filipino society into an exclusively Hispanic image. Much of preconquest culture survived the conquest. Indispensable to an understanding of how this result came about is an awareness of the way of life of the Filipinos on the eve of the arrival of the Spaniards.[1]

As we observed in Chapter I, the conquest was facilitated by the fragmentation of Philippine society. The only form of political and social organization was small kinship units known as barangays, a name derived from the sailboats which brought the early Malay immigrants to the Philippines. The barangays usually consisted of from 30 to 100 families. A few barangays, such as the ones of Manila, Vigan, and Cebu, contained as may as 2,000 people. In the barangay complex there were four distinct classes, with several gradations inside each one: (1) the chieftains, called *datus,* and their families, (2) *maharlika* or the nobles, (3) the freemen called *timagua,* and (4) the servile, dependent class whom the Spaniards misleadingly called slaves.

The precise nature of interbarangay relations is not always easy to determine. Frequently it was unmitigated hostility, which in the Philippines took the form of headhunting expeditions. There are also examples of interbarangay coöperation. Whether such cases deserve to be called confederations in which one *datu* was recognized as the overlord of a regional grouping of barangays is a moot question. In their understandable desire to ennoble the remote history of their land, some nationalist-minded Philippine historians have referred to the kings of pre-Hispanic times.[2] According to this opinion, the jurisdiction of the native leader Humabon extended over the whole island of Cebu at the time of Magellan and in 1570 all the barangays of central Luzon acknowledged the authority of one Soliman. Although some of the early Spanish chroniclers referred to the *reyezuelos* of Cebu and Manila, that title of kinglet was evidently synonomous for the *datu* of a large barangay.[3]

The following passage from Pigafetta, the chronicler of the Magellan expedition, suggests that the Spaniards did not find kinglets in the islands; hence they tried to create them.

The captain [Magellan] told the king [Humabon, the local chieftain] through the interpreter that he thanked God for inspiring him to become a Christian; and that now he would more easily conquer his enemies than before. The king replied that he wished to become a Christian, but some of his chiefs did not wish to obey, because they said that they were as good men as he. Then our captain had all the chiefs of the king called, and told them that unless they obeyed the king as their king, he would have them killed, and would give their possessions to the king. They replied that they would obey him.[4]

Pigafetta's account indicates that Humabon was nothing more than the *datu* of a large barangay. Magellan's policy was to promote him to the status of a kinglet subordinate to Magellan.

The introduction into the central and northern Philippines of a suprabarangay concept of political organization may have occurred as a result of Muslim influence during those very decades between Magellan's death in 1521 and Legazpi's arrival in 1565. Muslim traders from the islands of Malaysia introduced this notion into the southern Philippines sometime after 1450. In the sixteenth century Mohammedization advanced slowly northward, eventually reaching the bay of Manila. The communities that the Spaniards encountered in both Cebu and in Manila in the 1560's were superficially Islamized, but the principle of suprabarangay leadership apparently had not progressed beyond the embryonic stage.

The example of Mindanao, the largest island of the southern Philippines, is significant in that Mohammedization was allowed to unfold there without being checked by the Spaniards. A suprabarangay form of political organization, the *rajah* of Muslim origin, did emerge there. The same development probably would have occurred in the central and northern Philippines if the Spaniards had not halted the Muslim advance. Equally suggestive is the case of the mountain province of northwestern Luzon, which for three centuries was scarcely touched by either Spanish or Muslim influence. There no suprabarangay units developed.

The conquest did not destroy the "kinglets" of pre-Hispanic times, but merely arrested their rise. What did survive the shock of the conquest was the barangay. The Spaniards adroitly refashioned this patriarchal kinship unit into the cornerstone of local government. How they did will be examined in some detail in Chapter IX.

Geography does much to explain this state of political decentralization. The fact that the Philippines are an archipelago of more than 7,000 islands, each one varying in size from substantial land masses to uninhabited dots of land, obviously discouraged the formation of transinsular political units. Only eleven of the islands are as large as 1,000 square miles apiece. Mountain barriers in many cases made for intrainsular isolation. In the narrow valleys and along the rivers small clusters of population settled. In the mountains dwelt the fierce Negritos, perhaps the original inhabitants of the islands. They were driven into the highlands by the Malay invaders, who were in possession of the maritime lowlands when the Spaniards arrived.

Riparian geography in addition to the prevalence of mountain barriers made for geographical particularism and political decentralization. The latter in turn encouraged linguistic diversity. Although all the Philippine tongues go back to a common Malayo-Polynesian root form, the Filipinos spoke a bewildering variety of languages. On the island of Luzon there are six major languages, many minor ones, and a host of dialects. The Tagalogs of central Luzon where Manila is located formed the largest single linguistic group. In the Bisayan group of islands in the central Philippines there are three principal languages in addition to a confusing variety of minor languages and dialects. And the southern Philippines formed yet another Babel of languages.[5]

The Filipinos had an alphabet of their own consisting of seventeen letters, three of which were vowels and the rest consonants. The Tagalog text of the *Doctrina* of 1593, the first book printed in the Philippines, was printed in both the Latin and Philippine alphabets. Although the Philippine languages survived the conquest, not so the pre-Hispanic alphabet. The Philippine tongues were soon transliterated into the Latin alphabet. Pre-Hispanic literature, however, was scant. Only a few historical fragments have come down to us, and there is little evidence to suggest that the Spaniards deliberately destroyed Philippine manuscripts. The Filipinos had an alphabet, but they did not often use it for literary purposes, according to Chirino.[6] Their literature was largely oral.

Political decentralization and linguistic diversity notwithstanding, the cultures of the maritime provinces were sufficiently similar among themselves to justify our making some generalizations about the pattern of preconquest society. Philippine social organization did not extend beyond the immediate family and the extended family or kinship unit. Polygamy was not widespread among the Filipinos. Its practice was confined to the Bisayan islands of Samar, Leyte, and Cebu in the central Philippines. Probably introduced by Mohammedan traders from Borneo, it was a costly custom in which only the wealthy chieftains could afford to indulge. Divorce and remarriage, on the other hand, were more common. The failure to have children, a prolonged illness, or an opportunity to make a more advantageous marriage were sufficient causes to secure a divorce. Divorce was socially acceptable under certain conditions, but it was still the exception.

The marriage pattern was relatively stable. Parents negotiated the marriages of their children, with a view to cementing kinship alliances and property arrangements. The custom was for the groom, not the bride, to provide the dowry. Furthermore, the groom had to pay his future father-in-law "bride-price" or to perform "bride-service." The young man either paid his father-in-law a sum in gold (*bigay haya*) or he worked gratis for a period of time in his father-in-law's house (*maninirbihan*).[7] The engaged couple living under the same roof evidently had opportunities to indulge in premarital sexual relations. Circumstantial evidence suggests that for the Filipinos the authenticity of a marriage depended upon the birth of children. The final ceremonial formalities of the marriage might be postponed until after the bride gave evidence of her ability to become a mother.

The rationale underlying the Philippine customs of bride-price and bride-service never has been adequately explained. To fill this vacuum a few tentative hypotheses may be suggested. It may have been thought that the bride's father should be compensated for the expenses involved in rearing a daughter. Perhaps a more basic explanation is that with the bride-money obtained from his daughter's marriage a father could then provide for his son's marriage and thus insure the perpetuation of the kinship unit. Since the bride-gift was provided by the groom's kinfolk, the latter acquired a vested interest in the stability of the marriage. In case of divorce the bride-gift was not returned if the husband was the guilty party. Hence the husband's kinsmen were a potent force in stabilizing marriage.

The Spanish sources provide only a few clues about the precise nature of kinship ties other than to indicate in general terms their central importance. The only political unit in Philippine society, the barangay, was kinship-oriented. On Luzon patrilocal residence was the rule; in the Bisayas, however, there was a strong tendency toward matrilocal residence. Everywhere there was bilateral kinship descent with some emphasis placed on the paternal side. In this respect the Philippine custom did not differ substantially from that of the Spaniards.

In preconquest times landowning was communal in character, with the actual title vested in the barangay. Wealth was determined by how many dependents a chieftain could muster to cultivate the communally owned lands. Essentially a self-sufficient agrarian economy in which commerce with one's neighbors played only a minor role, Philippine agriculture was based upon the cultivation of rice and root crops and was supplemented by fishing and the raising of swine and fowl.

To call the pre-Hispanic system of labor organization slavery, as the Spaniards invariably did, is misleading. The whole arrangement had much more in common with debt peonage and sharecropping than it did with the European conception of chattel slavery. The term "dependent" is a more accurate designation of this class. Among the Filipinos many judicial sentences took the form of fines. This custom offers a partial explanation for the existence of a large group among the dependent class, the debt peons. Those who were unable to pay judicial fines or who found themselves in stringent circumstances could secure loans only at a usurious rate of interest. Loans were payable at each harvest season at 100 per cent interest. In addition to debtors the dependent population was swelled by those captured in raids on neighboring villages, those convicted of poaching on a *datu's* land, or those guilty of committing adultery with the wives or concubines of the *datus.*

The dependent population was divided into two principal categories. Among the Tagalogs the *mamamahay* could own property, and they could marry without their superior's consent. As compensation they usually received one-half of the harvest. The *tumaranpuh* was the Bisayan version of the Tagalog *mamamahay.* Enjoying the freedom of their persons, including the right to acquire and dispose of property, their obligation was to work for their superior one day out of every four. Both the Tagalog *mamamahay* and the Bisayan *tumaranpuh* were sharecroppers rather than chattel slaves.

The second division among the dependent population, known as the *guiguilir* in Tagalog, were not precisely chattels. To be sure they could not marry without the consent of their superiors. If they were not household servants, they could be sold. They did receive some compensation for their labor services, but their share of the crop was much less than that of the *mamamahay*. The Bisayan *ayuey* corresponded to the Tagalog *guiguilir*. The *ayuey*'s obligation was to work gratis three out of every four days. Nor could they contract matrimony without the consent of their superior. Yet they could own and dispose of property. The *guiguilir-ayuey* resembled to some extent debt peons.

The Spanish administration recognized the difference between the two classes among the dependent population. The more prosperous *mamamahay-tumaranpuh* were responsible for paying their own tribute. The tribute of the *guiguilir-ayuey*, on the other hand, was paid by their superiors.[8]

Dependent status was hereditary. There were two alternatives, differing according to local usage. Either the individual children of a free man and a dependent woman were half free and half dependent, and their descendants became progressively one-fourth, one-eighth or one-sixteenth dependent, etc., or the children might be divided, with half of them free and the other half of dependent status. An indication of the bewildering complexity of the system is the fact that the labor services of one dependent might be distributed among ten or twelve superiors.[9] Part-dependents but not whole-dependents enjoyed the privilege of purchasing their manumission at a set price. Before the conquest the price of manumission for a Bisayan *tumaranpuh* was the equivalent of twelve Spanish pesos. By 1635 it varied between sixteen and twenty pesos. When the number of dependents was already on the decline, in 1660, the price of manumission fluctuated between thirty-two and forty pesos.[10] Although the Filipinos could buy their way out of dependent status, it was far easier for them to sink into that class by borrowing at a usurious rate of interest.

Although the Spaniards misleadingly called this institution *esclavitud*, knowledgeable Spanish observers candidly recognized that the "peculiar institution" of the Philippines lacked the harshness and brutality of European slavery. In a system combining features of sharecropping and debt peonage, the dependents were linked to their superiors not only by the obligation to perform certain labor services but also, in many cases, by close ties of consanguinity.

The refinements in, and the evident expansion of, the dependent class might suggest at first glance that kinship ties were being replaced by social and economic differences by the eve of the conquest. Although no certain answer is available, the evidence seems to point to the conclusion that kinship ties were not disintergrating. On the island of Mindanao the Spanish conquest did not take place, and Muslim influence resulted in the emergence of quasi-political states in which kinship ties remained very strong. In the last analysis, kinship ties rather than political and economic differences remained paramount in that region.

At the top of the social pyramid were the chieftains and their families. Underneath them were the *maharlika* class, those born of noble blood, who served their chieftains in war and provided them with counsel in peace. There was also a numerous class of free men who possessed neither the privileges of the chieftains and nobles nor the obligations of the dependents. At the bottom of the ladder was the dependent population with a bewildering number of subdivisions. Each barangay, consisting of these three groups, was bound together in a kinship system of mutual dependence essentially patriarchal in character. Outside the umbrella of mutual security provided by the barangay, war of every man against every man was apt to prevail.

Of all aspects of preconquest culture the one that most aroused the curiosity of the Spaniards was the religion of the Filipinos, or to be more precise their religious rituals. The Philippine cults were a blending of monotheism and polytheism, with the latter tending to predominate. They had some conception of a Supreme Being, the creator of the universe and the ruler of men. In Tagalog he was called *Bathala* and in Bisayan *Laon* or *Abba*. This remote supreme deity was relegated to the background by a pantheon of gods and goddesses who were the specific protectors for all the activities in which men engaged.

The spirit world in Philippine religion was densely inhabited. The spirits were called *anitos* or *diwatas*. The good spirits were those of the Filipinos' ancestors and the bad spirits were those of their enemies. In order to placate their wrath and to acquire their good will, the Filipinos offered up prayers and sacrifices to them. The Spanish sources are full of detailed accounts of these ceremonies.

Many rituals concentrated on the cure of illness. Other ceremonies, in which ritual drinking was an integral part, stressed the need to propitiate the gods. The Filipinos drank copious libations of rice wine on certain ceremonial occasions, notably at betrothals, weddings, and funerals. Although these ceremonies might last as long as three days, they were not unadulterated alchoholic orgies. A Spanish worthy whose name has been lost to posterity put it succinctly when he wrote: "Although they are drunk, they do not entirely lose their senses, and I have never seen any of them fall down because he was drunk."[11] Alcina reported that the Bisayans might take as many as twelve cups of wine without losing their judgment or their senses. He did add that their color was "somewhat altered."[12] The duty of providing wine and food for the guests cast many a chieftain into the depths of poverty, but such largesse was periodically expected from those of that class. *Noblesse oblige*, Philippine version. Ritual drinking was more popular with the men than with the women, who drank separately from the men. The Ilokanos, the Tagalogs, and the Bisayans were the strongest imbibers. The Pampangans enjoyed a reputation for relative temperance.

Like the ancient Egyptians and the Assyrians, the Filipinos worshipped nature. They rendered divine honors to the sun, the moon, the rainbow, the rivers, the plants, the caves, the mountains, and the trees. They adored certain animals such as crows, sharks, and crocodiles. Perhaps as a reflection of Chinese influence the Filipinos were also ancestor-worshippers. Some of the spirits, or the *anitos*, were regarded as intermediaries between the living and the dead. To commemorate their ancestors they carved idols in stone, ivory, and wood. The Filipinos did have a conception of the afterlife, in which the good were rewarded with a heaven (in (Tagalog, *kalualhatian*, and in Bisayan, *ologan*) and the wicked in this life were punished by being committed to an inferno (*kasamaan* in Tagalog and *solad* in Bisayan). Interwoven into their religious beliefs were whole strands of magical practices and superstitions.

Some of the earliest Spanish observers expressed doubt as to whether there was a professional priestly class. Friar Juan de Plasencia's study of Tagalog customs (1589) settled this question affirmatively. Ritual sacrifices were performed by persons known as the *babaylan* or the *katalonan*. They were usually elderly women, the few men who practiced this priestly function ordinarily being transvestites.

What the Filipinos lacked were temples or buildings reserved for the exclusive use of religious functions. This situation puzzled some Spaniards, who seldom took note of the fact that as nature worshippers the Filipinos had a host of sacred groves and sacred caves which took the place of temples. There was no fixed calendar of religious celebrations. Functions occurred as specific occasions warranted. Although the majority of religious rituals consisted of offerings to the spirits, these sacrifices did not involve human beings. In Filipino mythology there was no conviction that the gods had to be nourished and propitiated by the constant flow of that most precious commodity, human blood. The Spaniards might dismiss these religious convictions and ceremonies as unadulterated superstition, but the Filipino pagan cults never aroused the degree of indignation that the sanguinary rituals of the Aztecs usually did.

Such are some of the principal features of the Filipino society which the Spaniards set out to remodel. They made a serious effort to acquire a moderately objective grasp of the character of pre-Hispanic culture, but the Spaniards also attached value judgments to the data they collected. Two of these value judgments merit special attention. One was that the religion of the Filipinos constituted the tyrannical enslavement of the devil over a pagan people; therefore, in spreading Christianity the Spaniards were "liberating" the Filipinos from the oppressive sway of the devil. The other value judgment was that the preconquest system of sharecropping and debt peonage based on usury was an unjust and tyrannical form of social organization. In conquering the islands the Spaniards were "liberating" the lower classes from the oppressive bondage of their chieftains. By this semantic exercise the Spaniards transformed themselves from "conquerors" into "liberators."

This concept owes its origin to the Valladolid debate between Las Casas and Sepúlveda (1550–51). In answer to the thesis of Las Casas about the illegitimacy of the conquest, Sepúlveda rejoined that the licitness of the conquest could be founded on the alleged injustices and tyrannies of the pre-Hispanic regimes. The viceroy of Peru, Francisco de Toledo (1569–81), authorized an elaborate historical investigation of Inca society in order to substantiate this thesis. In the Philippines, Spanish opinion, both ecclesiastical and lay, accepted this principle.

In various provinces of the Philippines native chieftains and freemen were assembled during the year 1599 in order to "elect" the Castilian king as their natural lord and sovereign. These election ceremonies were organized upon the urging of a royal cedula from Spain. The Filipinos based their voluntary submission on the contractual promise that the king and his new subjects would render each other certain services. In these documents the conquest was interpreted as a "liberation." The Spaniards were said to have liberated the Filipinos from the enslavement of the devil as well as freed them from unjust social abuses. The positive benefits that the king promised to render were religious instruction, the administration of justice, and protection against their enemies (Japanese, Chinese, and Mohammedan pirates, and hostile infidel neighbors).[13]

The amount of real freedom of choice that these Filipinos did have under these circumstances was probably negligible. Yet it would not be unreasonable to assume that some Filipinos accepted voluntarily the theory underlying this ceremony. This formula does illustrate one significant argument by which the Spaniards justified the conquest to themselves and to the Filipinos, and this argument was based upon a Spanish interpretation of preconquest society.

However the Spaniards may have interpreted the world of the conquered in order to rationalize their own actions, this indigenous culture was deeply embedded in the islands. Hence significant elements of the old culture blended into the new society emerging under Spanish auspices, and in many cases took forms contrary to the wishes of the new regime. The Filipinos were and still are tough and flexible, able to absorb new cultural influences without losing their own identity. They survived the "shock" of the conquest with far less psychological and material damage to themselves than did many native races of the Americas. Although partially Hispanized, they never lost that Malaysian stratum which to this day remains the foundation of their culture.

In this connection it is tempting to compare preconquest Philippine society with the civilized Indian peoples of America, in particular the Aztecs of Mexico and the Incas of Peru, and to examine the Spanish role in these different areas. The most obvious distinction is, of course, the fact that in America the Spaniards came in contact with civilizations that had developed in complete separation from the mainstream of Eurasian culture, while in the Philippines they encountered a culture long in contact with that mainstream, owing to the archipelago's proximity to China and Malaysia. While, therefore, in some respects the Filipinos were distinctly inferior to the Aztecs and to the Incas, in other areas the reverse is true. The American peoples had progressed far beyond the level reached by the Filipinos in political organization, and in science and art. The Incas, and to a lesser extent the Aztecs, had developed a political state, whereas the Filipinos were just emerging from the kinship stage. The artistic accomplishments of the Filipinos were aesthetically meager alongside the impressive temples and the magnificent sculptures of the New World. Yet one cannot avoid the impression that indigenous America was fossilized as a consequence of its isolation. These peoples lacked an alphabet, the use of metals, and, with the exception of the Incas, beasts of burden. Among the Aztecs, human sacrifice was practiced on a massive scale and cannibalism was not unknown. Here the advent of the Spaniards broke down the isolation and connected the New World with the Old.

In the Philippines, however, the Spaniards played no such role. The Philippine contact with Eurasian culture accounts for the existence of a system of writing in the islands, the use of metals, the prevalence of beasts of burden, and the absence of human sacrifice and cannibalism among the maritime peoples of the archipelago. All of this might suggest that the Filipinos were more capable of an independent cultural growth, without European influence, than were the Aztecs and the Incas.

This alternative existed, but its possibilities ought not to be exaggerated. That the Spaniards did not interrupt in the Philippines the flowering of a sophisticated and an advanced civilization of the same high quality as that of Japan or China may be seen by studying the case of the Moros. In the southern Philippines the Moros, who successfully resisted Spanish penetration for three centuries, were left to develop free from Spanish influence. Their cultural achievements were solid and modest but scarcely sophisticated or advanced. There are few grounds for assuming that the central and northern Philippines would, if left independent, have made much more progress than did the south. In fact, it was probably inevitable that the Philippines fall under some form of European domination. In contrast to Japan and China their society was not sufficiently well organized either politically or militarily to resist aggression, and the archipelago constituted an inviting prey to any European power anxious to secure a base of operations from which to extend its influence over the neighboring peoples of the Orient.

# THE SPREAD

## OF

## CATHOLICISM

### Chapter III

# The Spanish
# Missionaries

In the meeting of Philippine and Spanish cultures the regular clergy of the Spanish Church were leading protagonists. In order to evaluate their role, one must first understand the rather complex relations of the regular clergy with the episcopacy and the civil authorities. A clear and precise comprehension of the theocratic elements in Spanish imperialism is a necessary ingredient to any understanding of the impact of Spanish culture on Philippine society.

The Papacy transferred to the Spanish Crown the administration of the new Church of the Indies, and the Crown in turn entrusted to the regular clergy the specific task of Christianizing the natives. Taking perpetual vows of chastity, obedience, and poverty, the regulars lived according to a community rule (*regula*) under the jurisdiction of elected superiors. The religious of the regular orders, with their higher standards of discipline and asceticism, were better prepared for missionary work than were the members of the secular clergy. The latter, whose superiors were the bishops, formed the parish clergy in established Christian communities. Those regular orders who participated in the conversion of the Filipinos were the Augustinians (1565), the Discalced Franciscans (1578), the Jesuits (1581), the Dominicans (1587), and the Augustinian Recollects (1606).

The regulars received a generous grant of authority in the *omnimoda* bull of Pope Adrian VI (May 9, 1522) to administer the sacraments to the Indians and to perform the duties of parish priests independently of the local bishop. This arrangement, convenient though it was for the missionaries in the New World, violated one of the key reforms of the Council of Trent, which declared no priest might exercise care of souls over laymen without being subject to episcopal authority. Philip II secured from Pope Pius V the brief, *Exponi nobis* (March 24, 1567), in which the Pontiff gave the Crown discretionary power in enforcing this Trentine canon in the Indies. The canon was immediately applied to Peru. The same action was taken in 1583 for the viceroyalty of Mexico, to which the Philippines was nominally attached.[1] The cedula of December 7, 1583, gave the secular clergy outright preferential treatment for vacant benefices and made the regulars, in the capacity as parish priests, subject to episcopal visitation. The Crown looked with misgivings upon the regulars' disregard for episcopal jurisdiction as an implicit denial of many of the privileges the Crown enjoyed by virtue of its patronage over the colonial church.

Two issues were at stake. One was tenure of benefices by the regulars. The other was the claim of the bishops to supervise the conduct of regulars in their role as parish clergy, i.e., the right of ecclesiastical visitation. In most regions of the empire where well-organized Indian parishes emerged the secular clergy replaced the regulars. The latter often retired after an acrimonious rearguard action. The Philippines is an outstanding exception to this trend. Down to 1898 the regulars continued to hold the majority of benefices, and episcopal visitation was a hollow claim. Various archbishops of Manila met persistent failure in their attempts to enforce visitation. The most notable incidents in this long controversy were those involving Bishop Salazar (1581) and the

Natives of the Zambal province.

*This and the following illustrations from a manuscript circa 1590*
*in the library of C. R. Boxer.*

Natives of the Cagayan province.

Natives of the Bisayan islands.

Natives from the Tagalog provinces.

archbishops Vásquez de Mercado (1612), García Serrano (1621), Poblete (1654–56), Camacho (1697), and Sancho de Santa Justa y Rufina (1767–76).[2]

The opposition of the religious to visitation would have been as futile in the islands as it had been in Mexico, if certain conditions peculiar to the Philippines had not prevailed. The regulars in the islands were irreplaceable. They knew it, and they took pains to make everyone else aware of the fact. In 1655 there were not more than sixty secular priests in the whole archipelago, in contrast to 254 regulars.[3] The secular priests in most cases did not speak the Philippine languages, and the Filipinos did not speak Spanish. In every serious attempt to enforce visitation the religious resigned their parishes or threatened to do so and retired to their convents in Manila. A restoration of the old arrangement always ensued. The civil authorities hesitated to take the drastic step of ousting the regulars from their benefices. Every responsible officer of the Crown realized that the continuation of Spanish hegemony in the provinces largely depended upon the authority and prestige that the religious exercised over their parishioners.

Archbishop Sancho de Santa Justa y Rufina (1767–76) sought to break the deadlock by the novel expedient of replacing the recalcitrant regulars with Filipino clergymen. These ill-trained priests, many of whom were hastily granted holy orders by the determined Archbishop, rendered a lamentable account of themselves.[4] The only result was to deal a crippling blow to the growth of a native clergy.

A genuine fear on the part of the religious was that episcopal visitation would endanger their corporate unity and might compel them to violate their vow of obedience to their superiors. Regulars serving as parish priests would thus be subject to two equal and coördinate jurisdictions—the bishop and the provincial superior—either one of which might issue conflicting orders. In addition the obligation imposed on the provincial superior to present a list of three candidates (the *nómina*) to the vice-patron (the governor) for every vacant benefice might jeopardize the freedom to assign his subjects. Another infringement of the provincial superior's freedom of action was to compel him to indicate to the vice-patron his reasons for removing or transferring a subject. The *nómina* itself, the regulars asserted, was unenforceable in the Philippines. In view of the diversity of tongues a superior was indeed fortunate to have one priest familar with the language of a particular parish. If such confusion and limitation of freedom were allowed to prevail, religious in Spain might be discouraged from coming to the Philippines.

According to another argument of the religious, the Philippines was still an active mission, *en viva conquista espiritual*, as one missionary spokesman put it.[5] Only the maritime peoples had been converted, while the mountain peoples remained pagan. Even in the lowlands Christianization had been only partially completed. Scarcity of missionary personnel as well as the dispersal of the population was responsible. The missionary orders argued that under these circumstances the Filipinos were not yet ready to be turned over to the secular clergy.

The episcopacy and the secular clergy tacitly admitted the partial validity of the argument of the religious. The suffragan sees of Cagayan, the Camarines, and Cebu were indeed missionary fields. With only a handful of secular priests there was also an acute shortage of regulars in these dioceses. The serious attempts to enforce episcopal visitation were usually confined to the archbishopric of Manila, containing the largest concentration of people along with the best organized and the best indoctrinated parishes. What the secular clergy wanted to take over were the lucrative benefices of the metropolitan see, leaving the rest of the archipelago to the regulars. That kind of compromise the religious refused to make. They claimed that the resources of the more profitable parishes of the archbishopric were needed to support the less lucrative parishes of the outlying suffragan sees.

The jurisdictional conflicts between the archbishops and the religious orders produced periodic states of turmoil with demoralizing consequences for all parties involved. But the religious did de-

rive one indirect benefit from this tension. In defense of their common privileges the various orders retained an unusual degree of
unity of purpose among themselves. Differences between the
orders were kept at a minimum in the face of the common threat
posed by the issue of episcopal visitation.

If the regulars could make a solid case for their opposition to
visitation, the archbishops could also cogently justify its need. One
of their pertinent arguments was that some external authority was
required to investigate whether the regulars were performing their
parish duties satisfactorily. An investigation conducted by Archbishop Camacho in December and January of 1697 and 1698 un-
covered a whole series of irregularities requiring correction.
Delays in baptizing the newborn, the refusal of the regulars to
administer the last rites to the dying in their homes, excessive
sacramental fees, inadequate indoctrination in the catechism, and
undue pressure exercised by the regulars in extracting alms from
their parishioners were some of the glaring abuses which the investigation documented.[6]

A justification for the episcopal contention that the regulars
were unable to discipline themselves can be found in the demoralization which overtook the Augustinian Order. An episcopal in-
quest in 1593 unearthed evidence that some Augustinians were
engaged in profitable mercantile operations at the expense of
their parishioners. Nine Augustinians, including the then provincial superior, Juan de Valderrama, were charged with repeated
violations of clerical celibacy.[7] The Augustinians split into two
factions—the peninsular friars, who took their vows in Spain,
and the creole friars, who entered the Order in the Indies. The
specific bone of contention was the battle over which group was
to get the lion's share of the offices and benefices which were
voted upon in the triennial chapter meeting. The creole faction
gained control during the second administration of Friar Lorenzo
de León.[8] The provincial superior was accused of acting like a
"public merchant" and failing to take disciplinary action against
some of his subordinates' misdeeds, ranging from several amorous

adventures to the wholesale theft of church property. So scanda-
lous was this administration that under intense pressure from both
lay and ecclesiastical authorities the Augustinians took the drastic
step of deposing Lorenzo de León on January 7, 1607, midway in
his triennium. Upon being informed of this precedent-shattering
action, the king and the Augustinian superiors in Rome approved
the decision.[9]

The disciplinary crisis reached its nadir under the administration of Friar Vicente de Sepúlveda. As provincial superior,
Sepúlveda was driven by a single-minded purpose to remake the
Augustinian Order in his own ascetic image. His vigorous, but
unfortunately tactless, efforts to root out abuses drove his creole
opponents to desperation, and a cabal of these friars murdered
Sepúlveda in his cell on the night of June 31, 1617.[10] The atrocious
character of the Sepúlveda murder did result in some momentary
relaxation of the tension between the creoles and the peninsular
factions. But the conflict exploded again during the chapter meetings
of 1623, 1626, and 1629. The presence of some civil authorities
re-enforced by armed soldiers was considered necessary to maintain order during those turbulent chapter meetings.[11]

A study of the parish map of 1655 throws added light on the
underlying causes of the Augustinian crisis. That order was over-
extended in its commitments. The Augustinians held more
parishes than any other single religious community. They were
the first order to come to the islands, for five Augustinian friars
accompanied the original expedition of Legazpi. The remarkable
navigator of the fleet and its spiritual leader, Friar Andrés de
Urdaneta, had taken the Augustinian habit in middle age. His
crucial role in the expedition probably had much to do with
Viceroy Luís de Velasco's decision to dispatch the Augustinians.
As a consequence of their head start, the Augustinians acquired a
large number of the populous and lucrative parishes in the Tagalog
and Pampangan country. In order to staff these missions Mexican
creoles had to be imported. Some of these creoles had a dubious
religious vocation and were ill-trained. Hence a rapid decline in
discipline set in.

Although the feud between the Castilian and creole friars abated with the definitive victory of the former, the underlying issue posed by the conflict was never resolved. It is apparent that the inability of the orders to discipline themselves on occasion resulted from the decentralized character of their government. Provincial superiors and the definitors (the governing council), who held office for a three-year period, were often loath to take vigorous measures against malfeasance, since they themselves would soon return to the status of subjects. The inspection system, in which a visitor from Mexico or Spain was vested with broad powers of investigation and correction, did not prove very effective in rooting out abuses. The Franciscan visitors, for example, provoked considerable resentment in the Philippines, since they usually came from the Observant branch of the Order established in Mexico. The Philippine Franciscans were of the Discalced branch of the Order, and there was often ill-feeling between the two.[12] The power of the superiors in Rome was limited. The governmental structure of the mendicant orders goes back to the thirteenth century when the federal principle in ecclesiastical polity was in vogue.

Most observers exempted the Jesuits from the charge of ill-discipline. The Jesuits were more selective in choosing personnel, and they received a more rigorous training than did the friars of the mendicant orders. Furthermore the government of the Society was highly centralized. Rome appointed the provincial superiors, in contrast to the mendicants, who elected their superiors. Given the authoritarian character of the Jesuit organization, Rome could intervene in any province before abuses got out of hand. In the case of the mendicant orders Rome could step in only after the scandals had been publicly exposed.

Yet even among the Jesuits the maintenance of discipline posed serious difficulties. Alcina admitted that during his residence of twenty-six years in the Bisayas in the mid-seventeenth century fourteen Jesuits were expelled from the Society. Not all of these expulsions were caused by violations of chastity, but obviously the infractions of discipline provoking this action were serious.

In order to meet the deficit of their Bisayan missions, the Jesuits in that region engaged extensively in the beeswax trade. Their parishioners gathered from forests large quantities of beeswax, which in turn was shipped to and sold in Manila. While all the evidence suggests that the profits of the beeswax trade went exclusively to cover the deficit of the Bisayan parishes, Alcina noted a consequent decline in morale. Many of his confreres, he suspected, were giving too much attention to the administration of this enterprise at the expense of the more important business of Christianizing the Bisayans. He eloquently pleaded for a rededication to missionary enthusiasm.[13] Alcina's comments illustrate the kind of obstacles that the Jesuits constantly had to surmount in order to maintain as high standards as they usually managed to do.

The nature of the impasse is unmistakable. The regulars needed some external supervision of their parish work, but episcopal visitation probably would have destroyed their morale and their discipline as corporate entities.

Among the other mendicant orders there was no prolonged disciplinary crisis comparable to the one that demoralized the Augustinians. Yet the other orders were not entirely blameless. According to Salvador Gómez de Espinosa, a member of the Audiencia, abuses among all the regular orders were sufficiently widespread to arouse serious concern among the civil authorities. In his *Discurso parenético*, published in Manila in 1657, he meticulously documented these abuses in which the Augustinians were the most notable offenders. The book was suppressed and all known copies were destroyed. The reason for this drastic action was political. The author, a respected jurist and trusted bureaucrat, was never accused of publishing false or libelous information, but the Manila authorities feared that the very factualness of the account would provide to Spain's Protestant enemies ammunition with which to ridicule and to discredit the whole Catholic missionary enterprise.[14] Although abuses among all the orders cannot be glossed aside, neither should they be exaggerated. The majority of the religious apparently performed their duties conscientiously. The spectacular vices of the minority ought not to obscure the less dramatic virtues of the majority.

The important question is what effect this type of malfeasance had on the Spanish clergy and their Filipino parishioners. To the latter, sacerdotal celibacy was an innovation of the Spaniards. The pagan priests ordinarily were elderly women or effeminate men, and the average Filipino was probably not shocked at observing any violations of clerical celibacy. There is some evidence to indicate that parents may even have encouraged their daughters to make liaisons with the clergy.[15] Any children born of such a union would probably be well provided for in that a parish priest had potential sources of wealth far in excess of anything to which a Filipino could aspire. The conduct of erring friars, however, scarcely contributed anything to raising the moral tone of society. Such *donjuanismo*, in fact, created another obstacle in the realization of one major goal of the missionary enterprise, namely to make the Filipinos adhere more strictly to standards of premarital chastity and marital fidelity. From the point of view of the Spanish clergy the consequences of clerical laxity were even more serious. Flagrant violations of the monastic vow of chastity obviously set a demoralizing example to the rest of the regular clergy. The result was to diminish corporate morale.

Infractions of the vow of poverty, infractions in which some friars acted like public merchants with goods acquired from their parishioners for little or nothing, may not have provoked bursts of indignation among the Filipinos, who may in fact have thought it fitting that the clergy should profit materially from their elevated station. But here again such mercantile activities on the part of some religious acted as a source of discouragement to the rest of their brethren.

Throughout the Middle Ages the maintenance of ecclesiastical discipline posed a grave problem to the Church. Traditionally the monastic and conventual orders sought to resolve this difficulty by living together in a community. The safeguards and incentives of community life tended to fortify high standards of asceticism. Even so, communal controls were not always effective, as the history of medieval monasticism amply attests. In the Philippines the only effectively organized monasteries were in Manila itself. As we shall observe in greater detail in the following chapter, the vast majority of the religious were scattered in parishes all over the archipelago. In most of the parishes there were usually not more than two priests, and one of them was often travelling around the parish. The Spanish clergy set out to Christianize the Filipinos, but in so doing they ran the danger of "de-christianizing" themselves. Isolated from most social contacts with their own Christian culture and surrounded by temptation created by the power and the prestige of their sacerdotal status, only the strong-willed and the inflexibly dedicated could maintain the high standards of their calling. It was in the nature of things that some should go astray. The unusual fact in these circumstances is that more did not do so.

The clergy recognized the dangers inherent in their cultural isolation. Mid-triennial and triennial chapter meetings provided an opportunity to restore disciplinary fervor by the performance of community spiritual exercises. In their Bisayan missions the Jesuits congregated four times annually for this purpose.[16] Yet most of the time the regulars were isolated culturally and physically in their scattered parishes, and this condition had significant consequences for sacerdotal discipline.

The religious in the Philippines enjoyed a generous amount of autonomy. Unlike their colleagues in Mexico and Peru, they were never subject to episcopal supervision, nor were they ousted from their parishes by the secular clergy. In spite of these favorable circumstances the success of the regulars was limited. The explanation must be sought in the geographic and ethnic character of the Philippines.

# The "Spiritual" Geography
## of the Philippines

If the missionaries were leading protagonists in the story of Spain's efforts to remodel Philippine society, geography was a major antagonist in the drama. A powerful negative factor, geography played a major part in determining what the Spaniards could and could not do. Transoceanic geography determined to a large extent the number of Spanish religious who could be transported to the Philippines. Intra-Philippine geography played an equally significant role in shaping the ultimate effectiveness of the work of the religious.

The principal handicap of the missionary enterprise was the constant shortage of personnel. The number of ecclesiastics administering to the Filipinos varied between 254 and 400 priests. This number was pitifully inadequate. Most of the regular clergy came from Spain. The small Spanish colony in the islands could only supply a few candidates for the priesthood, and they were apt to join the secular clergy occupying the benefices of the cathedral of Manila. The overpopulated monasteries in Mexico could have furnished a substantial number of priests, but the Mexican regulars were predominately creoles, and the bitter dissensions between the creole and Castilian friars among the Philippine Augustinians discouraged the other orders from accepting more than a controllable minority of Mexican creoles in their ranks. Nor did the regular clergy favor the growth of a native Filipino priesthood, as we shall see in Chapter VI. Hence the monasteries in Spain had to provide the distant Philippine missions with the bulk of their personnel.

The fabled Manila Galleon was both the economic and the spiritual life-line of the Spanish colony. The galleons, which plied between Manila and Acapulco, brought the sinews with which to maintain Spanish power in the distant archipelago—silver and friars. Mexican silver was exchanged in Manila for Chinese silks— the trade which spelled either prosperity or ruin for the Spanish colonists. Mexican silver also provided the subsidy, the *situado*, which covered the chronic deficit in the annual budget of the Manila government. The loss of one single galleon spelled ruin for the merchants and bankruptcy for the government. Without the constant reinforcements of clergy, whom the galleons transported, the Spanish commitment to maintain and to spread the Faith in the islands could not be met.

To supply the Philippines by using the route around the tip of Africa was not feasible in the seventeenth century. For one thing, it was Mexico and not Spain which had the surplus silver to export. Spain's silver came from the New World. Secondly, the line of demarcation laid down by Pope Alexander VI and modified in Portugal's favor by the treaty of Tordesillas (1494) established that remarkable partition of the world between the two Iberian nations. The whole of Africa and India belonged to the Portuguese sphere of influence. Spain scrupulously respected this treaty commitment long after it had become outmoded by the colonial expansion into Asia of the Dutch, the English, and the French. Even during the period when the Habsburg kings wore the crowns of both Spain and Portugal (1580–1640), Spain observed the prohibitions of the treaty of Tordesillas. It was not until the late eighteenth century that the Spaniards began to use the Cape of Good Hope route. In the sixteenth and seventeenth centuries the use of the Cape route could not have modified the extreme isolation of the

Philippines from Spain. No matter what route was followed, nothing could have altered the fact that the Philippines were situated at the other end of the world from Spain. Furthermore, the hazards and hardships of navigating the tip of Africa were just as perilous as the trans-Atlantic and the trans-Pacific crossings.

It was a formidable problem in missionary logistics to transport Spanish clergymen from Spain to the Philippines. All the expenses incurred in the voyage as well as a complete clerical wardrobe were provided by the royal treasury, and the deepening bankruptcy overwhelming the Spanish state during the course of the seventeenth century further complicated the task. Although the actual amount of time for the trans-Atlantic and the trans-Pacific crossing was approximately eight months, the journey seldom took less than two years. Long delays at the terminal points of Seville and Acapulco were inevitable. The rigors of oceanic travel, including squalid living conditions breeding epidemic diseases, required that trans–Atlantic arrivals recuperate for at least six months in Mexico before undertaking the perilous crossing from Acapulco to Manila.[1] Death, illness, and discouragement meant that many priests originally assigned to the Philippines never reached their destination. Many remained in Mexico in violation of repeated royal ordinances to the contrary.[2]

Once these missionaries had survived all the hazards involved in reaching the Philippines, the problem was how to keep them in the islands. Nature itself was the first obstacle. The hot and humid climate evidently took a heavy toll among the new arrivals. The roster of invalids was usually numerous. In addition the Philippines seemed to many new arrivals a barren missionary field in contrast to the glittering prize that the ancient and fabled civilizations of China and Japan offered. Many of the early missionaries regarded the Philippines merely as a convenient resting station before setting out for Japan or China. Vigorous measures on the part of the authorities in Manila failed to stop the exodus.[3] What eventually did, within a few decades, was the adamant hostility of the Chinese and Japanese authorities to the spread of Christianity in their lands.[4]

## Villages and Parishes

If isolation from Spain created a serious handicap for the Spanish clergy, the geographical particularism of the islands offered them an equally formidable obstacle. This particularism, which had facilitated the military phase of the conquest, proved a barrier to the consolidation of the "spiritual conquest." How could a few hundred Spanish priests hope to reach 500,000 Filipinos scattered in tiny clusters adjacent to their rice paddies. There was only one feasible means of overcoming this difficulty. The Filipinos must be "congregated" or "reduced," to use the official terminology, into compact villages varying in size between 2,400 and 5,000 people. In Mexico and in Peru the Church and the state had acquired a wealth of experience in resettling the Indians.[5] These lessons could be profitably applied in the Orient. But the problem in the Philippines was even more arduous in view of the greater dispersal of the population. Inspiring the resettlement policies of the Spanish regime in all parts of the Indies was a common set of objectives. It was generally recognized that the natives could not be adequately indoctrinated in the Christian faith, nor could the Spanish program of societal reorganization be implemented or the material resources of the land be efficiently exploited unless the Indians were congregated into large villages.

The decentralization of Philippine society clashed with one tradition deeply rooted in Spanish culture. As the heirs of Greco-Roman urbanism, the Spaniards instinctively identified civilization with the city, whose origins go back to the *polis* of ancient Greece. For the Spaniards, man was not only a rational animal gifted with the capacity to receive grace. He was also a social animal living in communion with his fellow men. It was only through this daily social contact with other men that he might hope to achieve a measure of his potentiality. The Spanish chroniclers endlessly repeated that the Filipinos lived without polity, *sin policía*, and for them that term was a synonym for barbarism.[6]

An ambitious program of resettling the Filipinos into compact villages similar to those already organized in Mexico and in Peru was laid out in the 1580's and 1590's.[7] Progress toward reaching this goal was slow. By the end of the seventeenth century there were not twenty villages in the whole archipelago (excluding the suburban villages of Greater Manila) with a population of over 2,000 people.[8]

The Filipinos tenaciously resisted resettlement. Sentimental ties kept them close to their rice fields. Archbishop García Serrano observed in 1622:

Although it is impossible to deny that the natives would be better instructed and would live in more orderly ways if the small villages [barrios] were to be reduced to the capital [*cabecera* or población], making one or two settlements of each benefice, they consider it such an affliction to leave their little houses where they were born and have been reared, their fields, and their other comforts of life, that it could only be attained with difficulty, and little fruit would result therefrom. Thus has the experience of assembling the people into communities in Nueva España proved, and so has what little of it has been attempted here. However, in the visit that I shall make in this archbishopric, I shall try to reduce them to as few settlements as possible.[9]

In face of native hostility even the clergy, who had the most to benefit from rural resettlement, faltered. Furthermore, the traditional rice economy provided no compelling material inducement to move into the new settlements that the clergy were seeking to organize around the parish churches. The Filipinos were subsistence and not surplus farmers. Their traditional adaption to their environment required that they live adjacent to the land they cultivated. In addition, fishing and hunting were important sources of food, and the transfer to compact villages threatened to destroy the whole ecological balance of existence, a fact which does much to explain the hostility of most Filipinos to the resettlement policy of the Spaniards.

In the Bisayan islands the Moro raids created another obstacle. Several new villages were destroyed by Moro depredations. Bisayans were discouraged from moving into these new communities sponsored by the clergy, since these riparian and coastal villages were exposed to Moro raids. Furthermore, the encomenderos in the Bisayas were often hostile to the regrouping of the population. Resettlement meant that some encomiendas would lose tributes, which were collected on a territorial basis.

Only military coercion could overcome resistance to resettlement, and the Spaniards rarely exerted this kind of compulsion except in cases of extreme provocation. An outstanding example is the case of the Sambals. In 1680, in retaliation against frequent raids by the fierce Sambals on the villages of the fertile and loyally pro-Spanish province of Pampanga, a Spanish expedition of some three hundred soldiers pulled thousands of Sambals from their caves and huts in the mountains. They were resettled in three lowland villages, which some Dominican friars had laid out. The friars hired some neighbors to teach the Sambals the methods of sedentary rice agriculture. The whole project cost the Dominicans 10,000 pesos.[10] The case of the Sambals is unusual. Not all the Filipinos were so fierce that coercion seemed the only alternative. Nor was Spanish military strength so great that compulsion could be employed on a large scale.

Of all the regions in the Philippines the Bisayan islands proved least responsive to resettlement.[11] The Sambal country and the province of Cagayan in northwestern Luzon also lagged. A contributory cause for the unrest in Cagayan during the last years of the sixteenth century was native resistance to resettlement. The Dominicans, who administered the province, were compelled to abandon their ambitious plans to relocate the Ibanag people into large villages.[12] By the end of the eighteenth century the Franciscan parishes in the Camarines and Laguna de Bay were moderately successful examples of resettlement.[13] In the provinces of the central plain of Luzon the Tagalogs were more compactly settled than were peoples of other regions, and they were more subject to Hispanic influences radiating from Manila. Yet by Spanish standards population patterns left much to be desired. In 1768 the energetic *fiscal* of the Audiencia, Francisco de Viana, vainly proposed that the civil authorities, in coöperation with the clergy, undertake a wholesale uprooting of the inhabitants of the populous Tondo province and their resettlement into larger villages.[14]

Since most Filipinos could not be coerced into the new villages, they had to be enticed. And the principal inducement was the colorful ritual of the Church. The Filipinos did flock to the churches for such ceremonial occasions as Holy Week, the feast of Corpus Christi or the patronal fiesta of the locality. They might even build houses near the church, but these were "Sunday houses," vacated as soon as the religious celebrations ended. Many of these communities were intermittent rather than constant, forming and dissolving in response to the performance of certain rituals fixed by the Church. The *cabecera* was the capital of the parish and was designed to be the location of a compact village. Since the Filipinos were reluctant to move into these settlements in large numbers, every parish had a whole series of *visita* chapels. The latter were visited periodically by nonresident clergy whose headquarters were at the *cabecera*.

The *cabecera-visita* complex, whose origins go back to the early missionary enterprise in Mexico, gradually became the prevailing pattern of rural settlement in the Philippines. In 1583 Bishop Salazar could write Philip II: "Your islands are not like Nueva España [Mexico] where there is a chief village and many others subject to it. Here [the Philippines] all are small villages and each one its own head."[15] During the course of the seventeenth century a gradual but remorseless change occurred. The Mexican system, in which a string of subordinate clusters of population were attached to a principal village, took root in the Philippines. No chapels were built in the numerous sitios, which were units of usually not more than ten families. The inhabitants of the sitios attended religious services at the nearest *visita* chapel. The *cabecera-visita* system was a compromise, inadequate in many ways, but the only feasible alternative, given the shortage of ecclesiastical personnel and the scattered distribution of the population.

This compromise was destined to leave an enduring mark on the patterns of rural settlement in the Philippines. The modern pobla-

ción grew out of the early *cabeceras*. Many *cabecera* churches indicated on the 1655 map can be found on a modern map as the location of a población. The prototype of the contemporary rural barrio
can be traced back to the *visita* chapel of the early missionaries. The
change from *cabecera* to población and from *visita* to barrio is
largely a shift from an ecclesiastical to a civil nomenclature.[16]

The *cabeceras* were usually established in the lowlands adjacent
to the coasts and rivers. The *visitas* were apt to be located upvalley
and in the foothills. The area beyond the *visitas* formed a kind of
buffer zone separating the quasi-Hispanized peoples of the maritime lowlands from the pagan Negritos of the mountains. The
people of the buffer zone were only half-Christian. In the late
seventeenth century the regular clergy sought to stabilize the
frontier by founding in these areas what were called *misiones vivas*.
Staffed with small garrisons of soldiers, these "active missions"
provided some kind of defense in depth, protecting the Christian
peoples of the lowlands from raids of the pagan peoples in the
mountains.[17]

The physical layout of the *cabecera* villages usually followed a
gridiron pattern with a central plaza and rectangular street blocks.
Of Greco-Roman origins, the gridiron was revived as the ideal
urban layout by some Italian Renaissance theorists. Adopted
throughout the Spanish empire, the gridiron plan provided a feasible and simple masterplan for the multitude of new communities
founded by the Spaniards.[18] But in the Philippines this layout of
compactly situated houses was a distinct fire hazard, since native
dwellings were wooden frames with bamboo walls and palm tree
roofs. In Mexico, on the other hand, Indian houses made of adobe
were not highly inflammable. In the eighteenth century the wis-
dom of the compact, rectangular plan was questioned in favor of a
more decentralized grouping of houses. One of Governor Raón's
ordinances read: "They [the *alcaldes mayores*] shall not allow any
house to be more than one-half league [approximately one and one
third miles] from a church; and, on the other hand, shall not allow
them to be built so close together than there is danger of fire."[19] A

similar ordinance was issued for the province of Cagayan in 1739.[20] Edicts were probably issued for other provinces. The fire hazard provides a partial explanation for the slogan, seldom used before the eighteenth century, that the Filipinos should be resettled *bajo de campana*, that is, within hearing of the church bells.

These ordinances represent an admission of the failure of the seventeenth-century program of rural resettlement. The Manila government apparently sought a compromise between its traditional objective of bringing the Filipinos into direct contact with Spanish culture, institutionalized in the local church, and the profound unwillingness of the Filipinos to abandon their isolated dwellings. How effective was this modified resettlement program? No satisfactory answer can emerge until the archives for the eighteenth century are carefully studied.

Although the early Spanish town planners fell far short of their goal, their efforts did initiate a gradual transformation of settlement patterns in the direction of concentration in larger villages. The results certainly were not as sweeping as the missionaries wanted, but preconquest decentralization was sufficiently reduced so that Filipinos were brought into some social contact with Hispanic culture.

## Geoethnic Distribution of the Missionary Foundations

Given the triple handicaps of a shortage of ecclesiastical personnel, the scattered distribution of the population, and linguistic diversity, the geographical apportionment of the missionary foundations required careful advance planning; the lack of such foresight, prior to 1594, had led to the abandonment of several missions. But on April 27, 1594, the Council of the Indies in Spain instructed the governor and the bishop to divide up the Philippines into contiguous areas among the four religious orders. The resulting partition rigorously followed geoethnic lines. All the orders received some parishes in the Tagalog country, but the bulk of these parishes went to the Augustinians and the Franciscans, who were strongly entrenched there prior to 1594. A much smaller Tagalog area was given the Jesuits. The Dominicans assumed responsibility for the Chinese community, most of whom lived in the Parian of Manila.

In addition to their extensive holdings in the Tagalog country, the Augustinians received the provinces of Pampanga and Ilokos, the former being one of the most fertile and populous provinces in the archipelago. The Franciscans took charge of Bikol-speaking province of the Camarines. Hence the Augustinians and secondly the Franciscans administered the most populous and best organized parishes in the islands. Dominican territory included the provinces of Pangasinan and Cagayan. The Bisayan islands were divided along linguistic and geographical lines between the Augustinians and the Jesuits. The parishes of the Dominicans and the Jesuits were much less populous and lucrative than were the holdings of the Augustinians and the Franciscans. The Augustinian Recollects, as the last order to arrive in the islands, staffed only a small string of parishes widely scattered over the archipelago.

From the viewpoint of the Crown, this partition contained some disadvantages. A settled royal policy was not to allow any one religious corporation to dominate a large, contiguous, ethnic-territorial area. A notable exception to this policy was the Seven Missions of Paraguay organized by the Jesuits after 1630. The Crown allowed this territorial concentration of power because those missions acted as an effective barrier against further Portuguese penetration from Brazil toward the silver mines of Upper Peru. Standard policy was to build up the power of the episcopacy and the secular clergy and to balance one missionary order against the other in order to create a situation in which the Crown held the ultimate balance of power. The geographical distribution of the Philippine missions violated this principle, but the geoethnic diversity of the archipelago offered no feasible alternative.[21]

The outstanding practical advantage resulting from this partition was that it enabled each order to concentrate its linguistic studies in not more than four different languages. Only thus could the religious hope to train sufficiently competent linguists in the wide variety of Philippine languages, for a maxim of Spanish missionary policy was that converts should be indoctrinated in their own tongues. It was thought that the natives would respond more readily if the Faith were not preached in an alien language.

The four printing presses in the islands published approximately one hundred books during the course of the seventeenth century. Since all the printing presses were operated by the religious orders, the bulk of the Philippine imprints were bilingual catechisms, dictionaries, grammars, and confessionals. In addition to these printed works, many linguistic manuscripts circulated.[22] The linguistic studies of the missionaries were a laborious undertaking, but in many languages the research done was inadequate. Of all the native tongues Tagalog was the most rigorously studied. The Tagalogs were the largest single ethnic group, and these provinces formed the citadel of Spanish power. Bikol studies undertaken by the Franciscans were extensive. But only the minimum was done in the Bisayan tongues and in the other major languages of Luzon (Pampanga, Pangasinan, and Ilokos). Nothing was published in the Ibanag language of Cagayan, although some Ibanag manuscripts circulated in the Dominican convents. Little systematic research was done in the various languages of Mindanao, where effective Spanish control was confined to a few coastal areas.

These linguistic studies were of a utilitarian character. The religious did just enough research to prepare them to discharge their sacerdotal obligations, and in some cases they even fell short of this goal. Yet the majority of the Spanish clergy managed to speak the tongues of their parishioners with fluency sufficient to deliver an occasional "canned" sermon or to hear confessions.[23] How deeply they penetrated the linguistic barrier separating them from their flocks is a moot question. Some religious undoubtedly did, others much less so.

It is apparent that geoethnic factors had much to do with delimiting the impact of Spanish culture on the Filipinos. Isolation and consequent poor communications with Spain prevented the Church from adequately staffing its Philippine missions. Rural decentralization, which the Spaniards could only partially change, gave the Filipinos more freedom in selecting their responses to Hispanization than they would have had if they had been congregated into large, compact villages under the daily supervision of the religious. As we observed in the last chapter, the very effectiveness of the clergy was sometimes vitiated by the cultural isolation in which they spent most of their time. The dispersal of clergy, necessitated by the settlement patterns of their parishioners, sometimes contributed to a relaxation of sacerdotal discipline. Yet the work of the missionaries was not totally ineffective, as subsequent chapters will indicate. What success the religious did achieve may be ascribed in large part to the realistic adjustment they made to the limitations that geoethnic factors imposed on their activity.

### Chapter v

# The Imposition
# of Christianity

Spanish missionaries viewed themselves as soldiers of Christ waging with spiritual weapons a war to overthrow the devil's tyranny over pagan peoples. They envisaged their work as a "spiritual conquest" of the minds and hearts of the natives, a supplement to, and the ultimate justification for, the military conquest. A superb iconographical expression of the Spanish view of the complementary nature of the temporal and the spiritual conquests can be found in Friar Gaspar de San Agustín's chronicle of 1698, a reproduction of which serves as the frontispiece of this book.

Christianity was presented to the infidels not as a more perfect expression of their pagan beliefs but as something entirely new. Any resemblance between the two religions was dismissed as a diabolical conspiracy in which the devil deceived unbelievers by mimicking the rituals and the beliefs of Christianity. The policy of breaking abruptly with the pagan past explains the vigor with which temples and idols were destroyed. The Spanish missionaries have been much criticized for this practice. Yet the religious were not modern archaeologists. In their eyes pagan artifacts were but the visible symbols of the devil's tyrannical dominion, and hence they merited destruction.

In the Philippines there were no temples to demolish. But sacred groves were cut down by zealous Spanish religious who were determined to break the magic sway such groves exercised over the Filipinos. And pagan idols by the thousands were committed to the flames by iconoclastic religious in the presence of bewildered and fascinated Filipinos.[1] The dismantling of outward pagan observances was but the first step in the introduction of Christianity.

## Baptism

In most cases the missionaries were preceded by the encomenderos. The latter were supposed to teach their wards the rudiments of the Christian religion and to build chapels. That most encomenderos poorly performed their quasi-missionary responsibility is abundantly clear. Their principal concern was to pacify their wards in order to collect tribute taxes from them. The religious, fearing that the conquered would be repelled by the religion of the conquerors, often decried the forceful methods with which the encomenderos went about their task. Such fears, although plausible, proved in fact groundless. Actually by their very blood and fire methods the encomenderos rendered a service to the religious by breaking the backbone of native resistance. The indigenous peoples with whom the Spaniards came in contact seldom showed any desire to abandon voluntarily their own religious values. Compulsion of some sort had to be employed. Given their Christian humanitarianism, the clergy usually protested against the use of force; but without coercion, or the threat of it, the natives in many cases would have rejected the appeals of the religious to discard paganism.

Sullen distrust but not armed defiance usually greeted the newly arrived missionary. More than one friar woke up in the morning to a deathly silence only to discover that his would-be flock had stolen away to the mountains during the night. One Augustinian not only had his hut burned but also suffered from attempts to poison his drinking water. In some localities the distrustful inhabitants refused to supply the clergy with the necessities of life.

Wherever the religious met morose distrust, they did not attempt to impose themselves on the elders of the community. What the religious usually requested was that some of the children be committed to their care. The chieftains might shun the monastery for some time, but out of a combination of curiosity and fear they would hand over some of their children to be educated by the religious. Evangelization followed a standard pattern. The children of the chieftains were first indoctrinated, and then the chieftains themselves were persuaded. With the conversion of the leaders of the community, the baptism of their followers came as a matter of course. Although the indoctrination of ex-pagan adults was conscientiously pursued, it was realized that their adjustment to Christianity would be incomplete. Special attention, therefore, was concentrated on the children. The children proved enthusiastic and effective auxiliaries of the religious in winning over the parents to the new religion, reporting clandestine pagan rituals, and in catechizing the older generation.

A substantial aid to the early missionaries in removing the barrier of distrust was the impression which rapidly gained currency among the Filipinos that baptism not only wiped away the sins of the soul but also helped to cure the ailments of the body. The ecclesiastical chronicles are full of accounts of ill people who made "miraculous" recoveries after receiving baptism and cases of converts who "miraculously" avoided catching a local epidemic. Since their pagan cults had stressed the cures of illness, the popular conviction that baptism was corporeally efficacious did much to attract the Filipinos to the new religion.

The missionary enterprise in Mexico provided the Philippine clergy with a wealth of experience upon which to draw. Baptism without benefit of some preliminary instruction was seldom performed in the Philippines except in cases of serious illness. The early Franciscans in Mexico had been sharply criticized for administering baptism without benefit of prior instruction. From this controversy emerged an ideal definition of the content of prebaptismal instruction. Converts were expected to repudiate paganism and to affirm their belief in the efficacy of the sacrament. The marriage of a convert was required to be monogamous. Adult converts were supposed to be able to recite by memory the *Pater Noster*, the *Credo*, the *Ave Maria*, and the Ten Commandments. Finally, some idea of the meaning of the other sacraments and an awareness of the principal obligations of a Catholic (attendance at Mass on Sundays and holydays and mandatory annual confession) were considered desirable baptismal conditions. These standards were not always observed in the Philippines, but they did provide a yardstick which was often enforced.

The missionary enterprise got off to a very slow start between 1565 and 1578. During the first five years there were not more than one hundred baptisms. In 1576 there were only thirteen Augustinian friars, and their baptisms had been confined mostly to children. Linguistic ignorance, paucity of priests, and the missionary interest in China account for this lack of progress. The coming of the Franciscans in 1578 and the arrival of large contingents of Augustinians and Franciscans after 1578 produced a change in the scope and tempo of evangelical operations. The Franciscans were soon followed by the Dominicans and the Jesuits. The decisive decade was the one between 1576 and 1586. During this period the number of missionaries rose from 13 to 94, and by 1594 there were 267 regulars. The number of baptisms rose proportionately to the increase in missionary personnel, as the following approximate figures suggest:[2]

| | | |
|---|---|---|
| 1583................... | 100,000 | baptisms |
| 1586................... | 170,000 | " |
| 1594................... | 286,000 | " |
| 1612................... | 322,400 | " |
| 1622................... | 500,000 | " |

Thus it took some fifty years of intensive missionary activity to lay the foundation of Philippine Christianity.

The sacrament was seldom granted to anyone who expressed strong antipathy to the new religion. According to Catholic doctrine, the efficacy of the sacrament depended upon a sincere act of repentance on the part of the convert. Many indifferent Filipinos probably were, however, swept along in the baptismal current, which flowed swiftly during the 1580's and 1590's. Although there are some examples of obdurate natives refusing baptism, such cases were rare. Most religious held that infidels could be compelled only to listen to the preaching of the gospel. Las Casas rejected even this proposition, but his opinion was shared by few missionaries. No responsible Spaniard argued that pagans could be compelled to believe.

The religious may have respected the ultimately voluntary nature of baptism, but they did exert various forms of individual and social pressure which few Filipinos were able to resist. As one Jesuit observed in 1604: "It seems to me that the road to the conversion of these natives is now smooth and open with the conversion of the chiefs and the majority of the people, for the excuse which they formerly had saying, 'I will become a Christian as soon as the rest do' has now become their incentive toward conversion and they now say, 'We desire to become Christians because all the rest are Christians.' "[3] With the achievement of a Christian majority, serious outward opposition vanished.

## The Catechism

The effectiveness of prebaptismal instruction depended upon subsequent indoctrination in the catechism. The Christian doctrine taught to the Filipinos was dogmatic Catholicism reduced to its essential minimum. The Tagalog-Christian *Doctrina* of 1593, the first book printed in the Philippines, included the following: *Pater Noster*, the *Ave Maria*, the *Credo*, the *Salve Maria*, the fourteen articles of the Faith, the seven sacraments, the seven capital sins, the fourteen works of mercy, the Ten Commandments, the five commandments of the Church and the act of general confession.[4]

The *Doctrina* of 1593 closely followed the Nahuatl catechisms previously compiled for the Mexican Indians. In the seventeenth century, however, the majority of the Philippine *doctrinas* were adaptations or translations of the much used *Dottrina Cristiana*

(1597) edited by the prominent Jesuit theologian, Robert Cardinal Bellarmine. The overwhelming popularity of the Bellarmine catechism in the Philippines is an indication of the success of the Holy See in standardizing catechismal instruction throughout the Catholic world.[5]

The catechisms published in the various Philippine languages were not meant to be distributed to the Filipinos themselves, although they possessed a long tradition of literacy. The high costs of printing and the use of fragile rice paper ruled out the feasibility of instruction by means of written materials. Indoctrination was oral, and the catechisms were for the Spanish clergy, who required accurate translations into heretofore unfamiliar languages of complex doctrinal concepts which medieval theologians had taken centuries to define. In conformity with the policy of deliberate rupture with the pagan past, the key concepts of Christianity were never translated into the Philippine tongues. Lest the converts confuse or identify the Christian with the pagan, such terms were ordinarily left in the Spanish form. Sometimes the Latin term was used.[6]

The religious organized and instructed the first catechismal classes. They were usually held on Sundays in the *cabecera* villages and in the outlying *visitas* at whatever time the itinerant priest happened to be there. In response to the shortage of priests, all the orders devised some system in which the brighter students taught the less advanced. In this method the Spanish religious foreshadowed by three centuries the Lancastrian system of instruction. The Jesuits, for example, cast the prayers, the Creed, and the commandments into Bisayan verse adapted to the traditional planting and rowing chants of the region.[7]

The sons of the chieftains might board for a few years at the parish residence, called the *convento* in the Philippines, where they were given a more intensive training in the doctrine. Reading, writing, and music as well as Spanish were also on the curriculum. In contrast to the practice in Mexico, the Filipinos were seldom taught Latin. The aim of these monastic schools was to train an elite class who could act as intermediaries between the Spaniards and the Filipino masses. Although primary schools were founded by all the orders, the Franciscan institutions were the most effective. Such had previously been the case in Mexico. Primary education flourished from the 1580's onwards, but after the intensification of the Dutch war, from 1609 onward, the quality of instruction fell off noticeably.[8]

During the seventeenth century the burden of organizing and supervising catechismal instruction fell increasingly on the *fiscales*. An important personage in the community, the *fiscal* was more than a sacristan. He was the intermediary between the clergy and their parishioners. Among his other duties were those of organizing the village's patronal fiesta, arranging for the ornamentation of the church, and cajoling if not compelling, his scattered charges to attend Mass and catechismal classes.

The *fiscales* were brought to the Philippines from Mexico, where they were sometimes called *mandones*. The role of the *fiscal* reflects the inalterable conviction of the Spanish clergy that the Filipinos required external disciple to compel them to perform their religious obligations. As one Jesuit observed: "They [the Filipinos] readily receive our religion. Their meager intelligence does not permit them to sound the depths of its mysteries. They also have little care in the fulfillment of their duties to the Christianity which they have adopted; and it is necessary to constrain them by fear of punishment and to govern them like school children."[9]

Informed observers agreed that most Filipinos had memorized, parrot-like, the catechism and the prayers. Reflective missionaries sometimes expressed doubts about the degree of the natives' comprehension. Alcina, for example, was discouraged in the face of his repeated failure to explain to his Bisayan parishioners the meaning of paradise. The brighter ones, he wrote, were willing to grant the plausibility of a heaven for the Spaniards, but they refused to believe that the Bisayans would be allowed to share it with the Spaniards. The Christian notion that worldly differences of race, wealth, and education did not exist in the sight of the Almighty shocked the earthy realism of the Bisayans. For them the inequalities of this world would be perpetuated in the next. Alcina confessed that after sixty years of missionary activity in the Bisayas very few of the converts had acquired a clear comprehension of the basic mysteries of the Catholic creed. Other thoughtful missionaries expressed equally searching doubts.[10]

The degree to which the Filipinos understood the meaning of the doctrine was often in proportion to the density of population. The inhabitants of the maritime provinces of Luzon were settled in larger units and were cared for by a greater number of priests than were those of the Bisayan islands. Hence the former tended to be better indoctrinated than the latter. On Luzon itself the Tagalog provinces, Pampanga and the Camarines, were better instructed than the outlying provinces of Ilokos, Pangasinan, and Cagayan. Natives living nearer the *cabecera* church, where there was a resident priest, usually acquired a firmer grasp of the doctrine than those living in the vicinity of the outlying *visita*, serviced only by an itinerant priest.

Although the methods of indoctrination varied considerably from order to order, these variations were not always exactly reflected in the quality of instruction in particular areas. The Augustinians, for example, were the least effective teachers of the doctrine, a fact which may be ascribed to the prolonged disciplinary crisis in that order. Yet the level of instruction in their Tagalog and Pampangan parishes was not appreciably inferior to that in the parishes administered by the other orders. These Augustinian parishes were some of the most compactly settled in the archipelago. The Augustinian parishes in Ilokos and the Bisayas, however, were probably the worst instructed in the islands, for in addition to the mediocre quality of the clergy there was widespread rural decentralization. Of all the orders the Jesuits had developed the soundest pedagogical methods. Nevertheless, the scattered population of their Bisayan parishes were no more intensively indoctrinated than the Tagalog and Pampangan parishes of the Augustinians. Not more, and often fewer, than thirty itinerant Jesuit priests administered to between 50,000 and 70,000 Bisayans.[11] Where Jesuit pedagogical skill did produce impressive results, however, was in their residences of Antipolo and Silan adjacent to Manila, where there was considerable density of population. The Dominicans in their parishes in Cagayan and in Pangasinan faced the same handicaps of rural decentralization confronting the Jesuits in the Bisayas. Given the obstacles, the sustained zeal of the Dominicans achieved maximum results with the limited means available. Instruction in the Franciscan parishes was of the highest quality in the islands. Not only did the Franciscans retain a respectable degree of discipline among themselves, but also they enjoyed the good fortune of holding a series of populous and compactly organized parishes in the Tagalog and Bikol country. All of which suggests that the level of instruction depended not so much on the quality of the clergy as it did on the density of the population. Given the difficulties involved in maintaining ecclesiastical discipline, and the decentralized character of settlement patterns, catechismal instruction could only meet minimum standards. But this result was remarkable in view of the internal and external obstacles confronting the clergy.

## The Sacraments

By virtue of baptism the Filipinos entered the Church. Instruction in the catechism gave them a modicum of knowledge about the doctrine of their new religion. The reception of three other sacraments was necessary before the Filipinos could become practicing Catholics. They were matrimony (for the married ones), penance, and Holy Eucharist.

Polygamy and the prevalence of divorce among the Filipinos were obstacles to the introduction of the Catholic sacrament of matrimony. Both customs were the prerogatives of chieftains. And both traditions created hindrances to the spread of Christianity in that missionary policy was to concentrate initially on the conversion of the chieftains. Since polygamy was a custom derived from recent Muslim influence in the Bisayas (Samar, Leyte, and Cebu), it was easily liquidated.[12] More formidable, however, was the task of the missionaries to teach the Christian doctrine of the indissolubility of marriage to the members of a society accustomed to the principle of divorce.

The first problem confronting the missionaries was to Christianize those marriages already performed according to pagan usages. Recognizing the existence of natural marriages among the Indians, Pope Paul III in his bull, *Altitudo divini consilii* (1537), declared that the legitimate wife was the first woman that a man had espoused. In case of doubt as to which one was the first, the Indian might chose any one of his wives and be married to her *in facie ecclesiae*.[13] The Holy See's dictum had as one aim to prevent natives from becoming Christians in order to exchange an older wife for a younger one.

The papal solution proved unworkable in the Philippines, and some of its provisions were quietly disregarded. Converts were allowed to chose for a Christian spouse any one of their present or former wives. In practice, this meant the present wife and her children. Hence few Filipinos were compelled to exchange a younger wife for an older one and thus leave the children of the younger wife fatherless and destitute. The Philippine religious flexibly interpreted canonical principles in order to avoid undue economic and emotional hardships on the neophytes.[14] Later on in the seventeenth century, after the majority of Filipinos had become Christian, a more literal interpretation of Paul III's bull prevailed. The right of choice could be exercised only in cases where the first pagan wife had disappeared or had refused baptism.[15]

The penchant of the Filipinos for divorce was a habit not easily suppressed. On occasion they displayed considerable ingenuity in exploiting canon law to gratify their desire for a marital change. In 1621 the archbishop of Manila was plagued by numerous requests for annulments. These petitions bore a suspicious resemblance to one another. They all alleged that the interested parties had had intercourse before marriage with relatives of their wives. The archbishop accused the plaintiffs of intentionally concealing these facts, which canon law recognized as an obstacle, until the husband desired to marry someone else. The archbishop urged the king to request from the Pope a bull giving the Philippine prelates broad powers to grant absolution for this type of impediment in cases where a marriage had already been performed.[16] The monarch instructed his ambassador to the Roman curia to make such a request. Mentrida's manual, published in Manila in 1630, granted parish priests the very authority that the archbishop had requested in 1621.[17]

This episode illustrates the degree to which functional Hispanization had progressed within fifty years of the conquest. These Filipinos were sufficiently Hispanized to attempt to continue inside the framework of canon law the preconquest tradition of easy divorce.

The transition from the pagan marriage pattern to the Christian one was not always smooth. Many marriages violated some principle of canon law. There were cases of baptized natives marrying infidels according to pagan rites, or of a man marrying his widowed step-mother, or of someone else marrying a cousin within the prohibited third degree, without securing a prior dispensation.[18]

The actual sacrament of matrimony did not have to be performed inside the church itself. A priest could marry a couple in the parish residence or in the home of the bride, but the solemnities of the nuptial Mass, followed by the nuptial blessing, could be performed only inside the church, at any time of the year but during the season of Lent. Such services were, however, rare. Some contemporaries blamed the relative infrequency of nuptial Masses on the high fees charged by the clergy.[19] Although such fees were a standard custom throughout Catholic Europe, the Crown sought to delay their introduction into the Indies. It was thought that these fees might discourage the Indians from receiving the sacraments and that the Indians might be confused about the spiritual nature of the sacraments. In 1596 Philip II ordered that no sacramental fees be collected from the Filipinos.[20] These mandates went unheeded. Nor would the regulars abide by a set of tariffs, one drawn up by Bishop Salazar in the 1580's and another by Archbishop Camacho in 1698.[21] As we have already observed in the last chapter, the religious defied episcopal authority with impunity. The Augustinians and the Franciscans, but not the Jesuits and the Dominicans, charged substantial sacramental fees.[22] In short, most Filipino Christians were married in the Church but not inside the churches. Nuptial blessings were for the well-to-do.

The introduction of Catholic matrimony implied certain changes in sexual mores. Some erotic practices, which provoked vehement opposition among the Spaniards, were gradually suppressed.[23] In discussing changes in sexual mores following the conquest, another issue is pertinent. Did the Chinese, who did not settle in the islands until after the arrival of the Spaniards, introduce sodomy to the Filipinos? Although this allegation was made by observers whose testimony on other matters has proved reliable, the evidence they adduce on the question of sodomy is something less than convincing.[24]

Spanish policy was to tolerate many indigenous mores which did not brazenly conflict with basic precepts of Spanish Christian morality. As early as 1599, Tagalog dowry and inheritance practices as codified in Plasencia's study received recognition in the Spanish law courts as customary law in all inter-Filipino litigations.[25] The Spaniards did not object to the pre-Hispanic tradition of the groom providing the dowry, although this custom differed from Spanish usage. The Spaniards did, however, view with hostility the twin customs of bride-gift and bride-price, in which the groom rendered either labor services or a payment to his future father-in-law. To the Spaniards it smacked of fathers selling their daughters, perhaps against the latters' will, to the highest bidder. Although it was the accepted practice in Spain for parents to arrange the marriage of their children, Catholic doctrine insisted that the ultimate decision to marry must be a voluntary act of the couple concerned.[26] Bride-service also aroused the suspicions of the clergy. The engaged couple living under the same roof might have opportunities for premarital sexual relations.

Plasencia's study did not mention bride-service and bride-price. Hence these customs did not come under the protection of the

Spanish law courts. In 1628 a cedula of Philip IV ordered that no Indian in any part of the empire should make a payment or provide free labor services to his future father-in-law.[27] This legislation was not vigorously enforced in the Philippines. At the beginning of the eighteenth century Governor Zabalburu and Archbishop Camacho did in fact launch a campaign to wipe out bride-service and bride-price,[28] but just how successful they were cannot be determined until the manuscript sources for the eighteenth century are examined. For our immediate purposes the important conclusion is that many of the socioeconomic aspects of the marriage pattern in pre-Hispanic society were not materially altered during the first century of Spanish rule.

The spread and the eventual acceptance of the Christian ideal of matrimony among the Filipinos represents one of the most enduring achievements of the Spanish religious. A new standard of premarital and marital morality was set up. Like all such norms, this one was not always observed, but it was a standard destined to exercise continuing influence through the coming centuries.

The next step in the spread of Christianity was the introduction of the sacraments of penance and Holy Eucharist. Penance provided the Church with a potent weapon in the enforcement of moral and ethical standards. Nor could the introduction of this sacrament be long delayed, for all Catholics were required to confess once a year.

This sacrament could not be properly administered unless the clergy acquired a solid linguistic training. There are few references to Filipinos confessing through interpreters, as was sometimes done in Mexico. Hence a characteristic publication of the Philippine presses was the *confessionario*. These confessionaries were bilingual texts designed to aid the priests in asking the pertinent questions and in eliciting truthful answers. The first of these texts was published circa 1610 by the prolific Dominican Tagalist, Francisco de San José. By the end of the seventeenth century similar manuals circulated in several of the major languages of the archipelago.[29]

The shortage of ecclesiastical personnel was always a handicap. In the Jesuit church in Manila, for example, Filipinos had to wait from ten to fifteen days in spite of the formidable array of priests hearing confession.[30] In contrast to the concentration of people in the vicinity of Manila, the dispersal of the population in the provinces posed another set of problems. Three years might elapse before Christians had their confessions heard.[31]

The principle of confession was entirely new to the Filipinos. In their pagan cults there was nothing even remotely analogous to it. Many Filipinos first viewed the sacrament with some misgivings. They had to be persuaded that the confessor would not be angry with them if they recited all their sins.[32] Frequent rotation of regular priests, usually every three years, avoided the awkward situation of someone being compelled or refusing to confess to a priest whom he feared or with whom he had quarreled.[33] Under those circumstances a Filipino was apt to become reticent and thus endanger the validity of that particular confession. The religious scrupulously avoided imposing heavy penances, lest the people's initial distrust of the sacrament harden into opposition. Typical penances were hearing a few Masses, reciting a few Rosaries, or visiting a sick person.[34]

Once accustomed to the idea of confession, the Filipinos took to it with characteristic enthusiasm. Sharp differences of opinion, however, were expressed about whether they understood it. Ribadeneyra, the sanguine spokesman of the first generation of Franciscan missionaries, claimed that the Filipinos usually needed no prodding from their confessors. They came to confession with their consciences well examined. They recited their sins with a clarity based on a firm grasp of the doctrine. The chronicler recounted with zest cases of Filipinos not satisfied with the rigor of the penance assigned.[35] The more sophisticated Jesuit historian, Pedro Murillo Velarde, writing around 1750, was more skeptical than Ribadeneyra. He wearily complained that the inclination of the Filipinos toward quibbling and contradictions created labyrinths which confused even the most experienced confessors.[36]

In order to overcome the Filipinos' fear and embarrassment, the missionaries developed a simple question and answer technique. Brief questions were phrased, and the confessors sought to elicit truthful and succinct answers. Placing no faith in the veracity of their parishioners, and experienced in handling primitive peoples, the confessors asked the same question in a variety of ways. An example of this technique is Fernando Rey's Ilokano confessional. The manual is divided into ten sections, one for each of the Commandments, with a series of simply phrased questions for each section.

Evidently it was in the enforcement of the Sixth Commandment that the religious encountered their greatest difficulties. Intercourse with in-laws and future in-laws, incest according to canon law, seems not to have been uncommon. The Filipinos apparently could not be made to take very literally the prohibitions of the Sixth Commandment, and they sought to conceal such conduct from their confessors.[37] From a canonical point of view such prodding was necessary, for a confession in which some capital sins are deliberately concealed is not valid.[38] What all conscientious religious fought to overcome was the popular conviction that an annual absolution in the confessional gave the Filipinos license to gratify their passions and appetites during the rest of the year.[39] In enforcing standards of premarital chastity, the clergy had more success among the women than the men. The efforts of the religious were sometimes undercut by that minority in their own ranks who openly violated clerical celibacy.

The administration of penance was complemented by the introduction of the sacrament of the Eucharist. In the case of this sacrament the Mexican background must be taken into account. There was a spirited controversy in Mexico about the desirability of allowing the Indians to receive Communion. Many Spanish laymen voiced doubts as to whether the Indians were able to appreciate its spiritual meaning. Some Spanish colonists accused the Indians of being stupid, infamous sinners, and chronic alcoholics. Their understanding of the Christian doctrine was said to be insufficient. The regular clergy, on the other hand, were partisans of a course of action which avoided extremes. They did not refuse the Sacrament to all Indians, and yet the friars would not grant it indiscriminately to everyone. Candidates were carefully screened. The religious were particularly anxious that the candidates know the difference between ordinary and sacramental bread, and between the nonconsecrated and the consecrated Host. Ordinarily, a convert was not allowed to receive Communion until he had been confessing for four or five years. The selective policy of the Mexican friars received vigorous endorsement from Pope Paul III in 1537. Although the Mexican synods of 1539 and 1546 confirmed this course of action, latent opposition continued. As late as 1573 the Augustinian canonist, Pedro de Agurto, found it necessary to publish in Mexico City a treatise whose thesis was the obligation of the Church to grant Communion discriminately to qualified Indians.[40]

This same Pedro de Agurto was presented by Philip II in 1595 as the first Bishop of Cebu. He died in his see in 1608. Two years before that event his Mexican treatise was reprinted in the Philippines.[41] This may not have been a casual circumstance, for the viewpoint expressed in Agurto's work coincided with the policy that the Philippine religious followed. Communion was not refused to all converts, nor was it granted to everyone. The Dominicans defined the course of action of the other missionary orders when, at their chapter meeting held in April of 1592, they resolved to administer the Eucharist "in good time" to those Filipinos "sufficiently well indoctrinated."[42]

The religious sought to impress upon the Filipinos the meaning of the Sacrament, so that they could derive the maximum spiritual benefit from it. It was also hoped that as a result of preliminary preparation desecrations, or the Sacrament's misuse, might be avoided. Incidents recounted in the chronicles about misfortunes befalling natives who received Communion without making a worthy confession had an obvious didactic purpose.[43] Parish priests were admonished not to allow the keys of the tabernacle where the consecrated Host was kept to fall into the hands of any Filipino lest some desecration result. For the same reason the Host was never kept in the *visita* chapels, where there were no resident priests.[44]

There was striking uniformity among the orders in their methods. By the 1590's confession was open to most converts, but only a small minority received Communion, usually during the season of Lent. Only the seriously ill received the Sacrament during the rest of the year. As in Mexico, candidates were screened as to their habits and their knowledge of the catechism. During the week prior to taking Communion, those chosen heard Mass daily. Sometimes the men lived in the monastery during that week, participating in its liturgical exercises, including the midnight matins. Some religious fostered the custom that during the week prior to taking Communion husbands and wives not cohabitate. This act of abstinence, of course, was not obligatory.[45] As the seventeenth century advanced, more and more Filipinos were receiving Communion. With the falling off of missionary enthusiasm, however, the quality of preliminary instruction declined.

The introduction of the Eucharist into the Philippines did not provoke the lively controversy accompanying its previous introduction into Mexico. For that matter the same is true for the sacraments of baptism, matrimony, and penance. Sufficient precedents had already been established in Mexico so that these sacraments could be introduced into the Philippines with only a minimum of dispute.

Not many Filipinos received the sacrament of confirmation, whose administration was an episcopal prerogative. The frequently long vacancies in the suffragan sees, as well as the extensive areas covered by each diocese, made this sacrament an occasional occurrence. In the populous Laguna de Bay district adjacent to Manila no confirmations were administered for a period of twenty-five years.[46] On the islands of Samar and Leyte there were no confirmations for a span of twenty-six years.[47] The regulars were indifferent if not actively hostile to the spread of confirmation. Some bishops had used the administration of confirmation as a preliminary to enforce episcopal visitation.[48] The consequences for the Filipinos were not grave. Theologically, confirmation is a supplement to baptism. As such it is desirable but not essential for participating in the sacramental life of the Church. Much more serious was the fact that few Filipinos received either the sacraments of holy orders or extreme unction, a condition whose ultimate consequences will be examined in the next chapter.

The Christianization of the Philippines falls into three periods. The years between 1565 and 1578 were preparatory and exploratory. There was a scarcity of missionary personnel, and those available were without adequate linguistic training. The decades from 1578 until 1609, after which date the Philippines began to feel the full impact of the Dutch war, were the "golden age" of the missionary enterprise. Fired with apostolic zeal, this generation of missionaries was inspired by a seemingly boundless enthusiasm. A modest program for training a native elite was launched. Once the initial misunderstandings and the economic dislocations provoked by the conquest receded, the Filipinos in the main responded enthusiastically to the appeal of the new religion. The chronicles of the Franciscan, Marcelo de Ribadeneyra (1601), and the Jesuit, Pedro Chirino (1604), eloquently reflect the optimism animating this first generation of missionaries.

Juan de Medina's Augustinian chronicle provides a foil to the accounts of Ribadeneyra and Chirino. Serving in the Philippines from 1610 to 1635, Medina had what we might call a "second generation complex." He suffered from an acute disappointment born of his conviction that the sanguine if somewhat unrealistic hopes of the preceding generation were not materializing. Among the Augustinians the lowering of morale took place as early as the 1590's. In the other orders the falling off of enthusiasm never was as pronounced as it was with the Augustinians, but there was a decline in the seventeenth century.

The general pattern of missionary activity in the islands was similar to what had previously occurred in Mexico. The zeal of the first generation of missionaries gave way to a spirit of apathy, routine, and discouragement. The net result was the same in both regions, but the causes were dissimilar. The decline of missionary morale in Mexico was largely the result of the losing battle the regular clergy were waging with the bishops and the secular clergy.[49] In the Philippines, the falling off of missionary enthusiasm set in as the regular clergy became increasingly aware of the limits of their resources and the magnitude of their task. The crushing burdens of the Dutch war weakened Spanish resolve to push forward the ambitious program of cultural reorganization originally contemplated.

As the seventeenth century wore on, the inadequacies of the missionary effort became increasingly apparent. Three sacraments—confirmation, extreme unction, and holy orders—were of slight importance in the spiritual life of the Filipinos. In the case of penance and the Eucharist only the minimum requirements established by the Church were met. The same situation, we observed, existed for instruction in the catechism. Yet the Filipinos were Christianized in the face of the severe handicaps of a shortage of priests and a dispersed population speaking a bewildering variety of languages.

# The "Philippinization"
# of Spanish Catholicism

Given the disadvantages under which the Spanish clergy had to operate, their efforts would have proved abortive if the Filipinos had not voluntarily responded to some features of Christianity. As it happened, the Filipinos endowed certain aspects of the new religion with a ceremonial and emotional content, a special Filipino flavor which made Catholicism in the archipelago in some respects a unique expression of that universal religion. In this process of "Philippinizing" Catholicism the major role belonged to the Filipinos. They showed themselves remarkedly selective in stressing and de-emphasizing certain features of Spanish Catholicism.

## The Societal and Ritualistic Character of Philippine Christianity

Before the conquest, sacred and profane were often indistinguishable. The pagan religion permeated all phases of life. One of the aims of the Spanish religious was to create a Catholic community consciousness in which the teachings and the spirit of the Church would penetrate into the daily lives of the converts. The religious fostered a series of pious customs to provide daily reminders to their parishioners. The women and the children, for example, were gathered every day at the foot of the large wooden cross erected in the main plaza of each village to chant the Rosary, and in many parishes the children walked through the streets at sunset chanting the Rosary. In other parishes one of the altar boys rang a bell as he walked through the street at sunset, to remind the faithful to say one Our Father and one Hail Mary for the souls in Purgatory.[1] But these measures proved effective only in the *cabecera* villages, where there was a constant community. The majority of the Filipinos lived at some distance from the parish church.

The fiesta system and the founding of sodalities, on the other hand, reached out to embrace the whole scattered population of the parish. Although the majority of Filipinos preferred to live near their rice fields, they could be lured periodically into the *cabecera* village. The enticement was the fiesta. There were three fiestas of consequence to the Filipinos, namely, Holy Week, Corpus Christi, and the feast in honor of the patron saint of the locality. The parishioners flocked to the *cabecera* villages for these occasions. Not only did the fiestas provide a splendid opportunity to indoctrinate the Filipinos by the performance of religious rituals, but they also afforded the participants a welcome holiday from the drudgery of toil. The religious processions, dances, music, and theatrical presentations of the fiestas gave the Filipinos a needed outlet for their natural gregariousness. Sacred and profane blended together.[2]

The periodic visits which the provincial superior was obligated to make to parishes administered by his order were usually the occasion of another elaborate celebration. The visiting superior and his retinue made an *entrée joyeuse* into the *cabecera* village.[3] The European origins of this ceremony, the liturgical prototype for which was Christ's entry into Jerusalem on Palm Sunday, go back to the Middle Ages.[4] It is highly doubtful that the Filipinos were aware of the ceremony's elaborate liturgical symbolism, but they evidently relished the pageantry involved.

The founding of confraternities or sodalities of laymen and laywomen also contributed to the formation of a Christian community consciousness. Here is another example of a medieval Spanish institution which served different ends overseas. In the late Middle Ages confraternities (*cofradias* in Spanish) were voluntary associations whose religious function was the practice of piety and the performance of works of charity. Under the patronage of a particular saint or the Virgin these associations also provided a wide range of mutual aid benefits. Requiem Masses were sponsored for the deceased, their funerals paid for, and their widows and orphans assisted.

Confraternities were founded in many Indian parishes in America whence they were introduced into the Philippines.[5] In the islands the mutual aid benefits, a prominent feature of the institution in Spain, were de-emphasized. The Jesuits skillfully used their sodalities as instruments to consolidate Christianization. The members performed two acts of charity. The first was to visit the sick and the dying to urge them to receive the sacraments and to persuade the infidels to request baptism. The purpose of these visits was to discourage the ill from appealing to clandestine pagan priests for consolation. The other act of charity was for members to attend funerals. The presence of sodality members, it was hoped, might discourage ritual drinking, a custom which the clergy was anxious to suppress.[6]

The Filipinos did not respond to all forms of social indoctrination. The attempt of the Franciscans and the Jesuits to introduce processions of flagellants during the Holy Week ceremonies enjoyed, because of its novelty, some initial success. But since the principle of corporeal mortification was alien to their previous religious traditions, the Filipinos only occasionally showed any sustained enthusiasm for that typical expression of Spanish asceticism.[7] What the Filipinos did accept with gusto were the more sensual and graphic aspects of traditional Spanish observances during Holy Week. Candlelit processions of penitents dressed in hood and gown, large floats depicting scenes from the Passion, the thick

aroma of incense, and noisy music were some of the colorful ex-
ternals of Spanish Catholicism which flourished in a Philippine
setting.

Another act of penitence to which the Franciscans sought to
persuade the Filipinos was to deprive themselves periodically of
their daily bath. Ribadeneyra, the first Franciscan chronicler,
quoted with approval the pious legend that the Apostle, St. James
the Younger, never bathed during his lifetime, but he ruefully admitted that the Filipinos all too infrequently showed signs of
emulating that Apostle's example. No amount of ecclesiastical
eloquence could induce the Filipinos to give up their daily bath
at sunset, which they took for pleasure as well as for bodily
hygiene. In spite of their prejudice against bathing, the clergy had
the good sense not to interfere with this Philippine custom.[8]

Accustomed to the water since infancy, the Filipinos did, however, take enthusiastically to another aspect of Catholicism, that
is, the use of holy water. Their faith in its efficacy was almost
boundless, and their demand for it was insatiable.[9]

It is apparent that one of Catholicism's strongest appeals was
its splendid ritual and its colorful pageantry. In this respect the
Filipino attitude was not substantially different from most other
indigenous peoples of the Spanish empire. But there are special
features to the Filipino response. Singing played a prominent role
in the pre-Hispanic culture, hence the Filipinos proved eager and
talented pupils of liturgical music. They soon acquired proficiency
in singing Gregorian chants. They learned to play European instruments like the flute, the violin, and the flageolet with remarkable skill.[10] The Filipino love of pageantry expressed itself in a
variety of ways, one of which was the popular custom of shooting
off firecrackers as the Host was elevated at Mass.[11]

The pomp and pageantry of the Church's ritual contrast with
the simple edifices in which these ceremonies were ordinarily performed. Only in Manila and its environs were there many elaborate stone churches constructed in the baroque style. In the provinces the majority of the *cabecera* churches and virtually all the

*visita* chapels were plain, wooden structures built according to the principles of the folk architecture of the Filipinos rather than the monumental architecture of the Spaniards.[12] As a protection against the hot and humid climate these churches were built elevated on thick timbers. The walls were made of bamboo, and nipa palm leaves provided the material for the roofing. The unpretentious-ness of these churches apparently did not dampen the enthusiasm of the Filipinos for the colorful rituals of the Church.

The acceptance on the part of the Filipinos of the Catholic ritual pattern had much to do with the eventual suppression of pre-Hispanic ritual drinking. Without being outright hypocrites the Spanish clergy could not oppose moderate drinking as such. Excessive indulgence they could attack as a threat to public morality. What aroused their hostility was that drinking was identified exclusively with the pagan religious observances of be-trothals, weddings, and funerals. The missionaries took vigorous measures to wipe out this custom. One method was to denounce offenders from the pulpit. The culprits were ostracized for a cer-tain period of time.[13] Often less drastic measures sufficed. In order to disentangle betrothals from ritual drinking, the religious fos-tered the custom that the *fiscal* conduct the ceremony in the presence of the two families, without benefit of alcoholic stimulation.[14] The sodalities contributed to the undermining of ritual drinking at the celebration of funeral rites, as we recently observed. Such a tradi-tion could not be suddenly abolished by ecclesiastical fiat, but gradual progress was registered. Ritual drinking survived longest in the less Hispanized regions of the archipelago such as the Bisayas and Cagayan, but even there the custom was on the decline during the second half of the seventeenth century.[15] But the remarkable fact is that ritual drinking was eventually eliminated among the Christianized peoples of the islands. Ceremonial drinking dis-peared after the suppression of the pagan rituals with which, in the minds of the Filipinos, it had come to be identified. The custom withered away as the pagan ritual complex was overwhelmed by the elaborate ceremonies of Spanish Christianity, in which alcoholic stimulation had no necessary function. Thus the acceptance of the Catholic ritual pattern had much to do with making the Filipinos the sober people they remain to this day.

Since Philippine society before the conquest was kinship-oriented, the Catholic custom of ritual coparenthood provided an opportunity which the Filipinos eagerly grasped, namely, to bring kinship relations into the circle of Christianity. According to the Catholic ritual, each person at baptism is required to have two sponsors, a godfather (a *compadre* or *padrino*) and a godmother (*madrina*). Godparents were also required for confirmation, on the assumption that confirmation was a completion of baptism. At weddings, godparents were optional. The notion of sponsorship does not have a Biblical but rather a customary basis, according to canon law. Baptism was traditionally regarded as a spiritual rebirth at which ceremony spiritual, as opposed to natural, parents were considered necessary. Thus a spiritual and mystical relationship was formed between the godparents and the godchild. No marriage, for example, between them was possible.

Some interesting innovations resulted when ritual coparenthood (*compadrazgo*) spread to America and to the Philippines. In contrast to Spain, the tendency overseas was to expand the number of people involved. The "blanketing in" of relatives of the participants was common. The relationship between godparents and parents rather than between godparents and godchildren was stressed, thereby creating a functional relationship between age equals rather than an unbalanced relationship between two generations. In the colonies there were sometimes as many as twenty occasions when godparents were chosen, in contrast to the two obligatory occasions fixed by the Council of Trent. Coparenthood was often extended to include such mundane events as serious illness, the first shave of a youth, or the building of a new house. The trend was to chose godparents from a superior social stratum, for the participants in the relationship were under some moral obligation to aid each other. Ritual coparenthood promoted social stability, especially in regard to interclass and interracial relations.[16]

*Compadrazgo* rapidly spread in the Philippines. Conquistadores and early encomenderos frequently served as godfathers to native chieftains and their relatives. Magellan was Humabon's sponsor.[17] Legazpi was Doña Isabel's godfather. He also served in the same capacity at the baptism of Tupas, and the *Adelantado*'s grandson was the godfather of Tupas' son.[18] During the first generation of missionary activity, the *compadrazgo* served a symbolic purpose, a visible act of reconciliation between the conquerors and the conquered.

The actual spread of *compadrazgo* is exceedingly difficult to trace. The available sources contain very little information on the subject. A tantalizing indication of the rapid spread and the social significance of ritual coparenthood can be found in an ordinance of the Audiencia (May 17, 1599) prohibiting Chinese converts from serving as godparents. The edict accused the Chinese of "having a great number of godchildren, both Christian and infidel, in order to have them ready for any emergency that may arise, and to employ them as false witnesses—to which they lend themselves with great facility, and at little cost—and for other evil purposes and intents, exchanging with them favors and assistance in their affairs. . . ."[19] If more information of this sort were readily available, it would be possible to reconstruct the historical process by which ritual coparenthood blended into or destroyed preconquest kinship relations or created new kinship ties. Since this is not possible with the sources available, *compadrazgo* must be studied in a contemporary setting, with the tools available to the social anthropologist.

## Syncretic Elements in Philippine Christianity

The Filipinos' lack of a solid grasp of Catholic doctrine threatened to cause native Christianity to degenerate into outward ritual formalism. The line between veneration of the saints and idolatry was often crossed, and belief in miracles sometimes provoked a relapse into magic and superstition.

There emerged no one single cult of mass appeal comparable to the celebrated apparition of the Indian Virgin of Guadalupe in Mexico. Although there was no Philippine Virgin of Guadalupe, the Filipinos' belief in miracles was boundless and virtually uncontrollable. Few of these "miracles" received any official recognition from the Church, but such ecclesiastical discouragement did little to dampen the simple faith of the Filipinos in the ever-present powers of the supernatural. And to this day in the rural Philippines an atmosphere of the miraculous and the supernatural permeates popular Catholicism.

The suppression of outward pagan rituals did not entail the abolition of a whole accretion of superstitious customs of pre-Hispanic origin. Rather these folk customs were gradually if only superficially Christianized. Friar Tómas Ortiz's *Práctica del ministerio*, published in Manila in 1731, is an invaluable source for observing the development of this "Christianizing" process. Father Ortiz commented:

. . . the Indians [the Filipinos] very generally believe that the souls of the dead return to their houses the third day after their death in order to visit the people in it, or to be present at the banquet, and consequently, to be present at the ceremony of the *tibao*. They conceal and hide that by saying that they are assembling in the house of the deceased in order to recite the Rosary for him. If they are told to do their praying in the church, they refuse to comply because that is not what they wish to do . . . . They light candles in order to wait for the soul of the deceased. They spread a mat on which they scatter ashes, so that the tracks or footsteps of the souls may be impressed thereupon; and by that means they are able to ascertain whether the soul came or not. They also set a dish of water at the door, so that when the soul enters it may wash its feet there.[20]

One method for apprehending a thief turns out to be a classic example of the coexistence of pagan and Christian elements in which sacred and profane are interwoven. "It is reduced to placing in a *bilao*, sieve or screen some scissors fastened at the point in the shape of the cross of St. Andrew, and in them they hang their rosary. Then they repeat the name of each one of those who are present and who are assembled for this. If, for example, when the name Pedro is mentioned, the *bilao* shakes, they say that Pedro is the thief."[21]

The densely populated spirit world of pre-Hispanic Philippine religion was not swept away by the advent of Christianity. Some Filipino Catholics continued to ask permission from the spirits before doing certain things. The *nonos* had to be propitiated on occasions, such as before taking fruit from a tree or before crossing a river. Added Father Ortiz: "When they are obliged to cut any tree, or not to observe the things or ceremonies which they imagine not to be pleasing to the genii or the *nonos*, they ask pardon of them and excuse themselves to those beings by saying among many other things that the Father [the parish priest] commanded them to do it, and that they are not willingly lacking in respect to the genii, or that they do not willingly oppose their will, etc."[22] Thus did some Filipinos seek to reconcile their pagan superstitions with their Christian beliefs.

Father Ortiz's observations point up the syncretic element in Philippine Christianity during the early Spanish period. It would, however, be rash to postulate a "mixed religion" hypothesis by claiming that the Filipinos worshipped idols behind altars, adopting from Christianity only those elements which harmonized with the preconquest religion. Those preconquest rituals and beliefs which survived the conquest eventually lost their pagan identity and blended into popular or folk Catholicism. With the passing of time this process acquired increasing intensity. In the seventeenth century syncretic elements are often apparent, but in the nineteenth century they are much less so.

Toward the Spanish clergy the Filipinos were capable of showing on occasion a remarkable solidarity, even to the extent of burying, temporarily, personal animosities among themselves. An informal conspiracy of silence operated at times to keep the religious ignorant of the existence of some scandals or the continuance of clandestine pagan rituals. A Filipino who passed on such information to the priest was called a *mabibig*, a Tagalog word meaning informer or spy.[23] If his identity became known, ostracism by his fellow countrymen was apt to be his lot.

Various means of breaking through the conspiracy of silence were devised. One method was for the *fiscales* to keep the religious informed. But the *fiscales* could also be parties to the silent conspiracy. The clergy initially encouraged the writing of anonymous letters. This procedure proved not very helpful; charges made under the cover of anonymity often turned out to be false.[24]

The conspiracy of silence began to lose its effectiveness gradually, as the daily lives and customs of the Filipinos became somewhat more Christianized. The silent conspiracy continued longest in that sphere where Spanish Christianity could offer no satisfactory substitute for traditional pagan observances. Preconquest religion, for example, stressed the causes and cures of illness. Catholicism offered little specific help in this regard. There was no Catholic ritual for curing illness, other than the appeal to prayer. The Church could only provide sacramental consolations to the ill and the dying. But the majority of Filipinos died without receiving the sacraments of penance, Holy Eucharist, and extreme unction. The absence of the Church when death loomed was a salient characteristic of Philippine Christianity. Its causes and its consequences merit some attention.

## The Last Rites

Of all the sacraments that of extreme unction caused the greatest amount of controversy. Basic to an understanding as to how this controversy developed must be an awareness of the fact there were usually less than four hundred priests administering to about 600,000 Filipinos. Furthermore, the majority of the natives did not live in compact villages but in small scattered units near their rice fields. The shortage of clergy and the dispersal of the population were the two basic arguments that the regular clergy invoked to justify their refusal to administer the last sacraments in the dwellings of the Filipinos. They argued that a priest would not be justified in spending, for example, three days traveling to and from a sick person's home located in an inaccessible part of the parish, thereby depriving the remainder of his parishioners of his ministrations. In the early 1680's, Archbishop Pardo vigorously sought to enforce compliance with the canon of the Mexican Council of 1585 which ordained that the last rites be administered in the homes of the dying. That prelate's efforts, however, proved to be fruitless.

In their correspondence with Archbishop Pardo, the provincial superiors contended that they had trained the chieftains and the *fiscales* to bring the sick in hammocks to the *cabecera* church before illness had progressed too far. The provincial superiors concluded that few Filipinos died without the sacraments unless death occurred suddenly, in which case a priest could scarcely be expected to be present.[25] Independent evidence does not corroborate this claim. Not laboring under any such compulsion to rationalize as were the provincial superiors in the controversy with Archbishop Pardo, Alcina candidly admitted to his Jesuit superiors in Rome that seven out of every ten Filipinos died without the sacraments.[26]

The religious were sensitive to the charge that they had abandoned their parishioners on their deathbeds. The vacuum created by the scarcity of priests and the dispersal of the population was eventually, but only partially, filled by the growth of a custom peculiar to the Philippines. Specially trained natives visited the seriously sick and, reciting the Rosary and performing other pious devotions, did bring the ill some spiritual consolation to prepare them for possible death. These visitors were called *magpapahesus*, which in Tagalog means "one who makes another call on Jesus." The genesis of this custom goes back to the seventeenth century, but it was not prevalent then. The religious superiors in their correspondence with Archbishop Pardo did not mention it. It is inconceivable that they would have neglected to do so if this practice had then been customary. Such a makeshift substitute for the last rites certainly would have eased the task of justifying their refusal to administer the last sacraments in the homes.

The *magpapahesus* evidently had a Jesuit origin. One of the duties of the Jesuit sodality members was to visit the seriously ill. This obligation was originally envisaged as a means of destroying the influence of the pagan priests rather than as an imperfect substitute for the last rites.[27] Yet this substitute is precisely what it became in the eighteenth century and afterward, when the religious, sensitive about the accusations made in the Pardo period, felt compelled to do something toward consoling the sick and the dying.

The theological consequences of this neglect of the last rites may have been grave for many Filipinos. According to Catholic doctrine, a person dying in a state of mortal sin is destined for eternal damnation. In view of the fact that Filipinos ordinarily confessed only once a year, it is reasonable to suppose that some of the seriously ill were not in a state of grace. The most certain and direct means of winning grace is through the sacrament of penance. Because of the situation described above, this easier route was closed to most Filipinos. While it is true that even without the benefit of penance a believer can acquire grace by making what the theologians call an act of perfect contrition—an act of sorrow for sin based on the love of God—still, this act is more difficult of accomplishment for most people than is the act of imperfect contrition. The latter is an act of sorrow for sin motivated by fear of divine chastisement.[28] Considering the inadequacy of the average Filipino's doctrinal knowledge, it is certainly permissible to doubt whether many of them were capable of grasping the theological distinction between an imperfect and a perfect act of contrition. But here is where the task of the historian ends and that of the theologian begins. What can be said with certainty is that without the sacraments a believer's chances for salvation are made considerably more difficult but by no means impossible.

The more mundane consequences for the majority of Filipinos were as lamentable as were some of the theological implications. Spanish Christianity provided for the living a splendid liturgy and a colorful ritual which soon captured the imagination of most

Filipinos. The dying and their relatives, on the other hand, were deprived of the ceremonial consolations of their faith. Furthermore, the dead were usually buried without benefit of sacerdotal benediction. The dispersal of the population and the exorbitant fees charged by many priests made this ecclesiastical ceremony a privilege of the relatively wealthy. Burial fees often ranged from fifty pesos to five hundred pesos, varying according to the estimated wealth of the deceased.[29]

## The Question of a Filipino Clergy

Many of the characteristics of Philippine Christianity—outward ritual formalism rather than solid doctrinal knowledge, the tendency toward idolatry, superstition, and magic, the conspiracy of silence, and the infrequency of the sacraments, especially the last rites—are largely explainable in terms of two factors. There were not enough Spanish priests to administer the sacraments and the population was highly dispersed. These conditions enabled the Filipinos to be selective in their response to Christianity and to endow the new religion with a unique emotional and ceremonial content. From the viewpoint of the Spanish clergy, the "Philippinization" of Catholicism departed too often from the norms laid down by the Church. There was only one feasible means of checking this trend, namely to train carefully some Filipinos for the priesthood. Six or eight hundred well-trained Filipino clergymen obviously could have rendered invaluable assistance in consolidating the Church's hold over the people.

In principle, the Church recognized that one of its major responsibilities in a recently converted land was to train a native clergy which in time would be able to assume the administration and propagation of the Faith among their own people. And the Crown, from 1677 onward, urged that steps be prudently taken to train a Filipino clergy. But the Spanish regular clergy adamantly refused to grant ordination to any appreciable number of Filipinos.[30] This hostile attitude of the Spanish regulars rested on a selfish desire to preserve their privileges as well as upon genuine scruples of conscience. A numerous Filipino clergy obviously would have undermined the dominant position of the Spanish regulars. According to the administration of the *Patronato*, title to the parishes was vested in the name of the various orders. The regulars could only be ousted from their benefices by the determined action of the civil authorities. Such a drastic step no governor of the Philippines would undertake, for everyone was aware that the religious were a potent factor in maintaining Spanish hegemony in the provinces. Furthermore, there were no available replacements for the regulars.

The majority of the Spanish regular clergy genuinely believed that the Filipinos were congenitally unfit for the full responsibilities of the sacerdotal state. Friar Gaspar de San Agustín voiced the sentiments of many of his brethren when he wrote:

Rather, their [the Filipinos'] pride will be aggravated with their elevation to so sublime a state [the priesthood]; their avarice with the increased opportunity of preying on others, their sloth with their no longer having to work for a living; their vanity with the adulation that they must needs seek, desiring to be served by those whom in another state of life they would have to respect and obey . . . . For the *indio* [a native-born Filipino] who seeks holy orders does so not because he has a call to a more perfect state of life, but because of the great and almost infinite advantages which accrue to him along with the new state of life he chooses. How much better to be a Reverend Father than to be a yeoman or a sexton! What a difference between paying tribute and being paid a stipend! Between being drafted to cut timber [for the shipyards] and being waited on hand and foot! Between rowing a galley and riding in one! All of which does not apply to a Spaniard, who by becoming a cleric deprives himself of the opportunity of becoming a mayor, a captain or a general, together with many of the comforts of his native land, where his estate has more to offer than the whole nation of *indios*. Imagine the airs with which such a one will extend his hand to be kissed! What an incubus upon the people shall his father be, and his mother, his sisters, his female cousins, when they shall have become great ladies overnight, while their betters are still pounding the rice for their supper! For if the *indio* is insolent and insufferable with little or no excuse, what will he be when elevated to so high a station? . . . What reverence will the *indios* themselves have for such a priest, when they see he is of their color and race? Especially when they realize that they are the equals or betters, perhaps of one who managed to get himself ordained, when his proper station in life should have been that of a convict or a slave.[31]

An enlightened Spanish Jesuit, Juan Delgado, answered these declamations with wit and skill. Delgado's apologia for the Filipinos is permeated with the atmosphere of the Age of Reason. Like his contemporary, Montesquieu, Delgado stressed that the character of men is molded in large measure by their environment. Men do not inherit vices and errors but acquire them from experience. Hence such defects are susceptible to rational correction. After urbanely demolishing Gaspar de San Agustín's dismal characterology, Delgado concluded that whatever vices and defects the Filipinos might possess had an environmental rather than a congenital origin. Give some Filipinos a sound and well-supervised education and a conscientious and well-trained native clergy would emerge, according to him.[32]

Delgado's reasoned defense of the Filipinos was not shared by the majority of the Spanish religious. In the eighteenth century pressure from the Crown and the growth of the population compelled the regulars to use some native priests. Filipinos were not admitted into the regular orders, but some received training as secular priests in seminaries operated by the regulars. The Filipino priesthood, who numbered 142 in 1750, were trained to fill only subordinate positions as secular coadjutors to the religious.[33] These Filipino clergymen did a great deal of the laborious work of the parish, but they were denied the emoluments and the prestige of heading a parish. The regulars, believing the Filipinos were fit only for subordinate positions, gave them only a minimum of training.

The growth of a native clergy sustained a severe reverse during the administration of Archbishop Basilio Sancho de Santa Justa y Rufina, who arrived in Manila in 1767. In his attempt to enforce episcopal visitation, the archbishop ousted many of the religious orders from their parishes. He replaced them with Filipino priests. He also had to fill the parishes of the Jesuits, left vacant by the expulsion of the Society from the Spanish dominions in 1767. Poorly trained and half-educated, the Filipino clergymen rendered a deplorable account of themselves. Manila wits quipped "that there were no oarsmen to be found for the coastal vessels, because the archbishop had ordained them all."[34] The most lurid fears of Gaspar de San Agustín seemed to come to pass when these semi-illiterate priests were suddenly put into positions of authority which their lack of sound training did not qualify them to fill. The result of the fiasco was a restoration of the old order. The Spanish religious returned to their parishes, with Filipino priests merely serving as assistants.

In the eighteenth century the Spanish clergy rationalized that the Filipinos were temperamentally unfit for the full responsibilities of the priesthood. The justification for the perpetuation of the system in the nineteenth century was a political consideration. In the face of rising Filipino nationalism aiming at independence, Filipino priests were regarded as potentially if not actively disloyal. The task which the Spanish clergy should have undertaken was not begun until after 1898. Under the American regime, church and state were separated. This change paved the way for undertaking that arduous task of training a competent Filipino clergy, an enterprise supervised by the Catholic hierarchy of the United States.

The Spanish missionaries were not unmindful of the universal character of their own religion, a universality based on the premise that all men are created equal in the image of God, endowed with a common origin and with a common end. It was in the service of this ideal that the religious went to the Philippines in the first place. Nor did the Spanish clergy believe that God spoke only in Spanish. They preached the gospel in many Philippine languages. But Catholic equalitarianism and universalism were essentially other-worldly. All men were created equal in the sight of God but certainly not in the sight of their fellow men. This-worldly inequalities in wealth, status, and intelligence were justified as a necessary consequence of man's imperfect and sinful nature. In the Middle Ages the concept of social inequalities was applied to individuals but not to whole races as such. So it was with Thomas Aquinas, for example. Dante, both one of the last exponents of medieval universalism and one of the first spokesmen of modern statism and imperialism, extended the concept of social inequalities from individuals to races and nations by setting up a hierarchy of races, with Rome at the top of the pyramid. The Spanish humanist, Sepúlveda, molded this Dantesque argument into a justification for Spanish imperialism overseas—the Spanish race was congenitally superior and the Indians congenitally inferior.[35] This idea became a characteristic feature of the colonial mentality. Few Spanish religious in the Philippines could discard this colonialist notion that subject peoples were congenitally inferior. In deliberately stunting the growth of a Filipino clergy, they allowed their Spanish ethnocentricism to override the universal spirit of their creed.

The consequences for the character of Philippine Christianity were momentous. A well-trained Filipino clergy could have done a great deal to root out superstitions, to promote a firmer grasp of the doctrine, and to administer the sacraments with much greater frequency. As it was, there were virtually two religions. One was the Catholicism of the Spanish clergy and the Spanish colonists, and the other was the folk Catholicism of the Filipinos, a cleavage which was sharply delineated along racial and linguistic lines. A numerous Filipino clergy certainly could have done something to bridge the gap between these two expressions of Christianity. The Spanish clergy paid a heavy price for opposing the growth of a Filipino clergy. A trend toward "Philippinization" set in over which the Spanish clergy had little or no control.

If "Philippinization" was unfortunate from a Spanish and Catholic viewpoint, it had much to recommend it in a strictly Filipino context. It meant that the Filipinos absorbed as much Catholicism as they could easily digest under prevailing conditions but not as much as the Spaniards would have wanted them to do. That limited portion of Catholicism which the Filipinos did digest became an integral part of their way of life, and they found in the Church a new sense of human dignity. Catholicism forged powerful bonds of social unity, thereby creating a much needed cushion against the severe economic stresses and strains whose exact character will be discussed in subsequent chapters.

# LAND,
# POLITICS,
# AND
# SOCIETY

# Exploitation
# of Labor

In the Philippines, Christianization exerted an unusual influence over the political and economic developments of the colony. The Spanish were not unique among colonialists in their desire to exploit their conquered territories and peoples. But one should not overlook the fact that with the Spanish this desire was accompanied by a strong, if occasionally truculent, religious idealism. They genuinely believed that in bringing Christianity to the natives of the New World and the Philippines they were performing the ultimate service possible for one people to render another. The fact that the Spanish clergy on many occasions exploited their parishioners for materialistic ends, as has already been abundantly demonstrated, does not alter the ideal. And this religious idealism paid practical dividends. Christianization acted as a powerful instrument of societal control over the conquered people. While this spiritual ideal operated in all of the Spanish colonies, in the Philippines it was exaggerated because of the relative poorness of the archipelago's economy.

The maintenance of the Spanish regime in the Philippines was, in fact, a fiscal nightmare. The colony annually produced a substantial deficit, which was in turn met by the treasury of the much richer viceroyalty of Mexico. Although colonization had originally been inspired in part by grandiose commercial ambitions of exploiting the riches of the Orient, the hostility of the Dutch, the Japanese, and the Chinese eventually made a mockery of those dreams. Nonetheless, Spain did remain in the financially insolvent colony, a fact which is largely attributable to pressure exerted by the Church and which indicates the importance of altruistic motives in the actions of the Spanish government.

But imperialism, whatever the motive, is expensive, and it is inevitable that the price will fall upon the conquered themselves. Two irrevocable commitments of the Spanish colonial policy were first, that the natives, as "new Christians," merited some effective guarantees of their property rights and of the liberty of their persons, and second, that colonizing, based upon the exploitation of native labor, had to be made profitable for the Spanish colonists. The Crown seldom abandoned its restless attempt to reconcile these two aims. The purpose of this chapter and the next is to examine the nature of these Spanish economic and political experiments in the archipelago and to assess their immediate and more permanent consequences on the development of Filipino society.

The Spanish resorted to a wide variety of alternatives. Refusing to sanction the outright enslavement of the indigenous population, the Crown nevertheless did insist that the natives be made to work for the Spaniards. During the early years of the conquest the Spanish colonists enslaved some Filipinos, invoking a variety of legalistic pretexts. Bishop Salazar's Tondo Council (1581), legislation of Philip II, and a brief of Pope Gregory XIV (1591) provided for the immediate emancipation of all Filipinos enslaved by the Spaniards and for rigorous penalties against further enslavements. Henceforth Filipinos who accepted Spanish authority were effectively protected against enslavement. Those infidels who were actively hostile to the Spaniards (namely the Moros and the Negritos) were subject to enslavement, but they were too few in number to provide any appreciable source of cheap labor.[1]

## The Encomienda

The first workable compromise to emerge was the encomienda-tribute system. Originating in the Antilles, it spread to Mexico and to Peru and finally to the Philippines. This yearly tribute collected from the Indians in labor services, goods, or specie was justified on juridical grounds as a concrete recognition of Castilian sovereignty and an acknowledgment of the temporal and spiritual services rendered by the Spanish administration. Its economic justification was the need of the Spanish colonists to gain access to a supply of cheap labor. Encomenderos were supposed to protect their wards and to prepare them for baptism. All adult males between the ages of eighteen and sixty paid the tribute. Native chieftains and their eldest sons were exempt.

The *Adelantado* Legazpi soon apportioned the whole Filipino population into encomiendas. A third of the population was reserved for the Crown encomiendas. The alleged abuses of the early encomienda in the Philippines were the same catalogue of complaints that previously had come out of Mexico. Tributes far exceeded the official tariff, set at one peso (ten reales) in 1589. The tribute rolls were seldom kept up to date, with the result that sons often had to pay the tax on a dead father. The encomenderos were collecting their tribute with blood and fire methods without providing their wards with any of the protective services established by law. The agents of the encomenderos were harsh and brutal. Native chieftains, who frequently acted as tribute collectors, were a scourge. Many encomenderos compelled their wards to pay tribute in a scarce commodity, which goods the encomendero then resold at a handsome profit.[2]

What made the encomienda especially lucrative was that encomenderos sometimes collected their tribute in the form of labor services. During the 1570's and the 1580's the regular clergy articulately exposed the prevalence of these flagrant violations of the law. The virulence of the conflict between the churchmen and the encomenderos must be understood as a consequence of the severe economic crisis through which the new colony was struggling to stability. The consolidation of the Sino-Philippine trade, in which Mexican silver was exchanged for Chinese silks, and the gradual expansion of rice production did much to alleviate pressure on the Filipinos. This lucrative commerce with the Chinese merchants kept most of the Spaniards in the Manila area. These city-loving people lacked any pressing incentive to settle in the provinces and to carve out for themselves large landed estates operated by servile labor.

The principal abuse of the encomienda was remedied in 1595, when the Audiencia in Manila drew up a computation of payments (a *tasación*). Tribute henceforth was paid both in specie and in kind but with products which were ordinarily plentiful in each province. A junta convoked by Governor Acuña revised the *tasación* in 1604. In the provinces, encomenderos collected four reales in kind, one fowl, and the remaining six reales were payable in specie.[3] Evident is the influence of the clergy, who favored a monetary tribute because such an arrangement restricted the opportunities for extralegal exactions by the encomenderos.

The Acuña formula produced a result similar to what occurred in Mexico after the enforcement of the New Laws during the 1550's and 1560's. The encomienda was "tamed," to use Lesley B. Simpson's phrase.[4] It soon became a relatively light burden on the Filipinos, an annual head tax. The private encomienda could have been easily liquidated, but this step was not taken immediately, for its continuance provided the Crown with a cheap means of pensioning military personnel. There never was a dearth of pension-seeking soldiers in the islands. The Philippine encomenderos as well as their colleagues on the mainland repeatedly requested that succession be made perpetually hereditary. The Crown steadily rejected the request. Originally encomiendas in the islands could be inherited by two successive heirs, and after 1636 by three, before they reverted to the Crown for redistribution.[5] These rules of succession were usually violated in the Philippines by a variety of subterfuges.[6]

Since the private encomienda was ceasing to provide a sufficient

source of pensions for the military, the Crown set about to liquidate it, gradually and painlessly. The following statistics are revealing:

| Private Encomiendas | | Crown Encomiendas | |
|---|---|---|---|
| 1608 | 94,310 | | 32,395½ |
| 1621 | 97,422 | | 33,516 |
| 1655 | 61,308 | | 46,968½ |
| 1686 | 35,000 | | 86,000 |
| 1742 | 18,041¼ | | 165,773 |
| 1766 | 18,196¼ | | 160,775[7] |

The exact date of the abolition of the private encomienda is
not certain, but its decline began between 1621 and 1655. The
death knell was sounded in the cedula of September 17, 1721,
which provided that as encomiendas fell vacant they were to re-
vert to the Crown and were not to be reassigned to private persons or to charitable corporations.[8] The cedula was not always
observed, for as late as 1789 the governor granted an encomienda
to the hospital of San Juan de Dios in Manila for a period of four
years.[9] Although the private encomienda withered away during
the eighteenth century, the tribute tax now collected by the
Crown lasted as long as the Spanish regime. In 1874 the tribute
was fourteen reales, only four reales above the tariff established
in 1589.[10]

In both Mexico and the Philippines the Crown sought to fill
the vacuum created by the liquidation of the private encomienda
with free, paid labor. In the islands this development occurred
only in metropolitan Manila, whose suburbs contained some 20,000
Filipinos. They were paid wage earners who performed domestic
and manual labor for the Spanish residents of the walled city and
the Chinese residents of the Parian. Unlike the Indians in Mexico
City, the Filipinos did not produce a numerous class of craftsmen.
The skilled trades soon came to be a monopoly of the Chinese.
Filipinos in the Manila area did engage in petty retail operations,
but the more lucrative aspects of this trade were controlled by the
Chinese.

The Manila suburbs also had to provide gratis domestic service for the convents of the five religious orders. Each order maintained in the capital a large conventual establishment which served as an administrative headquarters, an infirmary, and a receiving station for arrivals and departures on the Manila Galleon. At its triennial chapter meetings, the Augustinian convent, for example, was temporarily staffed with 300 domestics.[11] Each of the convents had the exclusive use of the labor services of one of the suburban villages.

Although these domestics received no salaries, their obligations to the convent were not onerous. For one thing, they only had to work periodically. Furthermore, all these villages enjoyed the highly desirable privilege of being exempt from draft labor service. Most of the time they were able to offer their labor services for hire in a free market. They produced very little of the food they consumed, except by the raising of some fowl. An indication of their status as wage earners is the fact that metropolitan Filipinos paid their tribute in the form of nine reales in specie and one fowl. This concentrated population was attacked on occasion for being unproductive and parasitical. Commented one zealous bureaucrat: "These settlements have become dens of thieves and vagabonds, and of hucksters and retailers who buy provisions at wholesale for their retail trade, and hence their cost; and they commit many offenses against God."[12] He suggested that the metropolitan villages be disbanded and their inhabitants be sent back to the rice paddies in the provinces. The Filipinos of Manila in reality were no more parasitical than the metropolis itself, which never carried its own weight economically, living off the resources of the provinces. The Filipinos of Manila were an outstanding example of functional Hispanization in the economic sphere. They were urbanized wage earners.

In the provinces no such functional Hispanization occurred. There no numerous class of wage earners emerged. The Filipinos continued to engage in agriculture as in pre-Hispanic times under a complex system of debt peonage and sharecropping.

## The *Polo* and the *Vandala*

The relative economic equilibrium attained after the mid–1580's was shattered by the impact of the Hispano-Dutch war, which produced a severe strain on the Philippine economy between 1609 and 1648. The defense of the Philippines could not have succeeded if the government in Manila had not ruthlessly exploited the material and human resources of the islands. Since the conflict was essentially a naval war, the harshest burdens placed on Filipino labor were as woodcutters, shipbuilders, crewmen, and munitions makers.[13] Draft labor was recruited through a system known as the *polo*. Although draft labor existed in the Philippines in some form as early as 1580, its character changed radically after the coming of the Dutch war. The Philippine *polo* was modeled after the Mexican *repartimiento*.[14] All men in the community with the exception of chieftains and their eldest sons were obligated to serve periodically in the labor pool, but richer Filipinos could purchase exemption by buying a substitute for six or seven pesos.[15] *Polo* laborers seldom received even their token wages. The treasury soon fell into arrears. What kept *polo* workers alive was a monthly stipend of four pesos worth of rice provided by the village treasuries. The villages in turn levied a small annual assessment on their inhabitants for this purpose.[16]

The government did attempt to set up some safeguards to protect the interests of *polo* labor. Filipinos could not be drafted for private enterprises or for public works of a nonmilitary sort. Draft labor was not to be used when voluntary Chinese labor was available. Nor were Filipinos to be transported long distances or to different climates. Shipbuilding schedules were to be arranged so that labor drafts would not be necessary during the planting and the harvesting seasons. These humanitarian intentions of the Crown proved a dead letter in the face of the relentless exigencies created by war conditions. Working conditions for *polo* labor were usually appalling.

Perhaps more oppressive than the *polo* was the *vandala*. Meaning "purchase" in Tagalog, the *vandala* was the compulsory sale of products to the government.[17] Manila assigned an annual quota to each province, and the *alcaldes mayores* distributed this quota among the villages in their provinces.[18] In the poblaciónes and barrios the chieftains were held responsible for collecting the quotas. Since the hard-pressed treasury was in no position to pay, only periodically making token payments and generously distributing promissory notes, the *vandala* became in reality an extralegal form of taxation—and a burdensome one at that. Between 1610 and 1616 the treasury owed the Filipinos some 300,000 pesos.[19] By 1619 the sum had climbed to 1,000,000 pesos.[20] These sums include both labor services and enforced sale of goods. Although it is not possible to break down the figures between the *polo* and the *vandala*, the latter bulked much larger than the former in view of the nominal wages paid to *polo* workers.

Of all the provinces, Pampanga suffered the most acutely from the *vandala* and the *polo*. Adjacent to Manila, the products of its fertile rice fields and its excellent timber were in constant demand. Between 1610 and 1616 the treasury had accumulated a debt of some 70,000 pesos to the Pampangans. That figure had risen to 200,000 pesos by 1660, when the province was inflamed by revolt.[21] The Tagalog provinces also suffered acutely from the demands of the war effort. The resources of the Bisayan islands were not as densely exploited as were those of central Luzon. Yet the Bisayan area also sustained severe and continuous damage from the depredations of the Moros, as we shall see in Chapter X.

The demographic consequences issuing from the economic crisis provoked by the Hispano-Dutch conflict were not insignificant, as the following statistics of the total population under Spanish control indicate:

| | |
|---|---|
| 1606 | 580,820 |
| 1621 | 610,918 |
| 1655 | 505,250 |
| 1686 | 600,000 (rough estimate) |
| 1766 | 720,000[22] |

These figures come from the tribute rolls. In order to arrive at the total population, approximately one sixth must be added to the tribute statistics to cover the numerous statutory exemptions (*cabezas de barangay*, their eldest sons, elected officeholders, cantors, *fiscales*, etc.). One should use these tribute statistics with caution, but they do indicate a trend. Between 1621 and 1655 the Filipino population under Spanish control declined noticeably but not disastrously. An approximate loss of 35,222 male workers occurred out of a total population decline of some 105,688 persons. That the *polo* and the *vandala* took a heavy toll in lives is apparent. Filipinos, however, did have the alternative of fleeing to the pagan country in the mountains. Although the actual number of such fugitives cannot be determined, this practice was evidently not uncommon.[23] Such occurrences may partially, but not completely, account for the decline in the tribute rolls.

That the royal treasury had only a fraction of the funds it required to meet the mounting expenses of the war was due in part to the precipitous decline in the volume of the Manila-Acapulco trade. The prosperity of the Spanish colonists and the solvency of the treasury depended upon the safe arrival of the galleons in Manila and in Acapulco. A chain of calamities drove the treasury to the brink of bankruptcy. In 1636 no ships were dispatched from Manila to Mexico. The galleon, *Concepción*, en route to Manila was lost in the Ladrones in 1638. The Dutch in 1640 intercepted a large part of the Chinese junk fleet headed for Manila. Bad weather compelled one of the outgoing galleons to return to Manila in 1643. In 1645 the loss of the incoming galleon off the coast of Cagayan only compounded the tragedy of the disastrous earthquake of San Andrés, which reduced the proud and magnificent city of Manila to a pile of ashes and rubble. No ships came from Mexico in 1647, 1648, and 1652; and in 1654, 1655, and 1657 four galleons were lost.

The Dutch war was primarily responsible for the severe strains put on the Filipino population, and the string of calamities interfering with the galleon trade only aggravated an already desperate situation. After the treaty of Münster, which ended the Dutch

threat, and a run of better luck in the galleon trade, a gradual relaxation of the pressure on the natives resulted during the second
half of the seventeenth century. An official recognition of this improvement occurred in 1657, when the annual assessment paid by
all Filipinos to their village treasuries to provide rice for *polo*
workers was abolished.[24] Throughout this period there remained,
of course, the ever-present problem of Moro depredations. Nonetheless, the upward movement in the population curve after the
1650's substantiates the fact of gradual amelioration.

## Ecclesiastical Exploitation

As champions of native rights, the regular clergy were acutely
aware of the crushing impact of the *polo* and the *vandala* on the
Filipinos. Yet they seldom recommended the system's abolition.
They concentrated on mitigating some of its worst abuses, and
this was done in temperate language. Such an attitude on the part
of the religious in the Philippines contrasts sharply with that ot
their brethren in Mexico. The latter flayed the Mexican *repartimiento* in caustic language reminiscent of Las Casas' earlier denunci-
ations of the encomienda.[25] The religious in the archipelago realisti-
cally if unhappily recognized that the preservation of the Philippines as a bastion of Catholicism against the threat of conquest
from the Protestant Dutch entailed some substantial degree of exploitation of native labor. The very future of the missionary enterprise itself was linked to the success of the defense effort against
the Dutch.[26] In Mexico, on the other hand, there was no external
threat of conquest by a Protestant power. Furthermore, the Mexican economic crisis was of a more severe character than its Philippine counterpart, as we shall see in the next chapter. Hence the
mendicant orders in Mexico could not view the missionary enterprise and the exploitation of native labor as interdependent.

Although the clergy in the Philippines sought to place some
restraints on the civil power's exploitation of native labor, the
Church's record in this regard was not always blameless. Some
Augustinians, for example, showed an acquisitive instinct far at

variance with their monastic vow of poverty. They either cajoled their parishioners into selling products for a fraction of their true value, or they exercised undue pressure in extracting alms. Considerable quantities of rice, wax, and cloth were resold by the friars in a private and not a corporate capacity in the Manila market and abroad at substantial profits. The most notorious of these "clerical merchants," Friar Lorenzo de León, whose career was chronicled in Chapter III, was deposed as provincial superior by the Augustinians in 1607. While these practices cannot be glossed aside, neither should they be exaggerated. Only a minority of the clergy engaged in this type of flagrant exploitation. Actually the civil authorities in the provinces, the *alcaldes mayores* and their deputies, indulged in retail operations with the illegally acquired products of the natives on a much larger scale than did the clergy.[27]

The fact remains that most of the material burden for supporting the religious establishment in the islands fell on the Filipinos, the Crown assuming only the expense of the costly operation of transporting the clergy from Spain to the Philippines. Two reales of the tribute went to defray the stipend of 100 pesos and 100 bushels of rice paid to parish priests for every 500 families under their care.[28] Every community was required to furnish rowers and porters gratis to the clergy. Manual labor for the construction of ecclesiastical buildings had to be provided without payment.[29] Only the Dominicans and the Jesuits did not charge fees for the administration of the sacraments. The other orders collected fees which were considered excessive by the civil and the episcopal authorities. Periodic attempts of the latter to regulate the use of native services were not very effective. Customs such as the clergy requiring their parishioners to furnish rice, fish, and domestic service gratis were among the practices which came under attack.[30]

As a consequence of the prolonged war emergency, the *vandala* and the *polo* exacted a crushing toll from the Filipinos in goods, labor, and lives. The demands of the Church, some legitimate and others extralegal, as well as the impositions of the *alcaldes mayores*, added to the already heavy load. That the Filipinos managed to survive this "time of troubles" can be explained principally by the evolutionary character of the economic and ecological changes which transformed Philippine agriculture during the course of the seventeenth century.

# Ecological and Economic
# Consequences of the Conquest

A number of factors explain how the Filipinos managed to survive
those decades of strain and stress of the Hispano-Dutch war.
Underlying all these factors, however, is the comparative mildness
and the gradualness of the ecological and demographic changes
issuing from the conquest. In this fundamental respect the postconquest situation in the Philippines differs markedly from that in
sixteenth-century Mexico. The initial Spanish impact on the
Philippines was unquestionably less painful than on Mexico. The
conquest of the islands was relatively pacific. Few belligerents
were killed in military and postmilitary operations, a fact which
contrasts with the massive loss of life in the conquest of Mexico.
In addition, the Spaniards were never attracted to the Philippines
in such numbers as they were to Mexico. There was of course the
obstacle of distance, but there was also the absence of mining and
hence of the prospect of quick and spectacular wealth.

No mining industry developed in the islands. The mining of
precious metals on a massive scale would have caused an intensive
economic revolution, as it did in Mexico. There were precious
metals in the Philippines, but they were not discovered and

systematically exploited until the twentieth century. Had these mines been developed in the sixteenth or in the seventeenth centuries, Spanish colonization might have assumed a fundamentally different character. As it happened, the small Spanish colony largely consisted of merchants, civil bureaucrats, soldiers, and the clergy, for these activities corresponded to the only vested interests of Spain in the islands. Metallic wealth, on the other hand, would have attracted thousands of Spanish colonists. Vast numbers of Filipinos would have been conscripted to operate the mines, which in Mexico was one of the most grueling forms of exploitation the Indians had to endure. Thus the absence of mining in the Philippines intensified the evolutionary character of the transition from the preconquest to the Hispanic periods.

An increased Spanish population in the islands as the result of a mining industry might also have caused miscegenation on a large scale, and the Philippines might have become a mestizo nation, as did Mexico. *Mestizaje* was ordinarily confined to the Manila area, for few Spaniards except the clergy and a handful of bureaucrats settled in the provinces. Even in the capital Filipino women were more often the mistresses than the wives of Spaniards. In those days mestizo and illegitimate were synonymous terms.[1] In addition to informal unions between Spaniards and Filipinos, there were also various mixtures resulting from miscegenation with the Chinese community in the capital.

Spaniards preferred to marry their own kind, for marriage with a non-Spaniard seldom offered economic or social advantages. For this reason the establishment of the first convent in Manila in 1621, the Franciscan Poor Clares, caused a wave of panic and indignation to sweep through the ranks of Manila's eligible Spanish bachelors. Within a few years twenty-two young ladies from Manila's aristocracy, one-half of the eligible maidens of the capital, had taken the veil. Not with equanimity did the bachelors of the capital observe these dowries flowing into the empty coffers of the convent. Protesting loudly and vigorously, they pleaded with the Council of the Indies to close the convent. Their not impertinent argument was that these girls might best serve the cause of God and king in that exposed outpost of Christianity as the mothers of future Spanish citizens.[2]

In addition to the paucity of Spanish colonists and their concentration in Manila, some demographic factors help to explain the slow growth of a mestizo class. The effects of the Spanish conquest of the Philippines, demographically speaking, were also mild in comparison to those in Mexico. In the latter country there was a sharp and steady decline of the Indian population from approximately 11,000,000 in 1519 to 4,409,180 in 1565, and by the end of the sixteenth century to about 2,500,000.[3] The vacuum created by the disappearance of the Indians was rapidly filled by a fast-growing mestizo population.

One of the main causes of the Mexican Indian decline was the spread of contagious diseases—smallpox, influenza and measles—against which the Indians had no immunity. The Filipinos escaped this simple but devastating cause of depletion through the fact that they had acquired some immunity to such diseases as the result of their frequent contacts, before 1565, with the neighboring peoples of southeastern Asia. Furthermore, Philippine geography did much to limit the advance of contagious epidemics. Diseases were not apt to spread as rapidly from island to island as they might overland, and the mountainous terrain of the islands, together with the dispersal of the population, created additional barriers against the spread of disease. As was suggested in the last chapter, the basic cause for the decline in the Philippine population in the early part of the seventeenth century—and it never became a demographic disaster—was the dislocation produced by the Dutch war.

In Mexico, the severe demographic revolution provoked an ecological revolution. The preconquest system of sedentary agriculture based on the cultivation of maize was seriously disrupted by the rapid spread of a pastoral economy. Since nature abhors a vacuum, the lands vacated by the declining Indian population were filled by countless herds of cattle, sheep, and goats.[4] Although the demographic-ecological revolution created demoralizing social consequences on the surviving Indian population, not all the long-term results were harmful to the Indians. The massive production of beef created for them a new form of food more nourishing in proteins than the preconquest staple of corn. The non-Indian population of Spaniards and mestizos, increasing both relatively and absolutely, were determined to maintain their customary standard of living. Pressure on the rapidly diminishing Indians became almost intolerable. The Spaniards first resorted to draft labor under the form of the *repartimiento*. The long-range solution was the growth of latifundia based on Indian debt peonage.[5]

## Evolutionary Character of Ecological Changes

In the Philippines, on the other hand, the postconquest changes were evolutionary rather than revolutionary, most significantly as a result of demographic stability. During the seventeenth century the Filipino population under effective Spanish control varied between 500,000 and 600,000 people. In addition there may have been as many as one million Filipinos who were not Spanish subjects. The islands, in reality, were underpopulated in terms of what the land was capable of producing. What was required to stimulate production was that kind of external pressure that the war demands of the Spanish regime created. Although the initial process of expanding production imposed severe hardships on the Filipinos, long-term benefits may have resulted. As we have seen, once the strain of war conditions was removed, increased productivity facilitated the growth of a larger population, which increased steadily after 1650.

The Spaniards invariably accused the Filipinos of indolence. A frequent complaint was that they would not voluntarily grow a surplus.[6] Such an argument was, in part, a Spanish rationalization for coercion. Actually compulsion in the form of the *polo* and the *vandala* became necessary not because the Filipinos lacked industry but because the Spaniards would not adequately reward them for the toils of their labor. Although the preconquest Filipinos never were surplus farmers, they might easily have been induced to be-

come so if the Spaniards had paid them fair prices for their products. Since the Spaniards would not do so, they had to force the
Filipinos to grow a surplus. The *vandala* was an ill-camouflaged
form of confiscatory taxation. That it produced results may be
partly attributed to the bureaucratic system of enforcement extend-
ing down to the village level. Every *cabeza de barangay*, for example, had his annual quota. There were yearly allotments for rice,
fowl, coconut palms, and abacá plants. When these quotas were
not met, fines were imposed on both native chieftains and Spanish
officials.[7] Every community had its inspector of palm trees and its
inspector of the rice fields, both of whom enjoyed statutory exemption from the *polo* and the tribute.[8] Chosen from the Filipino upper
class, the responsibility of these officials was twofold. They had
to enforce the regulations of the central government in regard to
food production. An equally pressing obligation was to organize
protection against the various plagues of locusts which periodically
threatened to destroy the crops. Although it would be rash indeed
to assume that the coercive regulations of the central authorities
were always enforced, it would be equally unwise to take for
granted their total ineffectiveness. Production did expand in the
face of a decline in the total labor force.

All contemporary accounts credit the Chinese with being more
highly skilled farmers than the Filipinos. Although the majority of
Chinese preferred to engage in commerce and in the skilled crafts,
an appreciable number did enter agriculture. Those who did, accomplished much to raise productive efficiency. The Jesuits, who
were outstandingly successful in their agrarian enterprises, employed Chinese laborers on some of their estates.[9]

The most important agricultural region of the Philippines was,
and for that matter still is, the "rice basket" central plain of Luzon,
which consists of the present provinces of Bulacan, Pampanga, and
Nueva Ecija. The productivity of this area contrasts sharply with
that of the rest of the islands, much as the cultural and political
importance of Greater Manila vis-à-vis the archipelago as a whole
stands out in clear relief. Of all the provinces of the "rice basket"

Pampanga was the most fertile. Situated in a valley where the delta
of the Rio Grande was inundated during the rainy season, Pampanga produced two annual crops of wet rice. Of the peripheral
provinces on the island of Luzon only Ilokos sent an appreciable
supply of rice to Manila, usually during the months of February
and March, when the winds were favorable for the sea voyage.
The provinces of Cagayan and the Camarines at that time produced
no food surplus.

In the Bisayan islands Panay, with its dense population, produced a rice crop second only to that of central Luzon. Panay's
surplus was apt to move southward rather than northward. That
island served as the base of operations for supplying the fleets and
garrisons for Mindanao and the Moluccas farther to the south.
Cebu with its mountainous terrain was plentifully supplied with
game, but it had to import rice from the neighboring islands of
Leyte, Samar, and Bohol.[10]

Fish had always figured prominently in the diet of the Filipinos.
In the Spanish period the production of root crops, of which the
sweet potato became the most important species, greatly expanded.
Both the Filipinos and the Spaniards came to rely on it increasingly.
In fact, during those periodic rice shortages, especially before the
harvesting of the new crop, it was the availability of root crops
which prevented mass starvation.[11]

Although the Spanish regime sponsored a significant transformation of Philippine agriculture, the basic pattern of preconquest food production, based on the cultivation of rice and root
crops, fishing, and the raising of fowl and swine, was not over-
thrown. The agricultural innovations of the Spaniards were more
of a quantitative than of a qualitative nature. The exigencies of the
Dutch war required a rapid expansion of customary items. Those
qualitative changes sponsored by the Spaniards supplemented
rather than conflicted with preconquest patterns.

Notable changes occurred as the result of the introduction of
new crops and weeds, many of which were first brought to the Philippines from Mexico on the Manila Galleon. Flora from Brazil also

entered Papuasia at the same time by means of vessels coming from Brazil around Cape Horn to Guam. In 1912, E. D. Merrill made a study of the flora of a compact area of some forty square miles near Manila. Of the 1,000 known species of weeds, he identified 175 as having a Mexican or a Brazilian origin.[12]

Wheat was not cultivated in the Philippines prior to 1700.[13] Of cultivated plants the most significant novelty introduced by the Spaniards was Mexican corn, maize. It did not replace rice as the staple crop. On the contrary, all the available evidence suggests that maize production was not very large. The Filipinos did not like its taste, and they ate it only under duress. What is more to the point is that the preparation of maize for cooking required considerably more time than did the preparation of rice. Furthermore, the habit of some government officials to confiscate maize in the king's name scarcely encouraged the Filipinos to cultivate that crop extensively. Rice continued to be the staple of the diet not only of the Filipinos, but also of the heretofore grain-fed Spaniards. But maize production, small though it was, nonetheless contributed something to relieve the pressure of food shortages by creating a new form of nourishment.[14]

A revealing example of the mild character of the ecological changes in the islands is the story of cattle raising. There were no beef cattle in the Philippines before the Spaniards came. Cattle were first brought to the islands from Mexico on the Manila Galleon, but the Spaniards soon learned that the smaller variety of cattle from northern China and Japan acclimatized more easily than did the Mexican imports.[15] But the introduction of cattle was only a limited success. By 1606, some twenty years after the first shipments of cattle, there were only twenty-four ranches in the archdiocese of Manila. Each of these ranches contained herds of at least one thousand head of cattle, and some of them had as many as four thousand head. Cattle production was of limited scope, as suggested by the fact that in the fiscal year of 1632/33 the income from ecclesiastical tithes collected from cattle ranches in the archdiocese amounted to the paltry sum of 300 pesos.[16]

Cattle production supplied a limited market based on the traditional eating habits of the beef-consuming Spaniards. In the provinces the Filipinos seldom ate beef. What meat they did consume was apt to be pork and water buffalo, which were plentiful in the islands even before the conquest. Actually the Filipinos secured their proteins not from meat but from fish, which was usually varied and abundant. The fact that confessors often assigned as penance the task of bringing some meat to an invalid suggests that meat of any sort was a delicacy for most Filipinos.[17]

The Philippines never were and never could be a cattle country on the scale of Mexico, where the cattle industry grew rapidly. Only in the province of Batangas and in some other isolated areas was there the kind of succulent fodder upon which cattle could thrive. The coarse grass covering most of the unwooded land in the archipelago always has been a deterrent to extensive cattle raising. Intestinal diseases, such as hoof and mouth disease, liver flukes, and the generally hot and humid climate are other obstacles.

In addition to raising cattle the Spaniards made other experiments in animal husbandry, some of which were successful and others less so. The Manila Galleon brought several varieties of Mexican animals to the Philippines, but Spanish beasts of burden (donkeys and oxen), which had multiplied in Mexico, did not thrive in the Philippine climate. The water buffalo continued to be the beast of burden, as it had been before the conquest. Sheep and goats were relatively unimportant. Sheep could not be raised in the Philippines in spite of repeated attempts to do so. Goats and kids imported from Mexico acclimatized with difficulty. By 1650 there were only a few herds of goats and kids.

As in the case with cattle, the Spaniards found out that the Chinese and Japanese horses acclimatized more readily than did the Mexican variety.[18] There were no horses in the islands before the conquest, but their introduction did not produce a revolution in transportation.[19] The Philippine topography and climate, combined with the abundant and cheap supply of labor, assured that the rivers and coasts remain the principal highways during the Spanish regime. In the rainy seasons the trails were virtually unpassable for horses and mules, and furthermore these animals did not always thrive in that hot and humid climate. Overland transportation for the affluent was by hammocks or litters carried by native porters; the ordinary folk just walked. Because of these conditions, legislation issued in Manila designed to relieve the Filipinos of the harsh burdens of serving as porters and rowers, by requiring every community to maintain a supply of horses and mules, was seldom enforced and came to naught.[20] Not until the twentieth century have the Philippines undergone a revolution in transportation, one initiated by automobiles and highways.

The pastoral economy introduced by the Spaniards did not produce violent ecological dislocations. The Filipinos suffered from no widespread distress, for the encroachment of unfenced cattle on the landscape did not drive large numbers from their rice paddies.[21] A painful adjustment, such as occurred in Mexico, would have been required to superimpose a pastoral economy on top of the traditional agricultural economy of the islands. This adjustment proved unnecessary largely because of the fact that most of the unwooded land of the archipelago was unsuited to grazing. Thus the ecological changes introduced by the Spaniards supplemented, but they did not disrupt the preconquest agricultural economy.

## Native Servitude and Labor

The same pattern of continuity also prevailed in the systems of labor. Pre-Hispanic forms were modified gradually, but not radically altered, during the early Spanish period, despite the fact that both the Spanish clergy and the civil authorities were militantly hostile to the Philippine variety of debt peonage and sharecropping. The continuance of this system was in fact the major obstacle to the growth of free, paid labor in agriculture.

Spanish failure in this regard was as complete in the Philippines as it was in Mexico. The precipitous decline of the Indian population was at the root of Spanish failure in Mexico. The sustained war emergency in the islands crippled the innovating powers of the government. The immediate demands of the defense effort took precedence over more long-range reform projects, and the net result was to strengthen preconquest patterns based on debt peonage and sharecropping.

Applying a moralistic criterion, the Spanish clergy assailed the pre-Hispanic system of labor as wanting in what they considered to be elementary forms of justice and charity. War captives were cast into dependent status not in "just wars" but in raiding expeditions that seemed to the Spaniards like sheer brigandage. The churchmen attacked the usurious character of debt peonage. As the heirs of the medieval Aristotelian doctrine against charging interest, they regarded the Philippine form of usury, which was the primary cause of debt peonage, as unmitigated avarice and morally reprehensible.[22]

Profiting from its experience in Mexico, the Spanish government vigorously opposed in the islands the extension of any form of involuntary servitude, be it operated by the Spaniards or by the Filipinos. Consequently the colonists in the archipelago were not allowed to acquire Filipino dependents. The government's highly plausible supposition was that under the administration of the colonists such a labor system would quickly degenerate into overt slavery, which it never had been among the Filipinos.[23] Between 1565 and 1586 the Spanish missionaries made vigorous attempts to abolish native servitude, but everywhere they met tenacious resistance. This institution provided native chieftains with their principal source of wealth, and it was intimately bound up with kinship ties. Its abrupt abolition, in conjunction with other changes introduced as a result of the conquest, threatened to undermine the whole fabric of native society. The clergy actually found that their making emancipation of dependents a precondition for baptism was beginning to paralyze the missionary enterprise itself. By 1586 Bishop Salazar confessed to Philip II failure on the question of native servitude.[24] The ecclesiastical-inspired attempt in favor of immediate abolition was followed by a period of experimentation (1586–99). During this stage, legislation issued in Spain sought to determine how rapidly the institution could be liquidated without undermining the economic foundations of native society.[25] During the third period (1599–1679) the Audiencia, the highest tribunal of justice in the islands, conducted an operation to restrict the scope of the system gradually and thus to pave the way for its eventual extinction.[26]

The Audiencia's policy, however, encountered difficulties as a result of the severe economic strains produced by the Hispano-Dutch war. As we have seen, the war created an urgent need for manpower and supplies, and the requisitioning of these had to be delegated, on the local level, to the native chieftains. Hence the *cabezas de barangay* acquired new and lucrative sources of enrichment, and the tendencies toward debt peonage increased. The chieftains frequently confiscated the token wages paid to *polo* laborers.[27] Furthermore, in order to purchase a substitute for the *polo* some destitute Filipinos were willing to borrow money. That meant that they sold themselves into dependent status. Those who could not meet the burdensome *vandala* quotas had little alternative but to become debtors to their local *cabeza*.[28]

With the gradual improvement in the Philippine economy following the end of the Dutch war, however, the Audiencia's restrictive policy began to yield results. Between 1679 and 1692 the whole dependent system was ostensibly legislated out of existence. As of 1692 no dependent could be transferred from one superior to another, either through inheritance or through purchase. Those of dependent status as of 1692 remained under the control of their superiors until either one of them died. All children born after 1692 were free.[29] But all forms of pre-Hispanic debt peonage and sharecropping did not disappear within a generation after the settlement of 1692. The *guiguilar-ayuey* group, whose labor services were primarily monopolized by their superiors, disappeared.[30] The sharecropper group, the *mamamahay-tumaranpuh*, on the other hand, were abolished in law but not in fact. Sharecropping founded on debt peonage continued as the prevailing labor system.

During the eighteenth century it became the custom for the owner of a piece of land to enter into a partnership with a landless

native. The latter cultivated the land of the former, and the two
shared the harvest. Usually this system involved a loan from the
owner to the tenant at a usurious rate of interest. Toward the end
of the eighteenth century sporadic attempts were made to regulate
this arrangement, which was sometimes called the *casamajan*, a
Tagalog word meaning partnership. Ordinances restricting to the
old and the infirm the right to rent their lands and forbidding usurious interest on loans were difficult to enforce. The well-to-do
among the Filipinos preferred to rent their lands under the *casamajan*
system rather than to cultivate their own fields.[31]

An arrangement similar to the *casamajan* prevailed on estates
owned by ecclesiastical corporations. The tenant farmer paid a
nominal rent for his dwelling, and he shared the harvest with the
ecclesiastical owners of the land.[32] Chinese farmers were also
sharecroppers.[33]

From this discussion it will be seen that there has been a remarkable historical continuity in Philippine agricultural organization. Wealthy Filipinos have exploited their holdings by means of
tenant farming and debt peonage from preconquest times to the
present. The pre-Hispanic *mamamahay*, his seventeenth-century
successor, the *casamajan* farmer in the eighteenth century, and
the modern tenant farmer all have cultivated the land under various
systems of sharecropping and debt peonage that differ among themselves only in detail but not in substance.

## Land Tenure

The Spaniards introduced greater changes in the sphere of land
tenure than in either agriculture or the labor system. An ancient
myth, which has served only to obscure the true origins of land
tenure, is that Philippine latifundia grew out of the encomienda.[34]
For one thing, large-scale latifundia did not become significant in
the Philippines until the nineteenth century and not before. Even in
Mexico, where large estates owned by the Spaniards developed as
early as the sixteenth century, the connections between the
encomienda and land tenure have proved much more tenuous than

was commonly supposed.[35] In the Philippines the relationship seems to be virtually nil. Legally speaking, of course, the encomienda never was a land grant, but merely the right to collect tribute from a certain number of natives. The government did make efforts to keep the encomenderos near their wards as a means of consolidating Spanish political control in the provinces.[36] If these regulations had been observed, the encomenderos undoubtedly would have acquired the ownership of land near their tributaries. But events did not follow this course. Once the initial pacification had been consummated, Filipinos seldom saw their encomenderos. The *cabezas de barangay* collected the tribute and forwarded it to the encomenderos living in the capital. After the middle of the seventeenth century the decline of the private encomienda rapidly set in. Hence all the available evidence suggests that the encomienda as such had nothing to do with the origins of land tenure.

The Spaniards introduced one significant innovation in land tenure. It was the notion of land ownership as opposed to land use, the concept that individuals and not merely groups could own land, that land itself was a source of wealth. In preconquest times landowning was communal in character, with the actual title to the lands vested in the communal barangay. Wealth was determined by how many dependents a chieftain could muster to cultivate the communally owned lands. Although Spanish law recognized communal ownership, there was a tendency for chieftains in the early Spanish period to assume the formal ownership of that portion of the barangay land which their dependents ordinarily cultivated. During the seventeenth century the trend increased, more and more Filipino chieftains acquiring the actual title to the land that their dependents cultivated. This gradual adoption on the part of the Filipinos of the European principle of individual ownership of land is clearly one enduring consequence of economic Hispanization.

How extensive this development was awaits further archival research, but a well-documented example of its beginnings is the Jesuit acquisition of the lands of Quiapo, then a suburban village of Manila. The Jesuits purchased these lands from some local chieftains. By Spanish standards this seemed an equitable arrangement, but according to preconquest usages the ownership of the land belonged to the barangay, and therefore it was not the chieftains' to alienate. Protests of the villagers of Quiapo, vigorously seconded by Archbishop Benavides, were brought to the attention of the Audiencia, and an interminable litigation ensued. But it failed to expel the Jesuits from Quiapo.[37]

There were two types of land tenure, that of preconquest and that of postconquest origin. Under Spanish law preconquest usufruct of land became titles held in fee simple. Their owners could alienate such property.[38] All lands not owned either communally or individually at the time of the conquest belonged to the royal domain, the *realengas*. Some of this land was assigned by the Crown's representatives to those Filipinos who settled in or adjacent to the multitude of newly founded communities. These lands were held not in fee simple but in fee tail. Although such real estate could be transmitted to legitimate heirs, it could not be sold without the consent of the *fiscal* of the Audiencia. Title ostensibly reverted to the Crown after failure to cultivate this land for a period of two years.[39] How vigorously these laws were enforced is uncertain. For that matter many basic questions about the origins of land tenure cannot be clarified until the Spanish archival sources are more extensively examined.

It is evident that the bulk of all cultivated lands remained in the possession of the Filipinos. Ecclesiastical estates were the largest single item of Spanish-owned latifundia, yet the Church's holdings represented only a small fraction of the total land under cultivation. As of 1768 the religious orders owned only twenty estates in the Tagalog country.[40]

## Evolution of Philippine Society

Both the success and the failure of the Spanish efforts to introduce changes in Philippine systems of labor and land tenure left enduring consequences on the development of Philippine society. Here again the contrasts with Mexico are illuminating. Much though official Spanish policy desired the growth of free labor in agriculture, its attainment might have been highly inconvenient. Free labor in practice would have meant very small holdings of a subsistence variety. In such a situation there might not have been that agricultural surplus whose continuous flow provided the necessary economic underpinning of the colonial regime. The choice confronting the Spanish authorities was actually not one between free labor and debt peonage-sharecropping but rather between two forms of the latter—direct or indirect exploitation of the indigenous population. The former alternative, including Spanish-owned latifundia and Indian debt peonage, was what emerged in Mexico. The latter solution, involving smaller landholdings owned by a native upper class who were made responsible for delivering to the Spanish authorities labor and commodities, developed in the Philippines. Exploitation was of a direct variety in Mexico; in the Philippines it was indirect. The larger numbers of Spaniards in Mexico, the growth of large cities providing a market and hence an inducement for the rise of large estates, and the severe character of ecological and demographic changes account for this contrast.

The seventeenth-century crises in both Mexico and in the Philippines had much to do with shaping the character of society in both countries. Latifundia and Indian debt peonage were outgrowths of New Spain's "Century of Depression.[41] Subsequent events in the nineteenth century, such as technological changes and the abolition of ecclesiastical latifundia, served only to expand this system, whose origins go back to the seventeenth century. In the Philippines debt peonage and sharecropping, whose roots are pre-Hispanic but whose dominance was solidified during the Hispano-Dutch war, continue to this day to exercise a deep influence over that agrarian society.

Paradoxical though it may sound, the absence of Spanish latifundia in the Philippines was not an unmixed blessing. Although the leadership of the native chieftains, i.e. *principales*, may have facilitated the task of social adjustment, the Filipinos paid a price in the form of exploitation exercised by their own chieftains. Spanish latifundia would have diminished this abuse. Furthermore, Spanish landlords, if only for reasons of self-interest, would have protected their peons against excessive ecclesiastical exploitation.[42] The absence of Spanish landlords left the Filipinos virtually defenseless against the exactions of the clergy, for the native magistrates lacked the effective power to oppose the Church's demands.

In Mexico, on the other hand, latifundia of two varieties came to prevail. In the south, with its dense Indian population, Spanish landowning tended to be of smaller units than the extensive estates carved out of the northern country of the Chichimecas, where the Indian population was relatively sparse.[43] Although much of the communal property of the Indians survived intact, Spanish latifundia became increasingly predominant. The large-scale intrusion of Spaniards and mestizos into Indian Mexico weakened but did not destroy the leadership role of the native magistracy. Local administration continued to be in the hands of the caciques, but their capacity to provide creative leadership was enfeebled.[44] The role of the caciques as the intermediaries between the two races was gradually reduced in scope, since debt peons were under the direct control of the manager of the hacienda. Deprived of many sources of graft and exploitation, the wealth of the cacique class diminished. Although the Indian masses received some protection against the dual exploitation of their own chieftains and of the clergy, their lot as debt peons was scarcely enviable.

In the Philippines the class structure in native society remained more cohesive than in Mexico, for it was solidified by the performance of two kinds of services rendered by the *principales* to the colonial government. The native magistracy acted as intermediaries between the material demands of the Spanish regime and the productive capacities of the masses. Secondly, the *principales* were the local, political administrators. Heretofore attention has been concentrated on the economic role of the *principales*. What now must be explored is their complementary political role.

# Political
# Hispanization

Spanish legislation regarded the indigenous population of the empire as legal minors whose rights and obligations merited paternalistic protection from the Crown and its agents. For administrative purposes the natives were treated as a separate commonwealth, *la republica de los Indios*, with its own code of laws and its own set of magistrates. The segregation of the Indians from the Spanish and mestizo communities gave the Indian commonwealth a kind of ethnic-territorial reality. Among the natives there was a substantial amount of self-government. Spanish officialdom determined policy directives, but on the local level natives administered. Wherever the Spaniards colonized, they did not destroy the indigenous upper class. Rather they sought to transform such a group into a native nobility from whose ranks local magistrates could be recruited. The system of local self-government which the Spaniards introduced into the Philippines was largely of Mexican origin, with significant regional modifications. One of the most remarkable features of the whole Hispanization program was the degree to which the Filipinos acculturated to Spanish political usages. Their response was on the whole enthusiastic, rapid, and in many cases penetrating.

## The Barangay

The Spanish administration transformed the barangay into the smallest unit of local government. In pre-Hispanic times these kinship units, which were the only political entities, varied from thirty to one hundred families. In the interests of administrative efficiency the Spaniards sought to standardize the size of the barangay at a figure between forty-five and fifty families. Of the 6,000 barangays existing in 1768 the average size probably came closer to thirty families.[1] The actual number of people in a barangay was apt to vary considerably. The head of the barangay was originally called a *datu*, but this title was soon Hispanized to *cabeza de barangay*, best translated into English as headman.

As early as 1573 the Augustinian prelates urged Philip II to preserve this group as a privileged class. In 1594 Philip II granted two concessions to the headmen of the Philippines, privileges previously granted to the Indian caciques in America. Both the headmen and their eldest sons were exempt from the paying of the annual tribute as well as from participating in compulsory labor projects. They also enjoyed certain honorific tokens of prestige. They enjoyed honors similar to hidalgos of Castile, including the privilege of using the Spanish "don."[2]

The primary duty of the *cabezas* was to collect the tribute tax from the members of their barangay. In addition, as we noted in the previous chapter, their responsibilities in connection with the *polo* and *vandala* provided them with inviting opportunities for extralegal enrichment and tended to increase their power. No government regulations were successful in rooting out these abuses.[3]

Two notable features of the postconquest barangay were its stability and horizontal mobility. Leadership was hereditary, with succession passing from father to eldest son. In default of heirs, machinery existed for the selection of a new *cabeza*. Every Filipino subject of the Crown had to belong to a barangay. He could change his barangay when he moved from one locality to another. A baptized person, however, could not move from one locality with religious instruction to another settlement lacking it, nor could he change barangays within the same community. The post-Hispanic barangay provided for a greater degree of horizontal mobility than did the preconquest institution. Before 1565 the cost of moving from one barangay to another was prohibitive. Not only did such a person have to pay a large fee, but he also had to offer an elaborate fiesta in honor of his former barangay.[4]

During the reign of Charles III (1759–88) enlightened despotism was in vogue among the ruling circles in Spain. One of the political aims of this movement was to create a more rational, efficient, and uniform system of imperial administration. The monarch's energetic bureaucrats were also motivated by the practical incentive to increase the royal revenues, since the expenses for imperial defense were steadily mounting. This fiscal consideration prompted an abortive attempt to abolish the barangay itself. A proposal was made to replace the headmen, in their position as tribute collectors, with the elected magistrates of the villages, the *gobernadorcillos*. To encourage efficient tax collecting the *gobernadorcillos* were to receive one-half per cent of the tribute collected. The *cabezas* were to be deprived of their cherished privilege of tribute exemption. Thus it was hoped to add 11,250 pesos to the royal revenue.[5]

These changes proposed by Governor Raón were never enforced. In 1786 the barangay was modified and given the form it retained until the end of the Spanish regime.[6] This legislation was a less drastic reform than one contemplated by Governor Raón. The *cabezas* retained their basic function as tribute collectors. The regulations abolished hereditary succession in favor of the election of *cabezas* for a minimum term of three years by the leading members of the community. During his term of office the elective headman enjoyed all the privileges that the formerly hereditary *cabezas* once enjoyed, i.e., exemption from the tribute and forced labor services. If he served for a period of more than ten years, he retained these privileges for life.

## Village Government

The barangay was the smallest administrative unit. But there were also other units of local government, the most important being the *pueblo de Indios*. The latter was the forerunner of the modern *municipio* or township. A *pueblo de Indios* in the seventeenth century consisted of a principal settlement, the *cabecera*, where the main parish church was located. Attached to the pueblo was a whole series of outlying clusters of population, the *visitas* or barrios, serviced by an itinerant priest from the *cabecera*, in addition to various sitios (less than ten families). Every pueblo, which was an extensive territorial unit, was a collection of barangays. There might be more than one barangay in the *cabecera* if the population warranted it, but in the *visitas*-barrios there was generally only one barangay. Various sitios would have to be combined to form one barangay. The evolution of Philippine settlement patterns and administrative terminology may be clarified by the following chart.[7]

| | PRE-CONQUEST | EARLY SPANISH | LATE SPANISH | CONTEMPORARY ENGLISH |
|---|---|---|---|---|
| 1) | (no term) | Rancheria | Sitio | Sitio (hamlet) |
| 2) | Barangay | *Visita* | Barrio | Barrio (village) |
| | | Barangay | Barangay | |
| 3) | | *Cabecera* | Población | Población (town) |
| 4) | | Pueblo | *Municipio* | Municipality (township) |
| 5) | | *Cuidad* | *Cuidad* | City |
| 6) | | *Alcaldia mayor* | *Provincia* | Province |
| | | *Corregimiento* | | |

The chief magistrate of the pueblo was called the *gobernadorcillo*, meaning petty governor in Spanish. In the early seventeenth century all adult males nominated three candidates for the post, and a representative of the Crown selected one nominee who served for a term of one year.[8] This system proved unworkable, causing many disputed elections. The Filipinos evidently took their local politics seriously. Some politicans vigorously pushed their candidacy for the office of *gobernadorcillo* to the point of holding "political rallies."

Support was wooed by organized fiestas in which entertainment and rice wine were supplied by aspirants to office. These "rallies" were never held in the *cabecera* villages themselves lest the clergy interfere.[9] These facts do suggest that the Filipinos were rapidly responding to some Hispanic political practices, although in a manner that did not always meet with the approval of Spanish bureaucrats.

Governor Corcuera and Governor Cruzat in 1642 and 1696 drastically restricted the franchise. The democratic arrangement in which all married males voted was replaced by a more oligarchical franchise. In the presence of the retiring *gobernadorcillo* and the parish priest the twelve senior *cabezas de barangay* nominated three candidates at an annual election held between January 1 and February 28. The governor in Manila selected one of the three nominees for all communities adjacent to the capital. The *alcaldes mayores* chose one of the nominees in the outlying provinces.[10] Although Spanish officialdom retained the final voice in choosing the *gobernadorcillos*, Filipino leadership played a substantial role in this process of selection.

*Alcaldes mayores* were under standing orders not to interfere with the nomination of candidates except under rigorously prescribed conditions.[11] That Spanish bureaucrats sometimes did is evident, but it is doubtful if such interventions became wholesale practice. As a deterrent to maladministration and corruption, *gobernadorcillos* were required to submit to a judicial and public review of their conduct in office.[12] This review, known as the *residencia*, was a system initiated in the Indies, where all magistrates were required to undergo it. Its effectiveness is a moot question.[13] In the small Philippine communities the *residencia* was probably even less effective than in the larger administrative units staffed by professional Spanish bureaucrats. Petty peculations on the part of local magistrates usually went unpunished if these officials had an understanding with the *alcalde* of the province.

The Filipino upper class, the *principales*, largely consisted of two groups, namely, the hereditary *cabezas* and a whole series of elected officials. Officeholders other than the *gobernadorcillo* included his deputy, a constable, an inspector of palm trees, an inspector of rice fields, and a notary. Filipinos in the service of the Church also belonged to the upper class, in particular, the *fiscales* (the sacristans) and the cantors of the choir. All these magistrates enjoyed the statutory privileges of the *cabezas*. In practice there was much overlapping in the political functions of this class. *Cabezas* were apt to be the magistrates, and the *fiscales* ordinarily were ex-*gobernadorcillos*. The principle of rotation in office was observed. *Gobernadorcillos* could not succeed themselves, but they could be reelected to office after undergoing the *residencia*.[14] The possession of wealth and the participation in the local administration tended to coincide but perhaps not in all cases.

The political authority of the local magistracy was not negligible, although it was limited. The magistrates had to conform, outwardly at least, to orders from Spanish officialdom. Although policy decisions were not theirs to make, the enforcement of the law in the villages and in the countryside was in their hands. Procrastination and evasion on their part made the local magistrates not insignificant participants in the administrative chain of command. Nor could they directly oppose the expressed wishes of the priest, who was a "petty viceroy" of the Spanish king in his parish. The clergy could often be appeased by outward observance rather than inner acceptance. Within these limitations the Filipino magistrates exercised considerable power and prestige over their fellow countrymen, and a whole class of Filipinos acquired substantial political experience on the local level.

The growth of the *principalía* class in the early Spanish period has left a deep imprint on the subsequent political development of the islands. Although the Philippines did not achieve self-government on the national scale until very recently, the Filipinos had had extensive political experience on the level of local government since the late sixteenth century. New political practices introduced by the Spaniards, such as the principles of hereditary succession, representation, election to office, and rotation in office, were meticulously observed. This system of local administration was oligarchical rather than democratic. Political office was monopolized by a small group of "bosses" in each community. Venality, widespread but petty, flourished. In the Hispanic world this system has come to be known as "caciquism."

Its legacy has proved a major obstacle to the growth of sound democratic institutions in the modern Philippines. At times it looks as if the cacique tradition had been transferred from the village level, where it was confined in Spanish times, to the national level, where it now seems to be flourishing. Some contemporary politicians have acted like *gobernadorcillos* indulging in graft and favoritism. In Spanish times graft for the individual magistrate was petty, for an officeholder's authority seldom extended beyond one small village. Now the sphere of peculation has reached out to include the whole nation. It would be unjust not to recognize the solid progress that the Filipino people have made in recent years toward creating stable democratic institutions, an achievement which has been buttressed by the spread of popular education and economic growth. But candor requires that the obstacles toward the consolidation and expansion of democracy ought not to be glossed aside. One of the major barriers is just this legacy of caciquism.

In order to enable the *pueblos de Indios* to carry out their corporate responsibilities, legislation provided that every community establish a treasury called a *caja de comunidad*. A certain amount of land from the royal domain was assigned to every new pueblo in its corporate capacity. Every Filipino deposited one half bushel of rice in the village treasury at the time he paid his tribute. These funds were supposed to provide an agricultural surplus with which to relieve distress in times of famine, to make loans payable at harvest time, to pay the nominal salaries of local officials and to finance public instruction. The supervision of the *cajas* was entrusted to the officers of the royal treasury, the *oficiales reales*, who formed an autonomous branch of the imperial bureaucracy. The judicial protection of these funds was the responsibility of the Audiencia.[15]

Bishop Salazar was one of the first to suggest that the Mexican system of communal treasuries be extended to the Philippines.[16] This institution, however, did not prosper. The Audiencia estimated in 1609 that the total value of all the *cajas* in the islands did not exceed 10,000 bushels of rice.[17] No substantial surpluses could be accumulated. The *alcaldes mayores* repeatedly borrowed from these funds without troubling to repay the loans. The stewards of the *cajas* were unable to resist the combined pressure of the religious and the *gobernadorcillos*, both of whom were anxious to spend lavishly for religious fiestas. This practice, forbidden by royal edict, was widespread. Until 1657 the village treasuries also paid a monthly stipend to *polo* laborers from a separate fund accumulated from a special assessment.

The treasury officials in Manila evidently exercised little effective control over the administration of these communal funds. The *cajas* served to finance village fiestas, to pay the nominal salaries of local officeholders, and to provide sources of graft for Spanish and native officialdom.[18] The principal purposes for which the *cajas* were set up—the accumulation of surpluses for emergencies and the financing of a system of primary education—never were fulfilled. Reform legislation issued in 1642, 1696, and 1768 did little to alter the situation.[19]

The archipelago was divided into twelve provinces called *alcaldías mayores*. Some of the more extensive provinces were subdivided into *corregimientos*. There were eight of these subdivisions. The modern provinces of the Philippines grew out of these seventeenth-century *alcaldías* and *corregimientos*, just as the *cabeceras* and *visitas* are the genesis of the contemporary *población* and *barrio*.

The *alcalde mayor* or the *corregidor* was the principal executive, judicial, and military officer in his district, responsible directly to the authorities in Manila, the governor and the Audiencia. The alcaldes were scarcely able to provide for themselves, let alone for their families, on their modest salary of 300 pesos annually. The irresistable temptation was to indulge in a wide variety of peculations, mostly at the expense of the natives. Although these officers were required to submit to the *residencia*, this device evidently did little to diminish these abuses.[20]

The alcaldes and their deputies, the subdelegates, were the intermediaries between the central authorities in Manila and the *gobernadorcillos* in the villages. Occupying a middle position in the administrative chain of command, their primary responsibility was to enforce locally policy directives issued in Madrid and in Manila, not to formulate policy.

## The Administration of Justice

The Spanish regime provided the Filipinos with an elaborate machinery to enable them to seek redress of their grievances through the courts. A standard practice of the colonial administration throughout the Indies was to recognize the applicability of the customary law of the natives in those cases where it did not violate basic precepts of Spanish-Christian morality. In civil suits among the Filipinos, customary law applied in litigations dealing with pre-Hispanic dependent status, inheritances, and dowries. In 1599 the Audiencia defined as customary law for the whole archipelago Tagalog usages as codified by Friar Juan de Plasencia. In all criminal suits and civil cases not covered by customary law Roman jurisprudence applied.[21]

The transition from pagan to Spanish legal procedures was made as smooth as possible. Disputes antedating the conquest were settled on the basis of oral testimony. The Spanish monarchs issued repeated orders that native suits be adjudicated summarily and hence with the least possible expense to the Filipinos. As chief magistrates in the pueblos, the *gobernadorcillos* tried civil cases involving small sums. The alcaldes or their deputies heard appeals on these verdicts. In civil suits involving large sums, all criminal cases, and litigations in which the royal treasury was a party the alcaldes acted as the court of the first instance, with the Audiencia hearing appeals.[22] The Council of the Indies in Spain was the highest court of appeal for the colonies, but cases among the Filipinos were seldom referred to the Council.

Some restrictions had to be placed on the jurisdiction of the Audiencia in cases involving Filipinos. The government sought to discourage the Filipinos from spending their meager resources in needless litigations which, under the slow-moving Spanish legal machinery, were often interminable. Most observers felt that the Filipinos, like the Indians of Mexico and Peru, were all too prone to spend their time and their money in litigations merely for the sake of being embroiled in a legal controversy. As an appellate court the Audiencia reserved the right to refuse to hear cases at its discretion.[23]

Although the Crown sought to place some curbs on the litigiousness of the Filipinos, strenuous efforts were made to assist the Filipinos in their quest for justice before the Audiencia. The *fiscal* of the Audiencia, the Crown attorney, also held the post of protector of the natives and the Chinese. As such he defended them without fee. He was assisted by a solicitor and a staff of interpreters who performed their services gratis.

The regular clergy often questioned the desirability of applying Spanish judicial procedures to cases among the Filipinos. Most Spaniards, laymen and ecclesiastics alike, expressed nothing but contempt for the veracity of a Filipino's testimony. They shared the conviction, whether rightly or wrongly, that the capacity of the Filipinos for committing perjury was virtually limitless. What some religious criticized was the policy of the Audiencia of reaching decisions on the principle of *juxta allegata et probata*, without inquiring into the credibility of the witnesses. According to the religious, the Filipinos often exploited Spanish judicial processes to obtain vengeance in their feuds. Instead of murdering or assaulting his enemies, an accuser brought suit and presented false testimony, which usually produced the desired result. The accused languished in prison. The regulars claimed that the paternalistic system prevailing in the villages produced fewer miscarriages of justice.[24] Suits were settled on the basis of oral testimony, and the veracity of testimony could be checked against other local sources.

That the Filipinos sometimes exploited Roman law procedures to their ends is undoubtedly true. They used canon law for this purpose on occasion, as we observed in Chapter V. It should be realized, nevertheless, that the religious were not solely motivated

by a disinterested consideration in their criticism of the introduction of Roman law usages among the Filipinos. They felt that the
spread of Roman jurisprudence would tend to bring the Filipinos
under the increasing jurisdiction of the civil authorities and thereby
might lessen the influence and the power of the clergy.[25]

## The Nonlinguistic Character of Hispanization

The native commonwealth in the Philippines was no mere
legal or administrative fiction. It had more of a territorial and
socioethnic reality in the islands than it ever possessed in Mexico.
The vast majority of Filipinos in the provinces seldom saw any
Spaniard except the local priest, who usually spoke the local
language. The isolation of the Filipinos from Spanish-speaking
people provides the basic explanation for the strange fact that after
more than three hundred years of Spanish rule less than 10 per
cent of the population spoke Spanish.[26]

As we already know, the Crown originally encouraged the
clergy to preach the Faith in the native languages in order to
facilitate the transition from paganism to Christianity. In the
seventeenth century, however, royal policy became one of en-
couraging the Indians to become bilingual, and in the eighteenth
century frantic efforts were made to compel the natives to adopt
Spanish. Motivating this gradual shift toward "linguistic imperialism" was an ethnocentric prejudice of the Spaniards that the
native tongues were not sufficiently well developed to transmit
the mysteries of the Catholic creed. There was also a genuine fear
among the civil authorities that idolatries and superstitions would
persist until the natives abandoned the languages of their pagan
past.[27]

Every community was required to set up a primary school with
Spanish as the obligatory language of instruction. The monthly
salary of one peso paid to school teachers obviously did not provide any economic incentive for Filipinos to enter that perennially
underpaid profession.[28] Spanish-speaking school teachers were at a
premium, and students were scarcer still. Parents showed no en-

thusiasm for sending their children to school, since their labor services could be usefully employed in the rice fields or in domestic chores. Philippine geographical particularism also imposed considerable hardships on students, most of whom had to travel long distances daily to attend classes.[29] Hence few of these civil-operated primary schools, designed to take the place of the monastic-run schools which had long since decayed, actually functioned. Punitive measures in the eighteenth century produced no appreciable change. A royal cedula that no Filipino who did not read, write, and speak Spanish could be elected to public office was unenforceable. The Crown had to retreat behind the face-saving formula that Spanish-speaking Filipinos be "preferred" for public office. Since few Filipinos spoke Spanish, the phrase was meaningless.[30]

Bureaucrats during the time of Charles III (1759–88) were apt to accuse the regular clergy of deliberately conspiring to keep the Filipinos in linguistic isolation on the supposition that non-Spanish-speaking Filipinos would be more amenable to ecclesiastical control.[31] The regulars may have been indifferent if not hostile to the spread of Castilian, but they could not have prevented the Filipinos from learning that language if certain conditions had been present.

What the Filipinos lacked was a social and economic incentive to learn Spanish, the kind of incentive with which the American regime provided them to learn English. The Americans quickly recognized the practical necessity of throwing open most of the jobs in the civil service to qualified Filipinos. English was made the *sine qua non* for obtaining these positions. The creation of an educational system from the primary grades through the university level, with English as the obligatory language of instruction, spread the new *lingua franca* within a generation. Given the isolation of the Filipinos from most social contracts with the Spaniards, the slow growth of a Spanish-speaking mestizo class, and the total absence of any socioeconomic incentive, fluency in Spanish was confined ordinarily to Filipinos living in Greater

Manila. But even there Tagalog remained the "language of the hearth."

The failure of Spanish to spread among the Filipinos did not prevent a substantial measure of political Hispanization. The explanation of this anomaly lies in the character of the political and judicial forms which the Spaniards introduced. This system was a mosaic of preconquest and Hispanic features, with the latter elements tending to predominate. The post-Hispanic barangay, for example, was profoundly Hispanized without losing continuity with its preconquest antecedent. Out of the system of local self-government, in which the principles of hereditary succession, representation, election and rotation in office were meticulously observed, grew modern political caciquism. In the administration of justice pre-Hispanic usages and Roman jurisprudence originally coexisted, but they eventually blended together. Terminological Hispanization was in time followed by a substantial degree of functional Hispanization.

The enthusiasm with which the Filipinos adapted themselves to Spanish political forms attests to their capacity for creative social adjustment. Their response to political Hispanization was in many respects as positive and as penetrating as their acceptance of certain features of Christianity. The institutions of local self-government established in the islands were substantially similar to those the Spaniards had previously fashioned for Indian Mexico.[32] The long-term results in both regions, however, were somewhat dissimilar. As we observed in the last chapter, the Philippine magistrates remained relatively affluent, largely as a result of their role in organizing the material and human resources of the native population for the benefit of the colonial government. Continued prosperity in addition to the isolation of the Filipinos from the Spanish-mestizo community strengthened the political and societal leadership of the *principales*. These conditions enabled them to play a creative role as intermediaries between the two cultures.

The loss of wealth among the Mexican cacique class caused by the spread of Spanish latifundia and debt peonage weakened the societal role of the caciques as cultural intermediaries. Hispanization often took a more direct form, with Indian debt peons coming into close contact with some Spaniards but more especially with mestizos. In some respects the Mexican Indians may have been more completely Hispanized than the Filipinos. The intrusion of mestizos into the Indian countryside, for example, was an effective agent in spreading the Castilian language among the Indians. But this more direct form of Hispanization could produce confusion and demoralization. As is well known, the Indian consumption of pulque increased alarmingly all during the colonial period. Spanish pulque producers may have encouraged this trend in order to expand the market for their product. But the Indians' alcoholism can also be interpreted as a symptom of a state of demoralization caused by the cultural cross currents in which they lived.

In the Philippines, on the other hand, alcoholic consumption declined precipitantly during the seventeenth century. This result occurred in spite of the preconquest tradition of ritual drinking associated with the performance of certain religious observances. As was pointed out in Chapter VI, ceremonial drinking disappeared after the pagan ritual complex was overwhelmed by the elaborate ritual of Spanish Catholicism, in which alcoholic stimulation had no necessary function. The fact that alcoholic consumption during the seventeenth century declined to virtually nothing is indicative of a relative lack of demoralization.

While it is a valid generalization to describe Hispanization in the Philippines as indirect rather than direct, some reservations are in order. Outstanding among them is the case of metropolitan Manila. The large Filipino population in the capital was thrown into frequent contact with the Spanish community. They became urbanized wage earners who spoke at least a smattering of Spanish and hence were more Hispanized than their cousins in the provinces. Although a small class of mestizos emerged, miscegenation between the Filipinos and the Chinese was much more frequent than between the Filipinos and the Spaniards. The simple fact is that there were far more Chinese in Manila than there were Spaniards. Both the Chinese and the Filipinos were in an inferior social category to the Spaniards. The Chinese seemed to adapt themselves more easily to the Filipinos' way of life than did the Spaniards, who ordinarily insisted on the prevalence of Spanish cultural standards. Sino-Filipino miscegenation evidently produced far fewer psychological and cultural tensions than issued from unions between Spaniards and Filipinos.

In conclusion, it seems apparent that the cultural changes introduced by the Spanish regime were of a more orderly, a more selective, and a less demoralizing character in the Philippines than in Mexico. In the making of this result three factors seem decisive. The physical survival of the Filipino population was never threatened by any of the changes accompanying the conquest. The Filipinos in the provinces were isolated from most contacts with the Spanish and mestizo population except those provided by the clergy. Thirdly, continued prosperity enabled the *principales* to act in a creative and selective fashion as the intermediaries between the two cultures. A convincing demonstration of the inward cohesiveness of native Philippine society can be found in an examination of some of the disruptive pressures aimed at overthrowing this regime.

### Chapter x

# Patterns
of Resistance

The military phase of Spain's conquest of the Philippines must be thought of as a continuum, a movement which began in 1565 and one which was reaching its completion in 1898. The conquest falls into three principal periods. Within a decade after 1565 Spanish control was firmly established over the maritime provinces of the northern and central portions of the archipelago. During the first half of the seventeenth century the offensive was resumed against the two major groups who had rejected Spanish hegemony—the Moros of Mindanao and the inhabitants of the mountain province of northwestern Luzon. Spanish efforts in this period yielded few lasting results. It was not until the second half of the nineteenth century that the conquest entered its third and final stage. By 1898 the backbone of resistance in both regions was broken on the eve of the overthrow of the Spanish colonial regime by the combined efforts of a Filipino nationalist revolt and the more decisive intervention of the United States.

Thus two configurations of resistance emerged during the seventeenth century. One was the outright rejection of Spanish domination by some groups. The other was an occasional desire of the Christianized Filipinos of the maritime province to overthrow Spanish hegemony.

## Mindanao and the Mountain Province

The first contacts between Spaniards and Moros were sanguinary. The conflict was another clash between the Cross and the Crescent, for the inhabitants of the southern Philippines had been converted to the religion of Islam during the century prior to the Spanish conquest. Thus the Spaniards in their westward expansion to America and to the Orient had half-encircled the globe only to encounter in Mindanao the farthermost eastern advance of their ancient enemies, the Muslims. Spanish intervention in 1565 occurred just in time to halt the advance of Islam toward the central and northern portions of the archipelago. If the principal Spanish base of operations had remained in the Bisayas and had not been removed to Manila, Mindanao might have been conquered in the sixteenth century. However, early Spanish attempts at conquest and colonization, notably the expedition of Estebán Rodríquez de Figueroa (1596), failed.

The Moros vigorously retaliated against Spanish attacks. From their bases in Jolo and Lake Lanao the Moros conducted a series of devastating raids on the Christian communities in the Bisayas. These maritime and riparian settlements were an exposed and inviting prey for hit-and-run raids. Spanish efforts to defend the Bisayas from their bases at Iloilo and Cebu proved inadequate to stem the tide of Moro aggression. Jesuit missions on Leyte, Samar, Cebu, and Bohol sustained heavy damage.[1] This fact explains why the Jesuits vigorously demanded punitive measures to curb the depredations of the Moros. The enslavement of Moro raiders was authorized as early as 1570, but the Spaniards failed to capture many. As of 1606, for example, there were only fifty Mindanao captives serving as galley slaves in the Spanish fleet, whose total crew consisted of some seven hundred galley slaves.[2]

The primary objective of Spanish penetration into Mindanao in the seventeenth century was defensive in character. The

founding of a perimeter of coastal presidios had two strategic purposes. One was to protect the settlements in the Bisayas. The other
was to neutralize Mindanao and Jolo in the Hispano-Dutch war,
for the Moros frequently coöperated with the Dutch against the
Spaniards. Acting on the appeals of the Jesuit missionaries, Governor Cerezo de Salamanca dispatched an expedition in 1635 to
establish the fortress of Zamboanga in southeastern Mindanao.[3]
This site was strategic because leadership among the Moros had
passed from the Magindanaus to the Sulus, whose headquarters
were on the island of Jolo, from which they dominated the whole
Sulu archipelago. In order to combat the Sulu menace, the Spaniards chose Zamboanga as their principal offensive and defensive
base in that region.

An able general, Governor Hurtado de Corcuera, conducted
in 1637 and 1638 a twofold offensive in which he set out to destroy
the two principal centers of Moro power. At the battle of Lamitan
he defeated the Moro chieftain, Kudarat, and was thus enabled to
demolish the Moro citadel near Lake Lanao. Turning southward
the next year he led an expedition of some 1,000 Filipinos and 600
Spaniards against the sultan of Jolo, capturing the city of Jolo after
a fierce battle. Although Corcuera's campaigns momentarily re-
lieved the pressure from Moro raids, his victories, celebrated in
the Jesuit chronicle of Francisco Combés, turned out to be more
spectacular than solid. They were not consolidated by territorial
occupation of large areas.

It is possible, in fact, that Corcuera's expeditions against the
Moros on Mindanao had a more significant effect on the status of
Formosa than they did on the Moro problem. Under the influence
of his Jesuit advisers, Corcuera apparently neglected the Spanish
garrison on the island of Formosa, Spain's most northerly advance,
in favor of concentrating on the Moro menace to the south.
Corcuera's indifference may have contributed something to Spain's
losing her toehold on southern Formosa a few years later to the
Dutch, who were entrenched in northern Formosa. Also involved
in the loss of the island was the rivalry between the Dominicans

and the Jesuits. The Dominicans had set up a chain of missions in southern Formosa, which they regarded as a stepping stone to China. The Spanish Jesuits in the Philippines looked with disfavor on such a prospect. They feared Dominican encroachment on the modest but already flourishing Jesuit mission in the Celestial Empire.[4] However, in addition to these suspicions the Jesuits had the very real reason of the attacks their missions in the central Philippines had suffered from the Moros for advising concentration of military efforts in the south.

Corcuera's neglect of Formosa was a defensible decision. Given his limited resources, he had to concentrate on the most critical fronts, and the pressure of the Dutch in other areas and the depredations of the Moros required immediate attention. Formosa thus fell away from the orbit of the Philippines, to which it could conceivably have belonged because of the ethnic character of its indigenous population and because of geopolitical considerations. It is doubtful, however, whether the Chinese government would have tolerated Spanish control over Formosa for any length of time.

The tie-up between Formosa and Mindanao was to assert itself again in that critical year of 1662. No sooner had the Chinese condottiere, Koxinga, ousted the Dutch from Formosa in 1661 than he indicated aggressive designs on Manila. With Koxinga's sudden death the threat to the Spanish colony evaporated, but before the situation clarified Manila ordered the withdrawal of Spanish garrisons on the periphery, notably Zamboanga in Mindanao and the presidios in the Moluccas. The Dutch had long since won the "war of the spices," and the garrisons in the Moluccas were strategically obsolete and costly.[5] The decision to abandon Zamboanga, on the other hand, was the product of momentary panic rather than cool strategic thinking. In the eighteenth century the Spanish presidio was re-established there.

Accompanying Spanish soldiers to Mindanao were the Jesuits and the Augustinian Recollects. The first Jesuit mission, which was founded in 1596 and abandoned in 1600, was located at the mouth of the Butuan River. Re-established in 1611, the Jesuits handed it over to the Recollects in 1622. The two principal Jesuit missions were at Zamboanga and at Dapitan-Iligan. There were usually not more than eleven priests in both areas, administering to about 28,000 people. The Recollect missions were located along the coast adjacent to the mouth of the Butuan River and along the north-eastern coast of the Surigao peninsula. The Recollects administered to about 20,000 people.[6]

Spanish failure in the mountain province of northwestern Luzon was as complete as it was in Mindanao but for different reasons. The mountainous terrain of that interior province made it inaccessible. The area quickly aroused the curiosity of the Spaniards as a potential source of gold and as the home of the headhunting bands who occasionally raided coastal communities. Once the lowland provinces of Pangasinan, Ilokos, and Cagayan had been subdued, the Spaniards turned their attention to the mountain region, whose inhabitants they called *Ygolotes*. In the face of the uncompromising hostility of the mountaineers and the reluctance of Manila to underwrite the expenses of a prolonged and costly territorial occupation, various military expeditions in 1591, 1608, 1635, and 1663 proved fruitless.[7] Missionaries who ventured into the area without military escort often met a martyr's death at the hands of the headhunters. In the seventeenth century the Spaniards had neither the military nor the ecclesiastical personnel to conquer the area. Occasional uprisings by the maritime peoples, the endless depredations of the Moros, and the Hispano-Dutch campaigns sufficiently taxed the limited resources of Manila without the Spanish attempting the costly operation of subduing the determined resistance of the mountain peoples.

During the administration of Governor Manuel de León (1669–77) the Spaniards undertook to stabilize the frontier. The job of creating a buffer zone between the Christianized lowlands and the mountain country was assigned to the military in cooperation with the religious. The *misiones vivas*, or active missions, were organized in outlying areas. The natives paid no tribute, and many of them were not baptized. Each mission enjoyed the protection of a few soldiers. As of 1742 there were some twenty-eight religious stationed in these missionary outposts along the rim of the mountain country. Thirteen of these friars were in the province of Cagayan.

In the slow advance from the Cagayan valley the Dominicans took the lead. In the northeastern direction they reached the Isneg-Negrito country on the Abulog river, and by 1632 they had penetrated inland as far as the Isinai country in the southeastern part of the province. Eventually they opened a land route from the Cagayan valley to Manila.

The inhabitants of the mountain province had been expelled from the lowlands by the Malay invaders who were in possession of the maritime provinces when the Spaniards arrived. Hence there had been a long tradition of hostility between the people of the mountain province and those of the lowlands. This animosity was intensified in the seventeenth century, when the maritime peoples were converted to Spanish Christianity and the mountain province remained pagan. In spite of this traditional hostility, trade of a limited sort took place between the two regions, for each area had products the other needed. The semi-Christian buffer zone, the region of the *misiones vivas*, provided a convenient neutral ground where hogs, salt, iron, and cloth from the lowlands could be exchanged for gold, wax, and cacao from the mountain country.

The existence of this trade would suggest that the relations between these two diverse regions were not consistently hostile. Raiding expeditions organized by Christianized Filipinos against the mountain pagans sometimes degenerated into elaborate farces. The Christian raiders, who received a daily ration of rice from the royal treasury, sometimes forewarned their pagan neighbors of the impending attack.[8] Another significant example of coöperation between Christian and pagan Filipinos was that many of the former who fled to the mountains to escape the crushing burdens of the *polo* and the *vandala* were hospitably received by the pagans. Although there were deep historical roots antedating the conquest which help to explain the hostility between the people of the mountains and those of the lowlands, both groups on occasion were capable of coöperating against the Spaniards.

The mountain peoples of the other Christianized islands were equally unresponsive to Spanish efforts to subjugate them. They were the fierce and warlike Negritos, who were probably the original inhabitants of the islands. The mountainous terrain and the Negritos' passionate determination to preserve their independence proved effective shields against Spanish penetration.

The successful resistance of the Moros, the mountain province, and the Negritos cannot be explained solely in terms of a rigid analysis of the weakness and strength of the Spaniards. Numerical inferiority begs the question, for all the great Spanish conquests were achieved by a mere handful of conquistadores facing vast hordes of natives. The effectiveness of the tactical advantages of the Spaniards such as the horse and gunpowder was diminished by mountain barriers as well as the hot and humid climate in both regions. It is true that during their greatest concentration of military power in the first half of the seventeenth century the Spaniards were involved in a desperate struggle with the Dutch. Therefore they were able to concentrate only a fraction of their strength against their domestic Filipino enemies. Significant though these factors may be, these explanations border on the superficial.

In order to understand the successful resistance of these peoples it is necessary to explore their cultural development. Something in their way of life made resistance both meaningful and possible. After a few military encounters the peoples of the maritime provinces submitted to the rule of the conquerors. The Moros, the inhabitants of the mountain province, and the Negritos chose the alternative path of resistance. Why?

In the case of the Moros the factor of transculturation seems decisive. The creed of Islam gave them a religious belief, one which had amply demonstrated over the centuries its dynamic capacity to resist and even, in several cases, to overwhelm Christianity. Since Spanish nationalism had been born in the *reconquista* crusade against the Moors, the conflict between the Spaniards and the Moros in Mindanao became another clash between the Cross and the Crescent. Such a war seemed just and understandable to both belligerents. Islam's sway over the southern Philippines gave the Moros a political means of organizing successful resistance, for Muslim cultural influence introduced the suprakinship unit of the state. The new institutions of the *rajah* and the sultanates were superimposed on the pre-Muslim kinships units, which lost none of their vitality. Political-military authority was centralized sufficiently to organize effective resistance, but it never arrived at the point where the Spaniards could defeat and usurp it. What made the Moros unconquerable was the sound balance in their political-military organization between pre-Muslim decentralization and Muslim-sponsored centralization. Given their acceptance of certain features of Muslim culture, resistance became meaningful to the Moros. Hence resistance became possible by exploiting Spanish weakness in such a manner as to confine Spanish control to a few coastal presidios and even to carry the war into the territory of the enemy by means of devastating hit-and-run raids.

If transculturation illuminates the character of resistance in Mindanao, it provides no clues for understanding the successful resistance of the mountain province and the Negritos. Nor does the available evidence suggest that these peoples adopted certain features of Spanish culture in order to protect themselves against conquest. No trend away from the decentralized kinship units toward political-military centralization occurred. Spanish involvements with the Dutch or the fact that the mineral and manpower resources of the region provided no compelling inducement to the Spaniards are superficial explanations for Spanish failure to subdue the mountain province. The lack of success of the Spaniards had a preconquest origin. Built into the culture of the mountain province was the pattern of resisting encroachments from the lowlands. The Spanish conquest of the maritime peoples and the latter's subsequent adoption of Christianity merely fortified the traditional determination of the mountain province to resist conquest from the lowlands. Abandoning the idea of conquest, the Spaniards were forced to settle for a stable frontier which would afford protection to the maritime provinces. And the mountain peoples in turn wanted to be left alone. Military clashes occurred along the frontier from time to time, but the aims of both belligerents were essentially defensive in character.[9]

It was not until the second half of the nineteenth century that Spanish authority began to spread into these centers of resistance which for two centuries had tenaciously repulsed every effort at penetration. Ironically this development occurred during the very decades when Spain's ancient grip over the maritime provinces was being undermined by the spread of revolutionary and nationalist sentiment aiming at independence. Superior instruments of technology such as the steamboat, which opened up the interior river system of Mindanao, increased military strength, and the vigorous determination of the Spanish authorities, who then had the means of undertaking effective territorial occupations of pacified areas, partially account for the success of this last phase of the conquest. Equally decisive was the radical change which was taking place in Spanish methods. The Spanish were beginning to distinguish between the adoption of Catholicism and the acceptance of political control. Manila was willing to tolerate non-Christian beliefs in order to win the political allegiance of the newly conquered.[10]

Costly and inconvenient though the depredations of the Moros and the mountain peoples may have been in the seventeenth century, this very hostility strengthened the Spanish hold on the maritime provinces. The protective power of Spain was the only shield those Provinces had against the raids of their hostile neighbors, a condition which helps to explain their sustained loyalty to the Spanish regime.

## Revolts

The hard core of Spanish power was an area that included the central plain of Luzon (the Tagalog country), Pampanga, Pangasinan, Ilokos to the north, and the Bikol-speaking country of the

Camarines to the south. Spanish control over these regions was rapidly consummated during the 1570's. Uprisings such as the Pampanga revolt of 1585 and the Tondo conspiracy of 1587–88 were but the final stage of the conquest. No single item illustrates more concisely the firm grip of the Spanish regime over this area than the fact that between 1588 and 1762 there were only two periods of acute tension. They occurred in 1660–61 and 1745–46. Herein lies the principal explanation of why the Spaniards in the face of countless severe losses were always able to repulse their external enemies—the Dutch and the Moros. Nor were the Spanish authorities unaware of this fact. Acting on the suggestion of the procurator of the Philippine colony at the Spanish court, Philip IV in 1636 and 1642 instructed the *alcaldes mayores* to express his formal appreciation to the inhabitants of the Tagalog, Pampangan, and Bikol provinces for their fidelity.[11]

Manila itself, the very citadel of Spanish power, might have been a source of weakness in that it contained a concentrated population of some 20,000 Filipinos and some 15,000 Chinese. In response to famine conditions the same sort of floating population had twice looted Mexico City in the seventeenth century. In Manila, however, the crowds did not act in this fashion. The capital was adjacent to the "rice basket" of central Luzon. Food distribution never broke down as abruptly as it sometimes did in Mexico City, for, as we have seen, the ecological and economic changes introduced by the conquest were far less severe in the islands than in Mexico. Unlike Mexico City, where the Spanish town was exposed to the attacks of rioters, Manila was a walled and fortified town. Most of the Filipino community lived in the suburban villages encircling the walled city. The Chinese were settled in the Parian in wooden buildings within firing range of the guns of the fortress.

The resentments of the Filipinos in the face of economic hardships and dislocations had a visible scapegoat in the Chinese merchants who controlled the retail trade. The Filipinos enthusiastically coöperated with the Spaniards in periodic massacres of the Chinese community, the most notable of which occurred in 1603, 1639, 1662, and 1782. It is evident that Sino-Filipino hostility acted as a safety valve to unleash the pent-up resentments of the Filipinos. But it cannot be said that the Spanish administration cold-bloodedly fostered this racial-economic conflict in order to guarantee their hold over Manila. The Spaniards themselves were as genuinely afraid of the large Chinese colony in their midst as they were dependent upon it for a wide variety of economic services. Rather, the hatred of both the Spaniards and the Filipinos toward the Chinese created a situation favorable to the maintenance of Spanish control.

Hence Manila was a secure bastion from which the Spaniards continued to perpetuate their grip over the neighboring maritime provinces of Luzon. When revolt did sweep through the provinces of Pampanga, Pangasinan, and Ilokos in 1660, it did not represent a serious threat. The Pampangans were protesting against the crushing burdens placed on their material and human resources as a consequence of the Dutch war and its aftermath. Quick military action on the part of Governor Manrique de Lara saved Manila from the threat of invasion by the rebels. The governor negotiated with the leaders of the rebellion until his forces were sufficiently concentrated to undertake military operations. A small punitive expedition, a general amnesty for all rebels, the payment of 14,000 pesos as an initial installment on the *polo-vandala* debt of some 200,000 pesos, and a solemn promise to reduce the scope of woodcutting brought about a rapid cessation of the revolt.[12] Pampanga's fidelity to the Spanish regime up to 1660 was a partial outgrowth of the raids of the fierce Sambals who periodically terrorized that fertile valley. The Sambal threat made Pampanga as dependent on Manila as was the capital on the rice, the timber, the labor, and the soldiers of Pampanga.[13]

In Pangasinan and Ilokos the uprising of 1660–61 took on a more decided anti-Spanish character, with nativistic overtones. Malong in Pangasinan and Almazan in Ilokos proclaimed themselves kings of their respective peoples. Religious were killed, churches looted and their ornaments desecrated. Yet these provinces were rapidly pacified. Another general uprising in the Ilokano country did not occur until the period of the British invasion (1762–63).[14]

A revolt in the Tagalog provinces did not take place until the agrarian disturbances of 1745–46. In various localities the Filipinos took up arms to protest the alleged usurpation of their lands by some religious orders. The Jesuits, the Dominicans, the Augustinians, and the Augustinian Recollects among them operated some twenty large cattle ranches in the provinces of Bulacan and Batangas. Ten of these estates belonged to the Jesuits.[15]

The relative absence of revolts in the lowland provinces of Luzon is all the more remarkable in that these areas were the most densely exploited in the islands. From these provinces came in large quantities the agricultural products, the wood for shipbuilding, the labor services, and the soldiers that the Spanish administration required.

Spanish control over the Bisayas was never as penetrating as their domination of the maritime provinces of Luzon. Yet in a period of two centuries, between 1565 and the British invasion of 1762, only three major uprisings occurred in the whole Bisayan area. The Bisayans perhaps had as much need of the Spaniards as the Spaniards did of the Bisayans. The frequent raids of the Moros from Mindanao and Jolo terrorized the Bisayan settlements year after year. Spanish power was their only shield. When revolts did break out, they were apt to have a more pronounced nativistic content that the uprisings on Luzon. This trend was an outgrowth of the fact that the ecclesiastical establishment in the central Philippines was even more understaffed than were the parishes of Luzon.

In 1621 revolt swept through the island of Bohol, administered by the Jesuits. Led by a Filipino pagan priest, Tamblot, the rebels repudiated Christianity and aspired to return to the religion of their pagan ancestors. About 2,000 Boholanos joined the movement, but an expedition of fifty Spaniards and more than 1,000 Cebuans easily crushed the uprising, in January of 1622.[16]

The insurrection spread to the neighboring island of Leyte. Its leader was an aged chieftain, Bankaw, whose hospitable welcome of Legazpi was said to have evoked a formal acknowledgment from Philip II. A convert to Christianity and a loyal subject of Spain for many decades, he apostatized in his old age. Overthrow of Spanish control and the restoration of paganism were the twin objectives of the movement. Although the uprising plunged most of Leyte into chaos for a few months, a punitive expedition composed of a small detachment of Spanish soldiers and a much larger force of Cebuans quickly restored order.[17]

The year 1649, when the Hispano-Dutch war was drawing to its close, was another period of rebellious unrest in the Bisayas. The rebellion was precipitated by the order of Governor Diego Fajardo that a large detachment of Bisayan workers be sent to the shipyards in Cavite to relieve the hard-pressed Tagalogs. The religious in the Bisayas foresaw trouble and pleaded with the governor to revoke the order. The Bisayans were not accustomed to working in the shipyards, and the clergy stressed the hardships involved in Bisayans abandoning their homes and fields for distant Luzon. The fears of the religious were not groundless. When the governor's order was applied in Palapag on Samar, the standard of revolt was raised. The first act of the rebels was to liquidate an unpopular parish priest. The movement won initial successes as a consequence of the capable leadership of Juan Ponce Sumoroy. Before the insurrection was quelled the next year, it had spread to other islands. Its hard core, however, remained in Samar. The capture of the mountain citadel of Sumoroy brought hostilities to an end.[18]

An unusual revolt was one that broke out in Bohol in 1744. Under the leadership of Dagohoy, 3,000 of his followers fled to the mountains, where they repulsed all Hispano-Filipino expeditions sent against them. In fact, the rebellion did not end until 1829, some eighty-five years after its inception. Governor Ricafort pardoned the descendants of the rebels and permitted them to resettle in new villages in the lowlands. By 1829 Dagohoy's original 3,000 followers had multiplied to about 20,000 people.[19]

None of the five major uprisings which occurred prior to 1762 posed even a remote threat to Spanish hegemony over the lowlands. Each revolt was subdued by a handful of Spanish soldiers assisted by Filipino recruits, i.e., natives from a different province or island. In the absence of any clear-cut Philippine national consciousness, which did not begin to emerge until the nineteenth century, the Spaniards were able to play one ethnic group against the other.

The regular clergy played a key role. Some religious did lose their lives in the various uprisings. For this reason the clergy as a group were tireless in their efforts to pacify a recently revolted area. Their intervention usually secured a general amnesty, with the death penalty confined to a few leaders. The fact that more revolts did not break out may be traced to the appeal and authority the religious exercised over their parishioners. One bishop of Cagayan perhaps understated his case when he wrote Philip III that one religious was worth one hundred Spanish soldiers.[20]

The native constabulary was another reliable source of strength to the Spanish administration. A separate army modeled along the lines of the Spanish military organization was set up. Its officers were Filipinos, some of whom bore the high-sounding military rank of captain and master of the camp. Taught in the methods of European military science, they fought with distinction in every campaign along with Spanish troops. They were equally reliable against the regime's domestic foes and against its foreign enemies. Ordinarily a military expedition would consist of a small Spanish detachment and a much larger Filipino force. Pampanga furnished the bulk of these levies. The Spaniards usually expressed high regard for the courage and stamina of the Pampangan troops. Occasionally some uneasiness was voiced about putting arms into the hands of any native group. These fears, however, proved groundless.[21]

Along with the Church and the Filipino constabulary, the sys-

tem of local administration was another factor in the maintenance
of Spanish authority in the provinces. As we observed in the last
chapter, the *principales* were modest beneficiaries of the colonial
status quo. The preservation of the system was to their advantage.
The Filipino magistracy had to maneuver between the triple pressures exercised by the Spanish administration, their desire for self-
enrichment at the expense of their followers, and the discontents
of their fellow countrymen. Only under conditions of acute stress
did they desert the Spanish cause to lead their followers into
armed rebellion. Every insurrection that did take place resulted
from a case of such stress, and the *principales* provided the leadership for the revolt. Thus the class structure as well as the ethnic
divisions among the Filipinos provides a *divide et impera* explanation
of the long-enduring Spanish hold on the maritime provinces.

If the Filipino magistrates had to adjust to pressures exerted
by the Spanish administration, they also could not be indifferent
to the welfare of their followers. Only occasionally were they
driven to the desperate extremity of open rebellion, in most situa-
tions preferring to use peaceful means to protect their subordinates. The kinship character of Philippine society, which retained much of its cohesiveness in the seventeenth century as a
result of the survival of the barangays, made these magistrates
patriarchical and paternalistic leaders of their communities. In
dealing with the Spanish authorities, evasion and procrastination
were effective tactics, given the decentralized character of population patterns. The *principales* seldom put pressure on the Spanish
administration by means of memorials and petitions to the
Audiencia in Manila and the Council of the Indies in Spain de-
manding reform. This alternative was closed to them, for as a
class they had little formal education of the Spanish variety. They
were not illiterate, but few spoke or wrote Spanish. There were
no specially created schools where the sons of the chieftains could
acquire a Spanish education.

In Peru, on the other hand, special schools operated by the
Jesuits enabled some sons of caciques to acquire an excellent formal

education by the standards of the time and place. In the eighteenth century several caciques conducted a sustained program of political agitation, designed to improve the lot of the Indian masses, inside the framework of the Spanish bureaucracy. Periodically petitioning the Crown for reforms, this Inca nationalist movement culminated in a series of extensive rebellions whose well-organized character posed a serious problem to the Spanish authorities.[22] No comparable political activity was undertaken by the Filipino *principales*, lacking as they did the educational opportunities available to the Peruvian caciques. Yet it is apparent that the *principales* provided the Filipino masses with some modest protection against the worst excesses of colonial exploitation at the same time that they oppressed their subordinates for their own personal gain and for the benefit of the Spanish regime.

Understandably enough, the leaders of these early revolts have been enshrined in the pantheon of modern Philippine nationalism as heroic precursors of independence.[23] It should be realized, however, that none of these leaders was guided by an outlook that could be called even remotely Pan-Philippine. These revolts were local uprisings executed as protests against local grievances. It took two hundred and fifty years of the *pax hispanica* before a Philippine national consciousness could become articulate. The Spanish contribution toward the formation of the modern Philippine nation was substantial. The *pax hispanica* created conditions of law and order throughout the maritime provinces of Luzon and the Bisayas, Spanish forms of political organization spread, and Catholicism gave the Filipinos a new kind of spiritual and cultural unity. Nonetheless, if the Spanish contribution should not be overlooked, neither should the role of the Filipinos be underestimated. Their capacity for creative social adjustment to new cultural stimuli has been amply demonstrated. They selectively adapted rather than arbitrarily adopted Spanish forms to old patterns. If the Filipinos revere the leaders of the early revolts as the precursors of the modern nation, they should not disparage the laborious if undramatic efforts of those Filipinos in the seventeenth century who were confronted with the difficult task of synthesizing Hispanic and indigenous elements into a somewhat harmonious whole. The modern Philippine nation owes as much to the latter group as it does to the former.

# In
# Retrospect

Nietzsche was once supposed to have exclaimed, "Those Span-
iards! those Spaniards! Those are men who wanted to be too much."[1]
Spanish colonization in the Philippines is certainly a case in point.
Isolated from Mexico and Spain by the breadth of the Pacific and
the Atlantic, the small Spanish colony attempted to do too much.
As is now rather clear, the Spanish regime's ambitious program
of cultural integration was only partially implemented in the
Philippines.

Immediately apparent is the deep gulf separating legislation
formulated in Spain and its lack of enforcement in the islands.
Philippine colonization was modeled on Mexican precedents.
Conditions in the archipelago, however, did not always respond to
this Mexican-inspired legislation.[2] A Hegelian formula may clarify
matters somewhat. The thesis is royal legislation dispatched to the
Philippines based largely on Mexican models. The antithesis is
local conditions in the islands often at variance with the government's instructions. This gap was created by the Council of the
Indies' unawareness of the actual state of affairs in the distant
archipelago and by the instinctive impulse of the bureaucrats in

Spain to standardize practices throughout the empire. The synthesis was what actually happened in the Philippines. That may not always have been satisfactory, but it was usually a workable compromise between what the central authorities intended and what local conditions would permit.

Bureaucrats in Spain had a habit of treating the Philippine colony as if it were another province of Mexico. Administratively the islands did form an autonomous branch of the viceroyalty of New Spain, but local conditions often stubbornly resisted Mexican-oriented legislation. This proposition is true in many cases but not in all. There are two sides to the coin. Spanish activity in Mexico provided some experience that was profitably applied in the colonization of the Philippines. The relatively peaceful character of the military conquest itself is an outstanding case in point. In the organization of labor Mexican precedents proved helpful. Some of the worst excesses of the encomienda and the *repartimiento* were avoided when these institutions were transplanted to the Philippines. The Mexican experience also provided the clergy with a galaxy of pertinent models. The sacraments were introduced into the islands with a minimum of controversy largely because the lessons learned in Mexico were profitably applied. Political Hispanization among the Mexican Indians was equally useful to the Spanish authorities in setting up local self-government in the archipelago. It is apparent that previous experience in Mexico was both a help and a hindrance in the Philippines. It became an obstacle when special regional conditions were ignored.

In the Philippines the gap between the law and its observance was expanded by geographical isolation. Ordinarily it took two years to exchange communications between Manila and the Spanish court. In spite of the theoretical centralization of the Spanish monarchy, colonial magistrates often acted with a substantial degree of independence. They were able to disregard the injunctions of the authorities in Spain by invoking the "I obey but do not execute" formula. Royal orders whose implementation might create injustices or conflicts did not have to be enforced until the Council of the Indies had been made aware of the special circumstances of the area involved.³ In few regions of the empire was this formula more frequently invoked than in the Philippines. In many cases this procedure was followed with ample justification. Royal legislation was sometimes unenforceable. Hence both the civil and the ecclesiastical authorities in Manila did have considerable maneuverability in executing orders from Spain. These same conditions enabled the regular clergy in the provinces to pursue policies often in conflict with the wishes of the civil and episcopal authorities in Manila.

If Philippine isolation from the main centers of the empire gave Spanish magistrates a comfortable latitude of freedom in enforcing orders from Spain, local conditions also allowed the Filipinos to be selective in their responses to orders emanating from Manila. All the major participants in the transformation of Philippine society—the Spanish magistracy, the episcopacy, the regular clergy, and the Filipinos—each one had some freedom in which to maneuver. The paucity of large, compact villages of the type contemplated in colonial legislation, the scarcity of Spanish colonists, the slow growth of a mestizo class, the failure of the Spanish language to spread, and the shortage of religious limited the impact of Hispanic influences on the Filipinos. The range of Filipino responses varied all the way from hostility and apathy to curiosity and enthusiasm.

The Filipinos' hostility to resettlement greatly diminished its effectiveness and its extent. Settlement patterns did change in the direction of rural concentration but not as rapidly or as completely as Spanish officialdom desired. The población-barrio-sitio complex that emerged was a compromise between the preconquest pattern of geographical particularism and the Spanish ideal of compact rural concentration.

The Filipinos responded to some forms of Spanish political organization with an enthusiasm comparable to their acceptance of Catholicism. The system of local self-government established during the seventeenth century provided the Filipinos with a whole new range of political experience. Its ultimate consequences for the political structure of the modern Philippines ought not to be underestimated. The legacy of caciquism weighs heavily on the modern Philippine nation in its quest toward creating a stable democracy.

What facilitated a relatively orderly economic transition was demographic stability. Contagious diseases did not slaughter the Filipinos, who had previously acquired some immunity against these epidemics. The defenselessness of the Indians in Mexico against smallpox and measles made the economic transition there anything but orderly. In the wake of a severe demographic crisis there followed an economic and ecological revolution. The physical survival of the Filipinos was the *sine qua non* for the evolutionary character of the economic and the ecological changes introduced by the conquest.

The founding of the Spanish colony did not entail an overthrow of the preconquest economy based on fishing, the cultivation of rice and root crops, and the raising of swine and fowl. Rather, production expanded to meet new demands. This was accompanied by some significant changes that supplemented rather than destroyed the ancient pattern of economic organization. Among these changes were the influx of skilled Chinese labor and the introduction of new plants and animals. The mild character of ecological innovations spared the Filipinos the severe and painful dislocations which similar changes produced in Mexico. Although some forms of pre-Hispanic debt peonage were eventually extinguished, preconquest sharecropping continued under another name. In the sphere of land tenure the outstanding novelty was the gradual adoption of the European principle of individual ownership of land.

The Spanish administration sought to foster the growth of free, paid labor, but only in urbanized Manila did this objective meet with appreciable success. The Dutch war emasculated the reforming energies of the regime. In the absence of Spanish-owned latifundia, exploitation was of an indirect variety, and preconquest forms of labor therefore continued, with the chieftains responsible for delivering the required quotas of labor and goods to the Spanish authorities.

The economic underpinnings of the native upper class were not swept away by the conquest. On the contrary, colonial society provide the chieftains with additional means of enrichment. Their source of wealth was twofold. The pre-Hispanic system of sharecropping and debt peonage survived in a modified form in the face of vigorous Spanish efforts to abolish it. Secondly, the *principales* were both the economic and the administrative inter- mediaries between the material demands of the Spanish regime and the productive capacities of the masses. As such the opportunities of these chieftains for both legal and extralegal enrichment were various. The retention of both wealth and local political power enabled the *principales* to continue to play a role of moderately creative leadership as the intermediaries between the two cul- tures.

The absence of Spanish latifundia partially accounts for the more indirect character of Hispanization in the Philippines. Spanish landlords in the provinces and their mestizo managers would have dried up much of the modest wealth of the Filipino upper class, and the impoverishment of the *principales* would in turn have en- feebled but not eliminated their societal leadership. Acculturation to Hispanic norms would have become direct, with the natives being thrown into immediate and daily contact with Spaniards and mestizos. This is what happened in Mexico as a consequence of the intrusion of numerous Spaniards and mestizos into the Indian countryside.

That the Filipinos benefited in some significant respects from their indirect variety of Hispanization is apparent. It meant less Hispanization but better digested. The shocks of change and the stresses of adjustment were cushioned by the fact that continuity with preconquest culture was amply preserved. Under the leader- ship of their *principales* the Filipinos were able to absorb a modest portion of Spanish culture without suffering from an acute case of indigestion. Filipino adjustment to Hispanization was of an orderly variety, without causing the demoralization and confusion from which primitive peoples undergoing acculturation sometimes suffer.

The Mexican Indians in some respects may have been more Hispanized than the Filipinos, but their adjustment was of a more demoralizing and painful character. The prevalence of alcoholism among the Mexican Indians can be interpreted as a symptom of this demoralization. The most concrete manifestation of direct Hispanization was the rapid emergence of a numerous class of mestizos. The mentality of the mestizos was plagued by psychological insecurity, resentments, and frustrations created by their ambiguous cultural situation. Repudiating the world of their Indian mothers, the mestizos sought to identify themselves with the world of their Spanish fathers. There, however, they were not accepted as equals.[4]

Direct Hispanization made Mexico a mestizo nation. Although the process of miscegenation imposed severe psychological and cultural tensions on both the Indians and the mestizos which are visible to this day, the mestizo character of Mexico's culture offers promising and unique possibilities of development and growth. Indirect Hispanization of the Philippine variety, partially the consequence of the fact that there were not enough Spaniards in the provinces to produce a large mestizo class, created far fewer psychological tensions. This indirect form of Hispanization, moreover, did facilitate a more orderly adjustment to cultural change.

Indirect Hispanization presupposed two conditions. One was demographic stability. The other was the physical segregation of the majority of Filipinos from most Spanish and mestizo contacts. If the Filipino population had been decimated by the spread of contagious diseases or if the Philippine countryside had been overrun by Spaniards and mestizos, the type of indirect Hispanization which did occur would not have taken place. In surveying Hispanic colonization overseas, the Philippines emerges as a moderately successful experiment. The paradox is that Spanish success issued from Spanish failure. The Spaniards did not accomplish as much as they set out to do, and this result enabled the Filipinos to absorb a modest amount of Hispanic influence without breaking too abruptly or too completely with their preconquest way of life. The Filipinos were partially Hispanized with a minimum of psychological and physical damage. The same result did not occur in either Mexico or in Peru.

In the process of acculturation the *principales* played a key role. They had to find sufficient room to maneuver against the triple pressures exercised by the Spanish administration, their own ambition for self-enrichment at the expense of their followers, and the discontents of their own countrymen. Although the chieftains were the modest beneficiaries of the colonial status quo, the kinship character of the small barangays made them sensitive to conditions of acute stress. The *principales* both oppressed their subordinates and protected them from the worst excesses of Spanish exploitation. Yet the quotas of labor and material set by the *alcaldes* had to be met. When the pressure on the *principales* became unbearable, they led the masses into open rebellion. But these insurrections were not frequent.

Philippine society had its share of stresses and strains. That these tensions did not result in more frequent explosions may be ascribed in large measure to the influence of the Church. Catholicism provided the cement of social unity. The Filipinos responded enthusiastically to the multiform appeal of Spanish Catholicism. Knowledgeable in the psychology of primitive peoples, the missionaries knew how to capture the imagination of their parishioners. Alongside doctrinal or official Catholicism there also grew up a rich and varied folk Catholicism. The growth of these popular practices, beliefs, and superstitions indicates how deeply the new religion was taking root in the daily lives of the Filipinos.

From the viewpoint of the Church, the Catholicism of the Filipinos left much to be desired. The quality of indoctrination was not always adequate, nor did the converts always participate fully in the sacramental life of the Church. Outward religious formalism rather than sound doctrinal knowledge, the triple dangers of idolatry, superstition, and magic, added to the infrequency in the administration of the sacraments, were all defects which could have been partially remedied by a well-trained Filipino clergy. Motivated by an ethnocentric prejudice and by a selfish desire to preserve their privileged position, the Spanish regular clergy stunted the growth of the Filipino priesthood. By deliberately restricting the number of Filipino priests and the quality of their training, the Spanish clergy unwittingly sponsored the "Philippinization" of Spanish Catholicism in such a fashion that they virtually lost control over the direction and shape of folk Catholicism.

What the missionaries accomplished was nevertheless remarkable, in view of the severe handicaps under which they labored. There was a constant shortage of clergy administering to a numerous and dispersed population. The maintenance of high standards of ecclesiastical discipline, difficult under any circumstance, was aggravated in the Philippines by the fact that the clergy spent most of their lives isolated from social contacts with their religious culture. The regular clergy did manage to preserve their jurisdictional autonomy vis-à-vis the bishops, in contrast to what happened in Mexico and in Peru. Yet this advantage was largely vitiated by the considerable freedom of action that the Filipinos possessed in determining their responses to Christianity. The enthusiasm and the dedication of the first generation of missionaries was followed by a trend toward apathy and discouragement. Such a decline in morale, however, was almost inevitable, especially as the clergy became aware of the magnitude of the obstacles confronting them. It would be rash indeed to argue, without taking into account the handicaps under which they operated and the limitations of their own time and place, that the regular clergy could have done a more competent job than they actually did.

In that network of relations uniting Spaniard to Filipino, neither one always understood the other's aspirations and responses. Misunderstandings hardening into mutual deceptions abounded. In terms of their limited resources, the Spaniards actually attempted to do too much. Yet they accomplished a great deal. Judged by any objective standard, Spanish colonization in the Philippines was a remarkable episode in the global expansion of Europe. As an imperialist power the Spaniards did their share in exploiting the resources of their Philippine colony, but in all fairness to that colonizing power it should be realized that Spain gave the Filipinos something in return. The *pax hispanica* created conditions of law and order throughout the maritime provinces of Luzon and the Bisayas, Spanish political institutions took deep root and Catholicism forged powerful new bonds of cultural unity. Although dependent upon the products and the labor services of the conquered population, the Spanish administration made strenuous and sometimes effective efforts to place some restraints on the scope of exploitation. And finally, Spain brought the Philippines into the orbit of Western civilization, from which they have not departed since the sixteenth century. This is in contrast to China and Japan, for example, which have been subject to intensive Western influences for scarcely a century. As a direct consequence of Spanish colonization, the Filipinos are unique for being the only Oriental people profoundly and consistently influenced by Occidental culture for the last four centuries. In an Asia dominated by revolutionary and anti-Western nationalism, the consequences of this fact are a part of the world in which we live today.

Reference
Matter

# Glossary of Spanish and Philippine Terms

ALCALDE MAYOR—The governor of a province.
ADELANTADO—The governor of a frontier colony, a title granted to Legazpi by Philip II.
AUDIENCIA—The highest tribunal of justice in the islands. It also served as an advisory council to the governor.
AYUEY—Preconquest version of debt peonage among the Bisayans.
BARANGAY—In preconquest times a political-social unit; the Spanish term for a village.
BARRIO—Village.
CABECERA—A town or the capital of a parish.
CABEZA DE BARANGAY—Hereditary native chieftain who, in Spanish times, headed the smallest unit of local administration.
CASAMAJAN—A system of sharecropping prevalent in the eighteenth century.
CAJA DE COMUNIDAD—Village treasury.
CORREGIDOR—The governor of a province.
DATU—The preconquest term for native chieftain.
FISCAL—(1) Crown attorney; (2) a combined truant officer and sacristan of a parish church.
GOBERNADORCILLO—Literally meaning petty governor, the elected magistrate of a township.
GUIGUILIR—Preconquest debt peonage among the Tagalogs.
MAHARLIKA—The noble class in preconquest times.
MAMAMAHAY—Preconquest version of sharecropping among the Tagalogs.

165

Moros—The inhabitants of the southern Philippines who were converted to Islam.

Municipio—The modern term for a township.

Negritos—The pagan inhabitants of the mountains.

Población—A town.

Polo—A system of compulsory draft labor.

Pueblo de Indios—Township.

Principales—Upper classes among the Filipinos, including the hereditary *cabezas de barangay*, the elected officeholders, and people of means.

Principalía—The abstract form for the class of *principales*.

Ranchería—Seventeenth-century term for hamlet.

Sitio—Late Spanish and modern term for hamlet.

Timagua—Freemen in preconquest times.

Tumaranpuh—Preconquest system of sharecropping among the Bisayans.

Vandala—A system of compulsory sale of products to the government.

Visita—An seventeenth-century ecclesiastical term for a village serviced by a nonresident priest.

# Appendix

The following maps indicate the location of the *cabecera* churches of the regular clergy as of 1655. The first map is of the central (the Bisayas) and the southern Philippines (Mindanao). The second one includes the whole island of Luzon, and the third map is of central Luzon. The term, *cabecera*, refers to the capital of the parish, where the principal parish church was located and where ordinarily one or two religious were in permanent residence. Each *cabecera* had several *visita* chapels, usually located inland from the coast and serviced by an itinerant priest. The location of the *visitas* is not included on these maps.

These maps substantiate many of the conclusions contained in Chapter IV, which dealt with the geographical aspects of the Spanish missionary effort. The archipelago was partitioned among the five branches of the regular clergy along geoethnic lines. Spanish influence was deepest in the coastal areas, less intensive in the adjacent foothills and virtually non-existent in the central, mountainous areas of the islands. In the Bisayas the capital churches were often not located directly on the coast but a short distance inland. The frequent raids of the Moros were responsible for this trend, a problem which was discussed in Chapter X. These maps also suggest the relatively tighter grip the Spaniards held on central Luzon and the Camarines than they did on northern Luzon and in the Bisayas. Mindanao was just a frontier outpost with Spanish control confined to a few strategic coastal sites. And finally these maps constitute a convincing demonstration of the intimate relationship between the early Christianization of the archipelago and the historical development of settlement patterns in the islands. Virtually all of the *cabecera* churches of 1655 constitute important centers of population today, easily located on any large map of the contemporary Philippines.

A few words of explanation about the maps themselves are in order. Space made it difficult to include the parishes, which in 1655 were suburbs of Manila and which today constitute parts of Greater Manila. I include a list of these suburbs. The Jesuit parishes were San Miguel, Santa Cruz, and San Pedro Makati. The Augustinian parish suburbs were Tondo and Malate. Those of the Franciscans were located at Dilao, Tondo, Santa Ana de Sapa, and Sampaloc. The Dominican parishes in the suburbs were in the Parian and at Minondoc.

In order to indicate the geographical dispersal of the regular clergy different symbols have been chosen to indicate the parishes administered by the various orders. The following symbols have been used.

▲ Jesuit
● Augustinian
† Franciscan
✕ Dominican
▬ Augustinian Recollect

The parishes of each order are numbered consecutively, with each order having a separate sequence of numbers. The tables on the following pages identify the numbers. Older, historical names and spellings were used throughout, but the modern version follows in brackets.

# JESUIT ▲

| No. | Name | Province |
|---|---|---|
| | **ARCHBISHOPRIC** | |
| | *Residencia of Antipolo* | |
| 1 | Antipolo | Rizal |
| 2 | Baras | " |
| 3 | Taytay | " |
| 4 | Caynta [Cainta] | |
| | *Residencia of Silang* | |
| 5 | Silang | Cavite |
| 6 | Indan [Indang] | " |
| 7 | Maragondon | " |
| 8 | Cavite [Cavite City] | " |
| | *Marinduque* | |
| 9 | Boak [Boac] | Marinduque |
| 10 | Gasang [Gasan] | " |
| 11 | Marlanga (barrio of Torrijos) | " |
| 12 | Sta. Cruz de Napo [Sta. Cruz] | " |
| | **BISHOPRIC OF CEBU** | |
| 13 | Cebu [Cebu City] | Cebu |
| | *Bohol* | |
| 14 | Loboc | Bohol |
| 15 | Baclayon | " |
| 16 | Panglao | " |
| 17 | Inabagan [Inabanga] | Bohol |
| 18 | Malaboloc [Maribojoc] | " |
| | *Leyte* | |
| 19 | Carigara | Leyte |
| 20 | Leyte | " |
| 21 | Haro [Jaro] | " |
| 22 | Barugo | " |
| 23 | Alangalan [Alangalang] | " |
| 24 | Ocmug [Ormoc] | " |
| 25 | Baybay | " |
| 26 | Cabalian | " |
| 27 | Sorgor [Sogod] | " |
| 28 | Inundayan [Hinundayan] | " |
| 29 | Liboan [Liloam] | " |
| 30 | Dagami | " |
| 31 | Malaguicay [Malaguikay] (barrio of Tanauan) | " |
| 32 | Tambuco | " |
| 33 | Dulag | " |
| 34 | Bitto [Bito] | " |
| 35 | Abuyo [Abuyog] | " |
| 36 | Palo | " |
| | *Samar* | |
| 37 | Basey | Samar |
| 38 | Guiuan | " |
| 39 | Balanguigan [Balangiga] | Samar |
| 40 | Catbalogan | " |
| 41 | Caluigan [Calbiga] | " |
| 42 | Batan [Batang] (barrio of Hernani) | " |
| 43 | Capul | " |
| | *Samar y Ibabao* | |
| 44 | Catubig | |
| 45 | Biri | |
| 46 | Catarman | |
| 47 | Bobon | |
| 48 | Buri [Beri] (barrio of Oras) | |
| 49 | Tubig [Taft] | |
| 50 | Sulat | |
| 51 | Borongan | |
| | *Panay* | |
| 52 | Oton | Iloilo |
| 53 | Ylo-Ylo [Iloilo City] | " |
| | *Island of Negros* | |
| 54 | Ylog [Ilog] | Negros Occ. |
| 55 | Cabancalan [Kabankalan] | " |
| 56 | Suay | " |
| 57 | Ysiu [Isio] (barrio of Cauayan) | " |
| | *Mindanao* | |
| 58 | Residencia of Yligan-Dapitan | |
| 59 | Residencia of Zamboanga | |

# FRANCISCAN †

| Name | Province |
|---|---|
| **ARCHBISHOPRIC** | |
| 1 Polo de Catangalan [Polo] | Bulacan |
| 2 Meycauayan | " |
| 3 Bocaui [Bocaue] | " |
| 4 Binangonan | Rizal |
| 5 Morong | " |
| 6 Tanay | " |
| 7 Pililla | " |
| 8 Sta. Maria Caboan [Sta. Maria] | Laguna |
| 9 Mavitac [Mabitac] | " |
| 10 Siniloan | " |
| 11 Pangil | " |
| 12 Paete | " |
| 13 Lumbang [Lumban] | " |
| 14 Sta. Cruz | " |
| 15 Pila | " |
| 16 Nagcarlang [Nagcarlan] | " |
| 17 Lilio | " |
| 18 Mahayhay [Majayjay] | " |
| 19 Lugban [Lucban] | Quezon |
| 20 Mauvan [Mauban] | " |
| 21 Tayavas [Tayabas] | " |
| 22 Baler | " |
| 23 Atimonan | " |
| 24 Gurmaca or Silangan [Gumaca] | " |
| 25 Los Banos | Laguna |
| **BISHOPRIC OF NUEVA CACERES—CAMARINES** | |
| 26 Capalonga | Cams. N. |

| Name | Province |
|---|---|
| 27 Paracali [Paracale] | Cams. N. |
| 28 Labo | " |
| 29 Yndan [Vinzons] | " |
| 30 Daet-Tarisay [Daet and Talisay] | " |
| 31 Libmanan | Cams. Sur |
| 32 Quepayo [Quipayo] (barrio of Calabanga) | " |
| 33 Ciudad of Caceres [Naga City] | " |
| 34 Milaor | " |
| 35 Minalabac | " |
| 36 Bula (also Baao) [Bula] | " |
| 37 Nabua | " |
| 38 Yriga [Iriga] | " |
| 39 Buhi [Buhi] | " |
| 40 Libong [Libon] | Albay |
| 41 Polangui | " |
| 42 Ligao | " |
| 43 Oas | " |
| 44 Camalig | " |
| 45 Quipia [Jovellar] | " |
| 46 Albay (district of Legaspi City) | " |
| 47 Cacsaua [Cagsawa] (district of Legaspi City) | " |
| 48 Tabaco | " |
| 49 Milinao [Malinao] | " |
| 50 Casiguran | Sorsogon |
| 51 Sorsogon | " |
| 52 Bolosan [Bulusan] | " |
| 53 Calonga [Calongay] (barrio ot Pilar) | " |

# DOMINICAN ×

| Name | Province |
|---|---|
| **Cagayan** | |
| 1 Pata (barrio of Claveria) | Cagayan |
| 2 Abulug | " |
| 3 Potol [Pudtol] (barrio of Luna) | Sub-prov. of Apayao |
| 4 Cabagan | Isabella |
| Babuyanes islands (not included for limitations of space) | |
| 5 Masi (barrio of Buguey) | Cagayan |
| 6 Piat | " |
| 7 Camalanyugan [Camalniugan] | " |
| 8 Nasiping [Nassiping] (barrio of Gattaran) | " |
| 9 Iguig | " |
| 10 Tuguegarao | " |
| 11 Buguey | " |
| **Pangasinan** | |
| 12 Lingayen | Pangasinan |
| 13 Binalonan | " |
| 14 Calasiao | " |
| 15 Binmaley | " |
| 16 Magaldan [Mangaldan] | " |
| 17 Bagnotan [Bacnotan] | La Union |
| 18 Manaueg [Manaoag] | Pangasinan |

# AUGUSTINIAN ●

| Name | Province |
|---|---|
| **ARCHBISHOPRIC** | |
| 1 Tambobong (barrio of San Rafael) | Bulacan |
| 2 Bulacan | " |
| 3 Guinguito | " |
| 4 Vigua [Bigaa] | " |
| 5 Malolos | " |
| 6 Quinqua [Plaridel] | " |
| 7 Calumpit | " |
| 8 Hagonoy | " |
| 9 Paranaque | Rizal |
| 10 Pasig | " |
| 11 Taguig [Tagig] | " |
| 12 Bay | Laguna |
| 13 S. Pablo de los Montes [San Pablo City] | " |
| 14 Lipaa [Lipa] | Batangas |
| 15 Baguang [Bauan] | " |
| 16 Batangas | " |
| 17 Taal | " |
| 18 Tanaguang [Tanauan] | " |
| 19 Salaa [Salao] (barrio of Rosario) | " |
| *Pampanga* | |
| 20 Bacolor | Pampanga |
| 21 Guagua | " |
| 22 Macaveve [Macabebe] | " |
| 23 Lubao | " |
| 24 Mexico | " |

| Name | Province |
|---|---|
| 25 Candava [Candaba] | Pampanga |
| 26 Sesmoan [Sexmoan] | " |
| 27 Betis (barrio of Guagua) | " |
| 28 Porag [Porac] | " |
| 29 Minalin | " |
| 30 Apalit | Nueva Ecija |
| 31 Gapan | Pampanga |
| 32 Arayat | " |
| *Ilokos* | |
| 33 Agoo | La Union |
| 34 Baguan [Bauang] | " |
| 35 Tagurin [Tagudin] | Ilokos Sur |
| 36 Santa Cruz | " |
| 37 Candong [Candon] | " |
| 38 Navara [Navarcan] | " |
| 39 Bantay | " |
| 40 Sinay [Sinait] | " |
| 41 Dinglas [Dingras] | Ilokos N. |
| 42 Batac | " |
| 43 Ilagua [Laoag] | " |
| 44 Bacarra | " |
| **BISHOPRIC OF CEBU—BISAYAS** | |
| 45 Panay [Roxas City] | Capiz |
| 46 Dumalag | " |
| 47 Mambusao | " |
| 48 Batang [Batan] | " |
| 49 Pasig [Passi] | Iloilo |
| 50 Dumangas | " |

| Name | Province |
|---|---|
| 51 Haro [Jaro] | Iloilo |
| 52 Octon [Oton] | " |
| 53 Tibaguan [Tigbauan] | " |
| 54 Guimbal | " |
| 55 Carcar | Cebu |
| 56 S. Nicolas de Cebu [San Nicolas] (district of Cebu City) | " |

# AUGUSTINIAN RECOLLECTS ■

| Name | Province |
|---|---|
| *Pangasinan* | |
| 1 Masinloc | Sambal |
| 2 Bolinao | Pangasinan |
| **ARCHBISHOPRIC** | |
| 3 Marivels [Mariveles] | Bataan |
| **BISHOPRIC OF CEBU** | |
| 4 Romblon | Romblon |
| 5 Calamianes islands (not included for limitations of space) | |
| 6 Cuyo | Palawan |
| *Mindanao* | |
| 7 Tandag | Surigao |
| 8 Butuan | Agusan |
| 9 Cagayan [Cagayan de Oro City] | Misamisor |
| 10 Siargao island [Dapa] | Surigao |
| 11 Bislig | " |

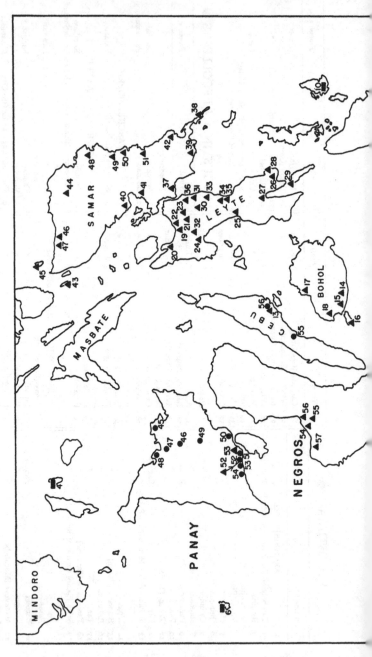

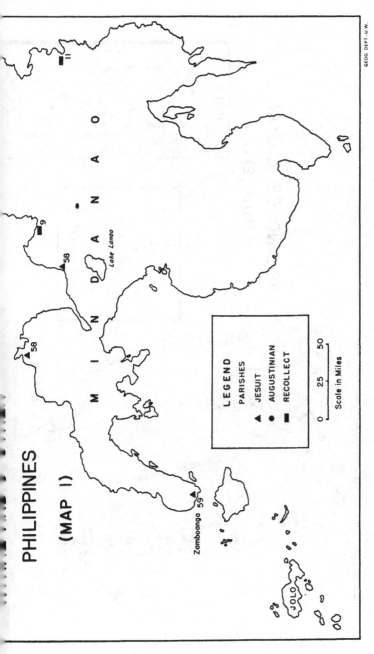

PHILIPPINES

(MAP 1)

MINDANAO

Lake Lanao

Zamboanga 59

JOLO

LEGEND

PARISHES

JESUIT

AUGUSTINIAN

RECOLLECT

Scale in Miles

0    25    50

GEOG. DEPT.-J.W.

173

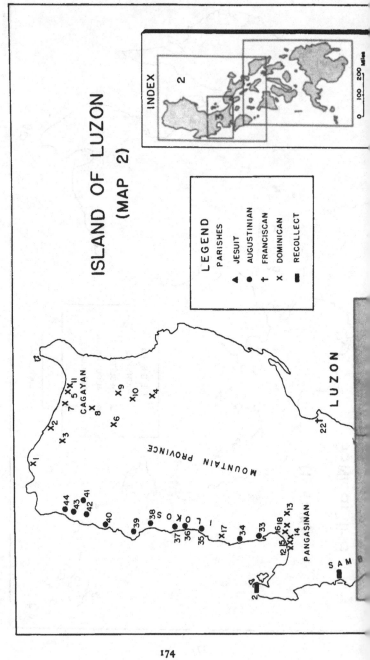

ISLAND OF LUZON
(MAP 2)

LEGEND

PARISHES

▲ JESUIT
● AUGUSTINIAN
† FRANCISCAN
✕ DOMINICAN
▮ RECOLLECT

INDEX

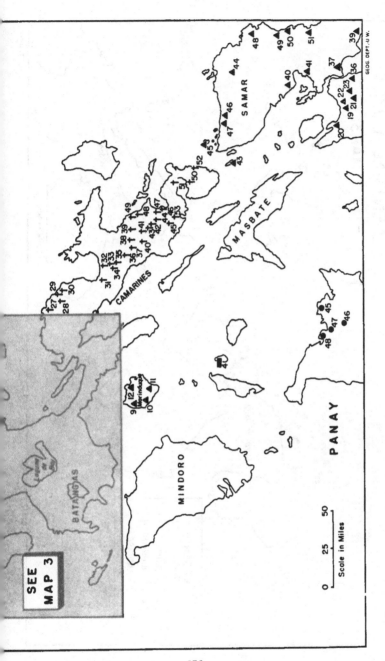

MINDORO

BATANGAS

CAMARINES

SAMAR

MASBATE

PANAY

Marinduque

GEOG. DEPT.-U.W.

Scale in Miles

0    25    50

175

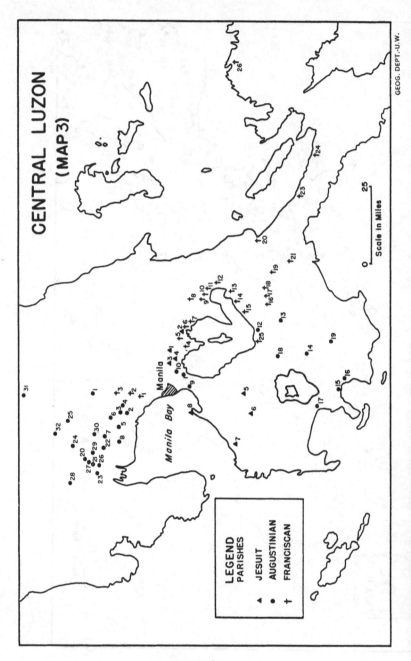

CENTRAL LUZON
(MAP 3)

Manila

Manila Bay

LEGEND
PARISHES

JESUIT ▲

AUGUSTINIAN ●

FRANCISCAN †

Scale in Miles

0                    25

GEOG. DEPT.-U.W.

# Notes

Abbreviations used in the Notes:

*AGI/AF:* The *Audiencia de Filipinas* section of the *Archivo General de Indias*, Seville.

*ARSI: Archivum Romanum Societatis Iesu*, microfilm collection at the University of St. Louis.

*BR:* Emma Helen Blair and James Alexander Robertson, *The Philippine Islands, 1493–1803* (55 vols.; Cleveland: A. H. Clark, 1903–9).

In addition, works frequently referred to that are listed in the Bibliography will be cited in shortened form in the Notes.

*Chapter I*

1. See my *Millennial Kingdom*, pp. 5–27.
2. For a more extended treatment of this topic see my article, "Some Ideological Aspects," pp. 221–39.
3. A detailed description of the imperial bureaucracy can be found in Clarence H. Haring, *The Spanish Empire in America*.
4. Philip II to Legazpi: August 28, 1569, *BR*, XXXIV, 252.
5. See my article, "Some Ideological Aspects," pp. 221 ff. The successfully executed pacific occupation of the Philippines was followed a few years later by the promulgation in July, 1573, of the "Ordenanzas hechas para los nuevos descubrimientos, conquistas y pacificaciones," the text of which is in the *Colección de documentos inéditos relativos al descubrimiento, conquista y organización de las antiguas posesiones españolas de América y*

*Oceanta* (42 vols.; Madrid: 1864–84), XVI, 142 ff.

6. Andrés de Mirandaola to Philip II: Cebu, 1565, *BR*, XXXIV, 201.

7. See my article, "Some Ideological Aspects," pp. 230 ff.

8. Horacio de la Costa, S.J., "Church and State in the Philippines during the Administration of Bishop Salazar," *The Hispanic American Historical Review*," XXX (August, 1950), 314–17, 324.

9. The standard work on Sino-Spanish trade is William L. Schurz, *The Manila Galleon* (New York: E. P. Dutton, 1939). Also see the suggestive article of Pierre Chaunu, "Le galion de Manille, grandeur et décadence d'une route de la soie," *Annales, Économies-Sociétés-Civilizations*, VI (October-December, 1951), 447–62.

10. Schurz, *Manila Galleon*, pp. 63 ff. Also see his "The Chinese in the Philippines," *The Pacific Ocean in History*, H. Morse Stephens and H. E. Bolton, editors (New York: Macmillan, 1917), pp. 214–22.

11. The population of the metropolis circa 1650 was divided as follows:

| | |
|---|---:|
| The Walled City (Spanish) | 7,350 |
| Parian (Chinese) | 15,000 |
| Suburbs (Filipino) | 20,124 |

*BR*, XXIV, 309; XXVII, 82; XXIX, 69, 305; XXXVI, 90–91, 203. Ventura del Arco transcripts, the Newberry Library, II, 402. Governor Vargas to Charles II: June 20, 1679, Pastells collection, St. Louis University, microfilm roll 14.

12. For a summary of the military aspect of the war see Schurz, *Manila Galleon*, pp. 342 ff.

13. W. L. Schurz, "The Philippine Situado," *Hispanic American Historical Review*, I (November, 1918), 461–64.

14. Woodrow W. Borah, *Early Colonial Trade and Navigation between Mexico and Peru* (Berkeley and Los Angeles: University of California Press, *Ibero-Americana:* 38, 1954), pp. 126–27.

15. Quoted in Schurz, *Manila Galleon*, pp. 43–44.

### Chapter II

1. The overwhelming bulk of our knowledge about the character of preconquest Tagalog society comes from a study of Tagalog customs composed by a Franciscan friar, Juan de Plasencia. Written in response to the orders of Governor Santiago de Vera, it was completed in 1589. Although it was not published until 1892, the manuscript circulated in various editions from the time of its completion. This work was regarded by the Spanish law courts as the definitive statement of customary law. For the Spanish text see Francisco de Santa Inés, O.F.M., *Crónica*, II, 592–603. There is an English translation in *BR*, VII, 173–96. Friar Juan came from Plasencia in Extremadura, a scion of the noble Portocarrero family. He arrived in Manila in March of 1578 along with the first mission of the

Franciscans. Elected custodian in 1583, Plasencia was the outstanding Franciscan in the Philippines until his death in 1590. The probable author of the first printed Tagalog-Spanish catechism, he also took a leading role in resettling the population into compact villages and in fostering the spread of primary education. His study of Tagalog customs is a short account remarkable for its factual and objective description. There are few moral judgments offered. Succeeding chroniclers such as Chirino, Ribadeneyra, Colín, Santa Inés, Morga, San Antonio, and Delgado added little factual information to Plasencia's account but merely indulged in value judgments of a moralistic and ethnocentric character on the data collected by Friar Juan de Plasencia.

For preconquest society in the Bisayan area, on the other hand, there are three distinct sources. Two of them were written by early encomenderos. Diego López Povedano's account of his trip through the island of Negros (1572) and his *Antiguas Leyendas* (1578) are brief accounts rich in ethnographic and linguistic material. See *The Robertson Text and Translation of the Povedano Manuscript of 1572*, E. D. Hester, editor, transcript number 2 of the Philippine Studies Program, Department of Anthropology, University of Chicago, 1954. Also *The Ancient Legends and Stories of the Indios, Jarayas, Jiguesinas and Igneines Which Contains Their Beliefs and Diverse Superstitions*, Rebecca P. Ignacio, editor, transcript number 3 of the Philippine Studies Program, Department of Anthropology University of Chicago, 1954. Another encomendero, Miguel de Loarca, composed a more extensive description of Bisayan society in 1592. For a bilingual text see *BR*, V, 34–185.

By far the most scholarly and detailed survey of Bisayan culture is the unpublished manuscript of Francisco Ignacio Alcina (1610–74). Spending nearly forty years in the Jesuit parishes on the islands of Samar and Leyte, Alcina provided an account equally rich in ethnographic material, Filipino responses to Hispanization, and natural history. This manuscript from the library of the *Palacio de Oriente* in Madrid is now being edited for publication by my colleague in the Philippine Studies Program, Dr. Paul Lietz. This work, which I consulted in Madrid, is one of the most informative of the unpublished sources of Philippine history. Francisco Alcina (Alzina), S.J., *Historia de las islas e indios de Bisayas . . . dividida en dos: la primera natural . . . la segunda eclesiástica y sobrenatural . . . .* For biographical information see Carlos Sommervogel, S.J., *Bibliothèque de la compagnie de Jésus* (11 vols.; Brussels and Paris: Alphonse Picard and Oscar Schepens, 1890–1932), I, 260. Also see the catalogues that the Jesuit prelates in the Philippines sent periodically to Rome, *ARSI*, roll 158.

A recent publication containing significant, primary source material about the preconquest and the postconquest culture of the island of Negros is *The Robertson Translation of the Pavón Manuscripts of 1838–1839*, Fred Eggan and E. V. Hester, editors, 4 vols., transcript number 5 of the Philippine Studies Program, Department of Anthropology, University of Chicago, 1957.

2. Gregorio F. Zaide, *The Philippines Since Pre-Spanish Times* (Manila: R. B. Garcia, 1949), pp. 67–70. Eufronio Alip, *Philippine Civilization* (Manila: University of Santo Tomas Press, 1936), pp. 75–81.

3. Povedano, *Antiguas Leyendas,* in *Robertson Text,* p. 22.

4. Antonio Pigafetta, *Magellan's Voyage,* I, 152.

5. On the island of Luzon there are six major languages: Tagalog, Ilokos, Bikol (the Camarines), Pangasinan, Pampanga, and Ibanag (Cagayan). There are three major languages in the Bisayas. They are: Samar-Leyte, Hiligaynon (Panay and eastern Negros), and Cebuano.

6. Chirino, *BR,* XII, 263. One of the most useful sources of ethnohistorical material is the various accounts of early Bornean settlements on the islands of Panay and Luzon commonly referred to as the "Maragtas." See the following articles: Fred Eggan, "Bisayan Accounts of Early Bornean Settlements in the Philippines," Tom Harrisson, "Bisaya: Borneo-Philippine Impacts on Islam," and R. A. Bewsher, "Bisayan Accounts of Early Bornean Settlements in the Philippines," in the *Sarawak Museum Journal,* VII (No. 7, 1956), 22–52. Also see James A. Robertson, "The Social Structure of and Ideas of Law among Early Philippine Peoples; and a Recently Discovered Pre-Hispanic Criminal Code of the Philippine Islands," in *The Pacific Ocean in History,* H. Morse Stephens and Herbert E. Bolton, editors (New York: Macmillan, 1917), pp. 160–191.

7. *BR,* L, 216–17.

8. Morga-Retana, *Sucesos,* pp. 210–11. Antonio de Morga, a high-ranking civil bureaucrat, published his informative account in 1609.

9. *BR,* X, 303–04.

10. Alcina, *Historia,* Bk. IV, ch. 5. Before the conquest the value of a Tagalog *mamamahay* was set at six pesos and the Tagalog *guiguilir* at twelve pesos. By 1593 the price of manumission for the *mamamahay* had risen to fifteen pesos, partially the reflection of the price inflation following in the wake of the conquest. Loarca, *BR,* V, 145.

11. *BR,* XXXIV, 378.

12. Alcina, *Historia,* Bk. III, ch. 22.

13. For the Spanish interpretation of the conquest as a "liberation" see my article "Some Ideological Aspects," pp. 237–39.

*Chapter III*

1. For a general survey of the *Patronato* see Clarence H. Haring, *The Spanish Empire in America,* pp. 179 ff. For the primary documentation see Francisco Colín, S.J., Colín-Pastells, *Labor evangélica,* III, 671 ff. Pastells' edition of Colín, first published in 1663, contains in the notes a rich collection of primary sources dealing with Church-state relations.

2. For the Salazar period see Gaspar de San Agustín, O.S.A., *Conquistas de las islas Philipinas . . .* (Madrid: 1698), pp. 394–95. Juan Francisco de San Antonio, O.F.M., *Chrónicas,* II, 49–55. Juan de la Concepción, O.R.S.A., *Historia,* II, 47–58. For Archbishop Vásquez de

Mercado see his letter to Philip III: July 8, 1612, in *AGI/AF* 74. For the García Serrano period see Colín-Pastells, *Labor evangélica*, III, 688 ff. For Archbishop Poblete see Casimiro Díaz, O.S.A., *Conquistas*, pp. 532–34, and Colín-Pastells, *Labor evangélica*, III, 697 ff. For Archbishop Camacho see Díaz, *Conquistas*, pp. 534–36, and *BR*, XLII, 25–117.

3. Archbishop to Audiencia: June 28, 1655, Colín-Pastells, *Labor evangélica*, III, 718. In 1697 there were only sixty secular priests. *BR*, XLII, 73.

4. See the Archbishop's pastoral letter of June 14, 1772, in Juan Ferrando, O.P., and Joaquín Fonseca, O.P., *Historia de los pp. dominicos en las islas filipinas* (6 vols.; Madrid: 1870–72), V, 54–59. Father Horacio de la Costa has discussed some phases of the visitation controversy with admirable clarity in his article, "Episcopal Visitation in the Philippines in the Seventeenth Century," *Philippine Studies*, II (September, 1954), 197–216. Charles H. Cunningham's "The Question of Episcopal Visitation in the Philippines," in *The Pacific Ocean in History*, H. Morse Stephens and H. E. Bolton, editors (New York: Macmillan, 1917), 223–37, is of limited usefulness in that the author fails to control his animus against the regular clergy.

5. Memorial of Juan de Polanco, O.P., to the Council of the Indies: October 6, 1666, Colín-Pastells, *Labor evangélica*, III, 732–39. This memorial of the procurator at the Spanish court for all the regular orders in the Philippines is a masterly statement of the viewpoint of the religious, exploiting to the fullest the strong points and glossing over the weaknesses of their case. Also see the joint letter of the Philippine provincial superiors to Philip V: June 30, 1708, *AGI/AF* 302.

6. The documentation of the Camacho investigation held in 1697 and 1698 is in the *AGI/AF* 302. As a result of the abuses exposed in this inquiry, the Archbishop issued a tariff of sacramental fees, *BR*, XLII, 56–64.

7. For the testimony taken on January 23, 1593, see "Algunos excessos de los frailes," *AGI/AF* 6.

8. The documentation on the creole-peninsular rift is mountainous, as the following list demonstrates. Bishop Benavides to Philip II: July 26, 1598, *AGI/AF* 76. Alonso de Vico, O.S.A., to Bishop Benavides: June 18, 1598, Morga-Retana, *Sucesos*, pp. 436–37. Governor Tello to king: July 14, 1599, *AGI/AF* 6. Cathedral chapter to Philip III: July 10, 1599, *AGI/AF* 77. Bishop Benavides to Philip III: July 31, 1601, *AGI/AF* 76. Juan de Garrovillas, O.F.M., to Philip III: December 19, 1603, *AGI/AF* 84. Dominican prelates to Philip III: December 15, 1603, *ibid.* Bernardo de Santa Catalina, O.P., to Philip III: June 1, 1605, *AGI/AF* 74. Ditto to Philip III: June 30, 1605, *AGI/AF* 84. Pedro de Arce, O.S.A. to Philip III: May 29, 1605, *ibid.* Miguel de Cigenca, O.S.A., to Philip III: May 24, 1605, *ibid.* Colín-Pastells, *Labor evangélica*, II, 466–67. *Fiscal* to Philip III: July, 1606, *BR*, XIV, 167–69. Juan de Tapia, O.S.A., to Philip III: June 20, 1605, *BR*, XIII, 301–6. The only letter of León defending

his conduct in office is apparently an undated one written between 1603 and 1605 in *BR*, XIV, 31–34.

9. Cathedral chapter to Philip III: June 24, 1604, *AGI/AF* 77. Audiencia to Philip III: July 19, 1609, *AGI/AF* 20. The Augustinian chroniclers are understandably reticent about the León crisis, since it was difficult for them to defend his conduçt. Juan de Medina, O.S.A., *Historia*, p. 175. Gaspar de San Agustín, *Conquistas*, p. 522.

10. Díaz, *Conquistas*, p. 71. Juan de Medina, *Historia*, p. 209. There is a sensationalist account of the murder with all the macabre details written anonymously, probably by a Jesuit, in *BR*, XVIII, 82–89. A more sober account is that of the *fiscal* of the Audiencia to Philip III: August 20, 1615, *AGI/AF* 20. When informed of the public trial of the assassins, the authorities in Rome voiced displeasure at what they considered to be the needless public scandal with which the whole matter had been handled. Ventura del Arco transcripts, Newberry Library, I, 476.

11. The documentation of the turmoil of the 1620's is the following. Juan de Medina, *Historia*, pp. 233, 239, 254–55. Augustinian prelates to the king: July 28, 1628, *AGI/AF* 85. Governor Silva to Philip IV: July 30, 1626, *BR*, XXII, 96. The Audiencia to Philip IV: July 23, 1629, *AGI/AF* 21. Audiencia to Philip IV: August 8, 1633, *ibid*. Díaz, *Conquistas*, pp. 384–88. Augustinian prelates to Philip IV: September 9, 1637, *BR*, XXVIII, 21–25.

12. Governor Corcuera to Philip IV: June 30, 1636, *BR*, XXVI, 131–36. Franciscan Commissary-General of the Indies to Philip III: May 11, 1612, *AGI/AF* 85.

13. Alcina's report of 1660, *ARSI*, roll 165.

14. I have not seen the Gómez de Espinoza text; very few if any copies survive. For a general description of its contents see *BR* XXV, 192–93; XXXVII, 103–4; XLII, 120.

15. For a compassionate and realistic analysis of this aspect of the problem see Sinibaldo de Mas, "Informe" (1843), *BR*, XXVIII, 244.

16. Colín-Pastells, *Labor evangélica*, II, 302–3, 406 ff. Ignacio Alcina, S.J., to the general of the Society: June 24, 1660, *ARSI*, roll 165.

*Chapter IV*

1. For a dramatic account of the rigors and perils of the transoceanic crossing to the Philippines see Diego Aduarte, O.P., *Historia*, pp. 13–16, 22–24.

2. *Recopilación*, Bk. I, tit. xiv, law 19.

3. Ordinance of the governor: March 2, 1582, *BR*, IV, 308–9; VII, 171–72; IX, 250–51. Colín-Pastells, *Labor evangélica*, I, 436–37. *Recopilación*, Bk. I, tit. xiv, law 30.

4. The standard works on Iberian designs on China and Japan are those of Arnold Rowbothan, *Missionary and Mandarin, the Jesuits at the Court of China* (Berkeley and Los Angeles: University of California Press,

1942), and C. R. Boxer, *The Christian Century in Japan, 1549–1650* (Berkeley and Los Angeles: University of California Press, 1951).

5. For the Mexican background consult the following. Robert Ricard, *La "conquête spirituelle" du Mexique* (Paris: Institute d' ethnologie, 1933), pp. 163 ff. Lesley Byrd Simpson, "The Civil Congregation," in his *Studies in the Administration of the Indians of New Spain* (Berkeley and Los Angeles: University of California Press, *Ibero-Americana:* 7, 1934), pp. 30–129. George Kubler, *Mexican Architecture in the Sixteenth Century* (2 vols.; New Haven: Yale University Press, 1948), I, 68–103. Howard Cline, "Civil Congregations of the Indians of New Spain, 1598–1606," *Hispanic American Historical Review*, XXIX (August, 1949), 349–69.

6. For clear-cut expressions of this attitude see San Antonio, *Chrónicas*, I, 375. Pedro Chirino, S.J. *Relación*, p. 178. Marcelo de Ribadeneyra, O.F.M., *Historia*, p. 32.

7. Juan de Plasencia, O.F.M. to Philip II: June 18, 1585, *Archivo Ibero-Americano*, II (May–June, 1915), 390–91. Acts of the ecclesiastical junta of 1582 in Valentín Marin y Morales, O.P., *Ensayo de una síntesis de los trabajos realizados por las corporaciones religiosas españolas de Filipinas* (2 vols.; Manila: 1901), I, 335. Philip II to Governor Tello: May 25, 1596, *BR*, IX, 239.

8. Alonso Sandin, O.P., to Charles II [1680's], *AGI/AF* 76.

9. *BR*, XX, 231–32.

10. Vicente de Salazar, O.P., *Historia de la provincia de el Santissimo Rosario de Philipinas, China y Tvnking* (Manila: 1742), pp. 138–52.

11. Alcina's report of 1660, *ARSI*, roll 165.

12. Cedula of Philip III to the bishop of Cagayan: September 8, 1603, Pastells collection, St. Louis University, microfilm roll 33. Bishop of Cagayan to Philip III: April 12, 1605, *AGI/AF* 76. The Dominicans were somewhat more successful in Pangasinan than in Cagayan, for in the former province the population was less dispersed than in the latter. Aduarte, *Historia*, pp. 114, 153. Bishop of Cagayan to Philip IV: May 24, 1636, *AGI/AF* 80.

13. Anda's memorial of 1768, *BR*, L, 176.

14. *Ibid.*, pp. 99, 128.

15. *BR*, V, 233.

16. Early Spanish observers tended to equate barrio and barangay. Bishop Salazar, for example, urged that tributes of the natives not be collected by "barangais que son barrios en lengua castellana." Salazar to Philip II: June, 1586, Colín-Pastells, *Labor evangélica*, I, 447. Chirino wrote: "El uso de estos pueblos para su mas comodo gobierno estar partidos en barrios a la traza de parroquias que alla llaman barangais." Chirino, *Relación*, p. 33, or *BR*, XII, 211. Chirino referred to the *cabezas de barrangay* as the *cabezas de barrios*. Chirino, *Relación*, p. 187. Also see Colín-Pastells, *Labor evangélica*, I, 117–18. In sixteenth century Spain barrio was synonymous with an urban parish. In the Philippines, barrio of necessity referred to a rural cluster of population usually grouped around

a *visita* chapel. The sitio or hamlet, the smallest unit of rural organization and usually consisting of ten families or less, was ordinarily called a *ranchería* in seventeenth-century sources. I have never encountered the use of the word "sitio" in the early accounts. For the meaning of "ranchería" in the seventeenth century see *ibid.*, II, 153; Chirino, *Relación*, p. 178.

17. Dominican provincial superior to Archbishop Pardo: October 20, 1682, Colín-Pastells, *Labor evangélica*, III, 116–17. Augustinian provincial superior to Archbishop Pardo: May 8, 1686, *ibid.*, pp. 118–21. Anda memorial of 1768, *BR*, L, 155. "Ordenanzas de alcaldes (Cagayan, 1739)," ms. in possession of Professor Lesley Byrd Simpson, pp. 28–29.

18. For the historical origins of the gridiron plan and its adoption in the Spanish empire see Kubler, *Mexican Architecture*, I, 97 ff., and "Ordenanzas" of 1573 in *Colección de documentos inéditos relativos al descubrimiento, conquista y organización de las antiguas posesiones españoles* de América y Oceanía (42 vols.; Madrid: 1864–84), XVI, 142 ff.

19. *BR*, L, 255–56.

20. "Ordenanzas de alcaldes," p. 20.

21. For the cedula of April 27, 1594, see *BR*, IX, 120–21. There is a clear statement of the Crown's instinctive distrust for the principle of ethnic-territorial partition in the letter of Viceroy Enríquez to Philip II: May 20, 1576, *Cartas de Indias* (Madrid: 1877), pp. 315–22.

22. There is an extensive evaluation of the linguistic studies of the clergy in my article, "Philippine Linguistics, pp. 153–70. The most complete list of early Philippine imprints can be found in the standard work of José Toribio Medina, *La imprenta*.

23. Camacho investigation of 1697–98, *AGI/AF* 302.

### Chapter V

1. A graphic description of iconoclastic activity on the part of the religious is in Francisco de Santa Inés, *Crónica*, II, 177 ff.

2. For the documentation regarding the introduction of baptism see my article, "Pre-Baptismal Instruction and the Administration of Baptism in the Philippines during the Sixteenth Century," *The Americas*, XII (July, 1955), 3–23.

3. Pedro Chirino, *Relación*, p. 233.

4. *Doctrina Christiana: The First Book Printed in the Philippines*, Manila, *1593*, Edwin Wolf, editor (Washington, D.C.: Library of Congress, 1947). Friar Juan de Plasencia (see Chapter II, note 1) is the probable author, according to Wolf's introductory essay. For background material about this *Doctrina* see my article, "Philippine Linguistics," pp. 155–56.

5. *BR*, XXIV, 268. Gerónimo de Ripalda's well-known catechism, first published in Burgos in 1591, was printed in the Philippines in only one Tagalog edition during the seventeenth century (see, J. T. Medina, *La imprenta*, II, 21). Hence it was no serious rival in popularity to the Bellarmine text.

6. In the *Doctrina* of 1593 the following key concepts were kept in Spanish: God, Trinity, Holy Ghost, Virgin Mary, Pope, grace, sin, cross, hell, church, Sunday, and the names of the sacraments. This principle of missionary policy was established in Mexico after a spirited controversy, decades before the conversion of the Filipinos. Robert Ricard, *La "conquête spirituelle" du Mexique* (Paris: Institute d' ethnologie, 1933), pp. 72–75.

7. *Archivo Ibero-Americano*, II (May–June, 1915), 393–94. Chirino, *Relación*, pp. 67–70, 97, 120, 123, 151, 184, 185, 231. Colín-Pastells, *Labor evangélica*, II, 118, 399, 409, 411. Ribadeneyra, *Historia*, p. 67.

8. For the Jesuit sources see Colín-Pastells, *Labor evangélica*, II, 127, 137; III, 135. Chirino, *Relación*, p. 242. For the Franciscans see Ribadeneyra, *Historia*, pp. 54–55. San Antonio, *Chrónicas*, II, 12–18. For the Dominicans see Adurate, *Historia*, p. 64. For the Augustinians see Juan de Medina. *Historia*, p. 75. Also see Morga-Retana, *Sucesos*, p. 206.

9. Diego de Bobadilla, S.J., "Relation of the Philippine Islands," 1640, *BR*, XXIX, 295.

10. Alcina, *Historia*, Bk. III, ch. 12.

11. There is a detailed census taken by the Jesuits of their Bisayan missions in *ARSI*, roll 158.

12. Chirino, *BR*, XII, 291–93, 295, 296, 299, 301, 317, 318; XIII, 52–54, 98–100, 134, 162, 163. Also *ibid.*, XXI, 21, 210, 221.

13. For a Latin text of the bull see Gerónimo de Mendieta, O.F.M., *Historia eclesiástica indiana* (Mexico: 1870), pp. 269–71.

14. Pablo de Jesús, O.F.M., to Pope Gregory XIII: July, 14, 1580, *BR*, XXXIV, 323–24.

15. Alonso de Mentrida, O.S.A., *Ritval*, pp. 92–98. His interpretation of Paul III's bull was derived from Alonso de Veracruz's *Speculum conjugiorum* (Mexico: 1556) written as a guide to aid the clergy unravel some of the matrimonial tangles created by the shift from pagan polygamy to Christian monogamy.

16. Archbishop García Serrano to Philip III: July 30, 1621, *BR*, XX, 86–87. Also see *Fiscal* to Philip III: July, 1606, *BR*, XIV, 158–59.

17. Mentrida, *Ritval*, pp. 88 ff. According to Rey's manual for confessors published in 1792 illicit intercourse with future in-laws continued to be not uncommon. Fernando Rey, O.S.A., *Confessonarios*, pp. 271 ff.

18. Colín-Pastells, *Labor evangélica*, II, 404–5.

19. *Ibid.*, I, 450. *BR*, VII, 317–18.

20. *BR*, IX, 225–26.

21. Camacho investigation of 1697–98, *AGI/AF* 302. For the tariff itself see *BR*, XLII, 56 ff. The Augustinians ordinarily charged two pesos for a simple marriage without the nuptial blessing. According to the episcopal tariff no fees were to be charged for this ceremony.

22. *AGI/AF* 302.

23. The most celebrated example of Philippine erotica was one first described by the famous chronicler of the Magellan expedition. Pigafetta

wrote: "The males, large and small, have their penis pierced from one side to the other near the head, with a gold or tin bolt as large as a goose quill. In both ends of the same bolt, some have what resembles a spur, with points upon the ends; others are like the head of a cart nail. I very often asked many, both young and old, to see their penis, because I could not credit it. In the middle of the bolt is a hole, through which they urinate. The bolt and the spurs always hold firm. They say that their women wish it so, and that if they did otherwise they would not have communication with them. When the men wish to have communication with their women, the latter themselves take the penis not in the regular way and commence very gently to introduce it into their vagina with the spur on top first, and then the other part. When it is inside it takes its regular position; and thus the penis always stays inside until it gets soft, for otherwise they could not pull it out. Those people make use of that device because they are of a weak nature." Pigafetta, *Magellan's Voyage*, I, 166–69. Also see Loarca, *BR*, V, 117, and Morga-Retana, *Sucesos*, p. 196.

24. Morga, Ribadeneyra, Archbishop Benavides, Archbishop Santibáñez, and Alcina, some of our most informative sources, claimed that the Chinese introduced sodomy to the Filipinos. Their principal argument was a linguistic one. They claimed that there was no word in the native languages for sodomy. The absence of a word does not necessarily prove the nonexistence of this practice, as the Spanish sources seemed to imply. Furthermore it is unprovable whether there was or was not a word for sodomy in preconquest times. The early seventeenth-century dictionaries are not now extant; and even if they were, the first vocabularies were certainly incomplete. Circa 1750 there was a Tagalog word for sodomy, *binabae*, meaning like a woman. Whether this word was of preconquest origin cannot be demonstrated. The few men who entered the pagan priesthood were effeminates and transvestites, but the Spanish sources deny that they were overt homosexuals. The linguistic argument is inconclusive, but the claim of these Spanish observers is suspect on other grounds: (1) if there was no sodomy in the Philippines before the conquest, that archipelago was one of the few regions in the world where it was unknown; (2) among the modern Filipino pagans sodomy is not unknown; (3) these Spanish observers were vituperative Sinophobes who hated the Chinese as intensely as they were dependent upon them for certain economic services. Spanish Sinophobia may be unconsciously responsible for inventing the charge that the Chinese introduced sodomy to the Filipinos. A more plausible conclusion might be that the incidence of homosexuality increased among the Filipinos as a result of the coming of the Chinese. Archbishop Santibáñez to Philip II: June 24, 1598, *AGI/AF* 74. Benavides to Philip III: July 5, 1603, and February 3, 1605, *BR*, XII, 107; XIII, 274, 278. Morga-Retana, *Sucesos*, p. 196. Ribadeneyra, *Historia*, p. 37. Alcina, *Historia*, Bk. III, ch. 21. Although placing the primary responsibility on the Chinese, Alcina does admit that a few Spaniards who

"ya no se contenta con la Venus ordinaria" were as guilty as the Chinese in introducing sexual deviations to the Filipinos.

25. Ordinance of the Audiencia: January 7, 1599, *BR*, XI, 31–32.
26. Mentrida, *Ritval*, p. 86.
27. *Recopilación*, Bk. VI, tit. i, law 6.
28. *BR*, L, 216–17.
29. For a list of these confessionals see J. T. Medina, *La imprenta*.
30. Pedro Murillo Velarde, S.J., *Historia*, pp. 5–6.
31. *Ibid.*, p. 28. Colín-Pastells, *Labor evangélica*, II, 409.
32. Aduarte, *Historia*, pp. 156–57.
33. Domingo Fernández Navarrete, O.P., *Tratados históricos*, p. 317.
34. Rey, *Confessonarios*, p. 344.
35. Ribadeneyra, *Historia*, pp. 51–52.
36. Murillo Velarde, *Historia*, p. 5.
37. Rey, *Confessonarios*, pp. 170, 208–10, 276–80, 284–87, 351–52.
38. Colín-Pastells, *Labor evangélica*, II, 409. Ribadeneyra, *Historia*, p. 51.
39. Rey, *Confessonarios*, pp. 221–24.
40. Ricard, *La "conquête spirituelle,"* pp. 148–52.
41. J. T. Medina, *La imprenta*, pp. 4–6. I consulted a photostat copy of the 1573 edition of Agurto's treatise.
42. Aduarte, *Historia*, p. 121.
43. Colín-Pastells, *Labor evangélica*, III, 113. Díaz, *Conquistas*, p. 239. Murillo Velarde, *Historia*, p. 36.
44. Mentrida, *Ritval*, pp. 48 ff.
45. Ribadeneyra, *Historia*, p. 67. Aduarte, *Historia*, pp. 74, 121, 158–59. Chirino, *Relación*, p. 140. Colín-Pastells, *Labor evangélica*, I, 361; II, 295, 343, 411.
46. *Ibid.*, III, 687–88. Bishop Salazar introduced confirmation as early as 1583. *BR*, V, 216–17.
47. Alcina's letter of 1660, *ARSI*, roll 165.
48. Colín-Pastells, *Labor evangélica*, III, 688. The infrequent references to confirmation in the chronicles of the regular orders suggests the relative lack of importance placed on this sacrament by the religious.
49. Ricard, *La "conquête spirituelle,"* pp. 285 ff. Charles Gibson, *Tlaxcala in the Sixteenth Century*, pp. 28 ff. Also see my *Millennial Kingdom*, pp. 52–55.

*Chapter VI*

1. Ribadeneyra, *Historia*, pp. 57, 67. Chirino, *Relación*, p. 70.
2. On June 18, 1677, Charles II dispatched a cedula to the Jesuit provincial superior (presumably to the superiors of the other orders also) ordering that each Philippine community have not more than one patron saint for whose festivities the natives were obligated to contribute. Pastells collection, St. Louis University, microfilm roll 28. This cedula apparently

meant that the Filipinos should not be required to contribute to the patronal fiesta of both the *cabecera* and the *visita*-barrio. Every male was required to make an annual contribution for this purpose at the time he made his obligatory annual confession. In 1697 this tax was fixed at three reales. *BR*, L, 218. For a description of how Holy Week was celebrated in a Jesuit parish see Chirino, *Relación*, p. 178.

3. Morga's letter to Philip II: June 8, 1598, Morga-Retana, *Sucesos*, p. 248.

4. Ernst Kantorowicz, "The 'King's Advent' and the Enigmatic Panels in the Doors of Santa Sabina," *The Art Bulletin*, XXVI (December, 1944), 207–31.

5. For general background see George M. Foster, "Cofradia and Compadrazgo in Spain and in Spanish America," *Southwestern Journal of Anthropology*, IX (Spring, 1953), 10 ff.

6. Colín-Pastells, *Labor evangélica*, II, 117. Murillo Velarde, *Historia*, p. 219. Although generally well informed, Morga showed no understanding of the effectiveness with which the religious used sodalities and fiestas as agencies of indoctrination and the enthusiastic response of the Filipinos to these techniques. Morga-Retana, *Sucesos*, p. 248.

7. The early Franciscan and Jesuit sources (Ribadeneyra and Chirino) claimed that the Filipino response was positive. This statement may be true, but the virtual absence of any references to flagellants in the later sources (San Antonio, Santa Inés, Martínez, and Colín) suggests that Filipino interest rapidly abated. Chirino, *Relación*, pp. 94, 137, 147, 176, 178, 186, 245. Ribadeneyra, *Historia*, pp. 49–50. Murillo Velarde, *Historia*, pp. 780–81.

8. Ribadeneyra, *Historia*, pp. 49–50.

9. *BR*, XXXIV, 380.

10. Ribadeneyra, *Historia*, pp. 54–55. San Antonio, *Chrónicas*, II, 12–18. Chirino, *Relación*, p. 242. Colín-Pastells, *Labor evangélica*, II, 127, 137; III, 135.

11. Acts of the First Provincial Council of Manila 1771, ms. at the Library of Congress, Manuscripts Division, Philippine Islands, Accession No. 6106–A, Box 1. Regarding the ms. see Schafer Williams, "The First Provincial Council of Manila, 1771," *Seminar*, XIII (1955–56), 33 ff. The Spaniards actually introduced a version of this theatrical custom into the Philippines. During the first Mass celebrated on Philippine soil, the guns of Magellan's ships roared a salute as the Host was elevated. Pigafetta, *Magellan's Voyage*, I, 121.

12. In the Manila area by 1620 there were only three wooden churches and twenty-seven stone churches. *BR*, XIX, 161–63. In the provinces the vast majority of *cabecera* churches and all the *visita* chapels were of wood. Alonso Sandin, O.P., to Charles II: May 20, 1685, *AGI/AF* 76. As of 1649 the Franciscans had some thirty-five *cabecera* churches in the Laguna de Bay area adjacent to Manila, eighteen of which were made of stone. The Jesuits constructed three magnificent baroque churches of stone at Silang,

Antipolo, and Taytay near Manila. Murillo Velarde, *Historia*, pp. 143–45. In the Bikol country, on the other hand, only three of the twenty-one parishes had stone churches. *BR*, XXXV, 278–87. Stone churches in the Bisayas and northern Luzon were uncommon, judging by the absence of references to such buildings. A few stone churches were built in the Bisayas during the eighteenth century.

13. See Chapter II for a discussion of ritual drinking in preconquest times. Aduarte, *Historia*, p. 65.

14. Colín-Pastells, *Labor evangélica*, II, 117.

15. Alcina, *Historia*, Bk. III, ch. 22. As late as 1739 *alcaldes* were warned to be on the alert for clandestine ritual drinking, but even in that isolated province the custom was evidently on the wane. "Ordenanzas de alcaldes (Cagayan, 1739)," ms. in possession of Professor Lesley Byrd Simpson, p. 6.

16. For the necessary background see Sidney W. Mintz and Eric R. Wolf, "An Analysis of Ritual Co-Parenthood (Compadrazgo)," *Southwestern Journal of Anthropology*, VI (Winter, 1950), 341–68. George Foster, "Cofradia and Compadrazgo," *ibid.*, IX (Spring, 1953), 1–28.

17. Pigafetta, *Magellan's Voyage* I, 153–55.

18. Juan de Grijalva, O.S.A., *Crónica de la orden de n. p. s. Augustín en las provincias de la Nueva España en quatro edades desde el año de 1533 hasta el de 1592* (Mexico: 1624), p. 125.

19. *BR*, XI, 75–76.

20. *BR*, XLIII, 105–6.

21. *Ibid.*, p. 109.

22. *Ibid.*, p. 105.

23. Letter of Gaspar de San Agustín published in Juan Delgado, S.J., *Historia sacro-profana*, p. 284.

24. *Ibid.*, pp. 314–15.

25. For the correspondence of the Dominican, Augustinian, and Jesuit superiors with the archbishop see Colín-Pastells, *Labor evangélica*, III, 115 ff. For the letters of the Franciscan and Recollect superiors see Pastells collection, St. Louis University, microfilm roll 14.

26. Alcina to General of Society, 1660, *ARSI*, roll 165.

27. Colín-Pastells, *Labor evangélica*, II, 117. Murillo Velarde, *Historia*, p. 28. Both Archbishop Camacho in 1697 and Simón de Anda in his memorial of April 12, 1768, criticized the religious for their refusal to administer the last sacraments in the homes of the sick. *BR*, XLIII, 55, and L, 175–76.

28. Hieronymous Noldin, S.J., *De sacramentis* (3 vols.; Rome: 1927), III, 253–55. Henry Davis, S.J., *Moral and Pastoral Theology* (4 vols.; London: Sheed and Ward, 1945), III, 335–57.

29. Camacho investigation of 1697–98, *AGI/AF* 302.

30. Cedula of August 22, 1677, Pastells collection, St. Louis University, microfilm roll 8. Archbishop Pardo opposed the growth of a Filipino clergy, alleging "their evil customs, their vices and their precon-

ceived ideas which made it necessary to treat them as children even when they were forty, fifty or sixty years old" *BR*, XLV, 182–83.

31. The translation is from Horacio de la Costa, S.J., "The Development of the Native Clergy in the Philippines," *Theological Studies*, VIII (July, 1947), 235–36. This discussion is lucidly presented and meticulously documented.

32. For San Agustín's letter and Delgado's reply see Delgado, *Historia sacro-profana*, pp. 273 ff. Delgado's "environmentalist" explanation of the character of the Filipinos is similar to the defense of the Mexican Indians formulated by Clavigero (1731–87). Francisco Javier Clavigero, S.J., *Historia antigua de Mexico* (4 vols.; Mexico: 1945), IV, 259. Both Jesuit historians were evidently under the spell of Enlightenment environmentalism, whose most articulate spokesman was Montesquieu.

33. A. Brou, S.J., "Notes sur les origines du clergé philippin," *Revue de l'histoire missionaire*, IV (1927), 546–47.

34. De la Costa, in *Theological Studies*, VIII, 242. For the archbishop's melodramatic confession of failure see his pastoral letter of June 14, 1772, in Ferrando and Fonseca, *Historia de los pp. dominicos en las islas fiilipinas* (6 vols.; Madrid: 1870–72), V, 54–59.

35. For some remarks on the Spanish and late medieval origins of this colonialist mentality see my *Millennial Kingdom*, pp. 61–63.

*Chapter VII*

1. In 1605 there were only 24 Mindanao galley slaves out of a total of 570 galley slaves. Audiencia to Philip III: June 30, 1605, *AGI/AF* 19. *BR*, VIII, 70–72; XXXIV, 325–31.

2. For the documentation of the early encomienda see my article, "Some Ideological Aspects," pp. 230 ff.

3. Audiencia to Philip II: June 15, 1595, *AGI/AF* 18. Governor Tavora to Philip IV: August 4, 1628, *BR*, XXII, 261–62. Morga-Retana, *Sucesos*, pp. 208–9.

4. Lesley Byrd Simpson, *The Encomienda in New Spain* (Berkeley and Los Angeles: University of California Press, 1950), pp. 145 ff.

5. Cedula of February 1, 1636, *BR*, XXV, 145–47; XIX, 273–74.

6. Dasmariñas to Philip II: June 20, 1593, *BR*, IX, 65–66. Philip III to Governor Tello: August 16, 1599, *BR*, XI, 130. *Fiscal* to king: July 21, 1599, *AGI/AF* 18. Philip III to Governor Acuña: Zamora, February 16, 1602, *BR*, XI, 272. *Fiscal* to Philip III: July, 1606, *BR*, XIV, 153.

7. The 1608 figure comes from a treasury report of August 18, 1608, *BR*, XIV, 247–48. The 1621 is Ríos Coronel's, *BR*, XIX, 285–87. The 1655 figure is another treasury report of July, 1655, Colín-Pastells, *Labor evangélica*, III, 730. The 1686 figure is from a letter of the Augustinian provincial superior to Archbishop Pardo: May 8, 1686, *ibid.*, III, 119. The 1742 figure comes from Pablo Francisco Rodríguez de Berdozido, "The Ecclesiastical Estate of the Aforesaid Philippine Islands," *BR*, XLVII, 140–42. For the 1765 figure see Viana to Charles III: July 10, 1766, *BR*, L, 78.

8. "Cédulas reales dirigidas a estas islas filipinas," ms., 2 vols., Newberry Library, II, 58–63.

9. Charles Henry Cunningham, *The Audiencia in the Spanish Colonies as Illustrated by the Audiencia of Manila (1583–1800)* (Berkeley: University of California Press, 1919), p. 110.

10. Rafael Moreno y Díez, *Manual del cabeza de barangay* (Manila: 1874), p. 35.

11. Agustín María de Castro, O.S.A., "Historia del insigne convento de San Pablo de Manila," *Missionalia hispanica*, VIII (1951), 91. It cost 12,000 pesos annually to meet the running expenses of this convent.

12. *BR*, XVIII, 311–13. In 1606 the Audiencia brought suit against the orders to compel them to restrict these settlements to the number of thirty servants per convent. The decision proved unenforceable. *Fiscal* to Philip III: July, 1606, *BR*, XIV, 169–70. Another attempt was made by the Audiencia, but again in vain. Audiencia to Philip III, July 19, 1609, *AGI/AF* 20.

13. The most informative account of Philippine shipbuilding is that of Sebastián de Pineda, *BR*, XVIII, 169–88.

14. For draft labor prior to 1609 see Morga-Retana, *Sucesos*, p. 211. For the post–1609 *polo* see cedula of Philip III: May 26, 1609, *BR*, XVII, 79–81. *Recopilación*, Bk. VI, tit. xii, law 40.

15. *BR*, XIX, 71–72.

16. The salary paid by the treasury to *polistas* was one peso monthly. Jesuit provincial superior to *fiscal*: August 21, 1616, *AGI/AF* 20. Governor Fajardo to Philip III: August 10, 1618, *BR*, XVIII, 130–31. Hernando de los Rios Coronel to king: 1619–20, *ibid.*, 297–98, 316.

17. *BR*, L, 221.

18. *Ibid.*, pp. 204–5. Fernández Navarrete, *Tratados históricos*, p. 304.

19. Provincial superiors to *fiscal:* 1616, *AGI/AF* 20.

20. Ríos Coronel, *BR*, XVIII, 309.

21. Augustinian provincial superior to *fiscal:* 1616, *AGI/AF* 20. Murillo Velarde, *Historia*, pp. 254–56. Circa 1650 Pampanga's annual rice quota was 40,000 bushels of rice payable in two installments. Fernández Navarrete, *Tratados históricos*, pp. 304–5.

22. The sources for these statistics were cited in note 7. The mid-century decline can be further demonstrated by statistics relative to the population of the Jesuit parishes in the Bisayan islands (Samar, Leyte, Bohol, and Cebu), who suffered as much from the depredations of the Moros as they did from the consequences of the Dutch War.

```
1622.................74,600 total population
1659.................52,269 total population
1679.................70,961 total population
```

The 1622 figure comes from Archbishop García Serrano's report. *BR*, XX, 230. For the 1659 and 1679 figures see the Jesuit census reports, *ARSI*, roll 158.

23. Provincial superiors to *fiscal:* 1616, *AGI/AF* 20. Fernández Navarrete, *Tratados históricos*, p. 304, 318.

24. *BR*, L, 210.

25. See my *Millennial Kingdom*, pp. 93–98.

26. This attitude of the Philippine clergy is clearly reflected in the correspondence of the provincial superiors with the *fiscal, AGI/AF* 20. For a characteristic example of the kind of moderate pressure exercised by the clergy to restrain the abuses of the *polo* see Philip IV's letter to the Audiencia: December, 17, 1639, *BR*, XXIX, 192–93.

27. Diego de Carate to Philip II: June 10, 1581 and Juan Pacheco Maldonado to Philip II: June 6, 1582, *AGI/AF* 34. Morga-Retana, *Sucesos*, p. 258. "Ordenanzas de alcaldes (Cagayan, 1739)," ms. in possession of Professor Lesley Byrd Simpson, p. 7.

28. *BR*, IX, 106–7. Rodríquez de Berdozido, *BR*, XLVII, 146.

29. Cedula of May 13, 1579, Colín-Pastells, *Labor evangélica*, III, 681–82.

30. "Ordenanzas de alcaldes," pp. 23–24. Memorial of Governor Dasmariñas, 1593, *AGI/AF* 6. Morga-Retana, *Sucesos*, p. 247. Rios Coronel, *BR*, XVIII, 317. Camacho investigation of 1697, *AGI/AF* 302. Cedula of March 17, 1608, *Recopilación*, Bk. VI, tit. xii, law 41, and cedula of June 18, 1594, *ibid.*, Bk. I, tit. xiv, law 81. Cedula of May 29, 1620, *BR*, XIX, 40–41; *BR*, L, 205–6, 218, 238.

### Chapter VIII

1. Only occasionally do we hear of a Spaniard petitioning the king to legitimize his mestizo children, i.e., to enable them to inherit their father's property. For one such request see the petition of Pedro Sarmiento: October 14, 1581, *AGI/AF* 34.

2. The founder of the first convent of nuns of Manila was the celebrated Gerónima de Assumpción, a lady of indomitable strength of character as well as outstanding spiritual qualities, whose candidacy for sainthood was ardently championed at the Papal court by Philip IV of Spain. Sister Gerónima needed all her will power to surmount the series of noisy controversies accompanying the founding of her convent in Manila. For a hagiographical account of her life see Ginés Quesada, O.F.M., *Exemplo de todas las virtudes y vida milagrosa de la venerable madre Gerónima de la Assumpción* (Madrid: 1717). For another Franciscan account see Domingo Martínez, *Compendio histórico de la apostólica provincia de San Gregorio de Philipinas de religiosos menores descalzos de n. p. San Francisco* (Madrid: 1756), pp. 169–74. The most level-headed discussion is that of Juan de la Concepción, *Historia*, V, 9–17.

3. Sherburne F. Cook and Lesley Byrd Simpson, *The Population of Central Mexico in the Sixteenth Century* (Berkeley and Los Angeles: University of California Press, *Ibero-Americana:* 31, 1948), pp. 1–48.

4. Lesley Byrd Simpson, *The Exploitation of Land in Central Mexico in*

*the Sixteenth Century* (Berkeley and Los Angeles: University of California Press, *Ibero-Americana:* 36, 1952).

5. Woodrow W. Borah, *New Spain's Century of Depression* (Berkeley and Los Angeles: University of California Press, *Ibero-Americana:* 35, 1951).

6. Governor Tavora to Philip IV: August 4, 1628, *BR*, XXII, 261–62. Hernando de los Ríos Coronel, *BR*, XVIII, 317.

7. *BR*, XVIII, 317; L, 199, 211.

8. *Ibid.*, p. 108.

9. Cathedral chapter to Philip III: July 4, 1603, *AGI/AF* 77. Archbishop Benavides to Philip III: July 5, 1603, *BR*, XII, 109. Tavora to Philip IV: August 1, 1629, *BR*, XXIII, 36–38.

10. *BR*, XVIII, 93 ff. Fernández Navarrete, *Tratados históricos*, p. 322.

11. *BR*, XXIX, 298; XXXII, 93; XXXIX, 98; XXXVIII, 24–25, 28, 34. Santa Inés, *Crónica*, I, 78–79. Morga-Retana, *Sucesos*, p. 174. Alcina to General of the Society, 1660, *ARSI*, roll 165.

12. Elmer Drew Merrill, *The Botany of Cook's Voyages* (*Chronica Botonica series*, XIV, numbers 5 and 6, Waltham, Mass.: 1954), p. 237.

13. *BR*, XVIII, 179. Before wheat was grown in the islands, flour for the Host was imported from Mexico. Communion wine also was imported, shipped from Spain via Mexico and the Acapulco galleon. *Ibid.*

14. Reliable statistics about maize production must await a careful examination of the ecclesiastical tithes, the records of which are in *AGI*. Occasional references in the printed sources indicate that maize production was not large. As of 1650 a bushel of maize was worth about ninety pesos, exorbitantly expensive in contrast to the value of rice whose price fluctuated between one and four pesos per bushel. Fernández Navarrete, *Tratados históricos*, p. 322. *BR*, XXIII, 36. Alcina, *Historia*, Bk. III, ch. 6.

15. Morga-Retana, *Sucesos*, pp. 178 ff.

16. *BR*, XIV, 156–57. Colín-Pastells, *Labor evangélica*, III, 125–26. *BR*, XXV, 81. Beef production was somewhat higher than these figures would indicate, for not included in the tithes was cattle production of the ecclesiastical estates. In the province of Batangas the religious owned twenty large cattle ranches. *BR*, L, 154.

17. Fernando Rey, *Confessonarios*, pp. 343–44. Alcina reports that Jesuit priests in the Bisayas ate pork or chicken at midday and fish in the evening. Apparently they rarely ate beef. Alcina's letter of 1660, *ARSI*, roll 165.

18. *Ibid.* Fernández Navarrete, *Tratados históricos*, p. 322. He also reports that the Spaniards crossed buffaloes with cows, "and the result has been a third and very strange appearing species." *Ibid.*

19. Morga-Retana, *Sucesos*, pp. 178 ff.

20. "Ordenanzas de alcaldes (Cagayan, 1739)," ms. in possession of Professor Lesley Byrd Simpson, pp. 1–3, 37–38. *Recopilación*, Bk. VI, tit. x, law 17. *BR*, L, 198.

21. That cattle did ravage the fields in those few areas where beef production was profitable is attested by the ordinance of the Audiencia issued in 1606 authorizing the killing of cattle trespassing on adjacent rice fields owned by the natives. *BR*, XIV, 156–57. One cause for the distress culminating in the agarian insurrection of 1745–46 in the province of Batangas was the encroachment of cattle from the ecclesiastical-owned ranches on the fields of the Filipinos. *BR*, XLVIII, 27–36.

22. The Augustinian memorial of 1573, *BR*, XXXIV, 280–81. Ribadeneyra, *Historia*, p. 70. Santa Inés, *Crónica*, I, 60–62. Chirino, *Relación*, pp. 148–49. Delgado, *Historia sacro-profana*, pp. 349–52. The moralistic tone of these accounts contrasts with the dispassionate description found in the writings of Plasencia, Loarca, and Alcina. See Chapter II, note 1.

23. *BR*, VIII, 70–72; XXXIV, 325–31.

24. Salazar to Philip II: June, 1586, Colín-Pastells, *Labor evangélica*, I, 449.

25. *Ibid.*, p. 435. Alcina, *Historia*, Bk. IV, ch. v.

26. Plasencia's text was adopted by the Audiencia as customary law in all cases concerning dependent status. *BR*, XI, 31–32. Filipinos who petitioned the Audiencia for manumission often met with a favorable decision. See two letters of the *fiscales* to the king: July 10, 1610, *AGI/AF* 20, and one of November 24, 1630, *ibid.*, 21. Other regulatory acts of the Audiencia were decrees that a dependent could have only one superior and that a dependent who had been sold could not be transported beyond a distance of five leagues from the place of his habitual residence. *Fiscal* to Philip III: July 10, 1610, *ibid.*, 20. *BR*, X, 303–4.

27. Ríos Coronel, *BR*, XVIII, 297–98, 316. Unsigned letter [1598], *BR*, X, 117.

28. *BR*, XIX, 72. Provincial superior to *fiscal:* 1616, *AGI/AF* 20.

29. Cedula: June 12, 1679, *Recopilación*, Bk. VI, tit. ii, law 16. "Testimonios de los autos seguidos en Manila entre el real fiscal y el cabildo eclesiástico . . . y principales y cabezas de barangay en Pampanga sobre la libertad de Indios esclavos (1683–1684)," Pastells collection, St. Louis University, microfilm roll 32. *BR*, L, 199.

30. Delgado, *Historia sacro-profana*, p. 358.

31. *BR*, LII, 294–98.

32. *BR*, XLVIII, 142–43.

33. *BR*, XXIII, 36–38.

34. The myth that encomiendas were land grants still crops up in places where it should not. See J. E. Spencer, *Land and People in the Philippines, Geographical Problems in a Rural Economy* (Berkeley and Los Angeles: University of California Press, 1954) p. 113.

35. François Chevalier, *La formation des grands domaines au Mexique* (Paris: Institute d' ethnologie, 1952), pp. 150 ff.

36. Colín-Pastells, *Labor evangélica*, I, 424–25. *BR*, VII, 156–57.

37. Archbishop Benavides to Philip III: July 6, 1603, *BR*, XII, 117–21. Petition of Miguel Banal to Philip III: July 25, 1609, *BR*, XIV, 327–29. Philip III to Governor Silva: December 7, 1610, *BR*, XVII, 151–52. Audiencia to Philip III: July 20, 1612, *AGI/AF* 20.

38. Ordinance of Governor José Basco: March 20, 1784, *BR*, LII, 295–98.

39. "Ordenanzas de alcaldes," pp. 14–15.

40. Anda, *BR*, L, 154.

41. Simpson, *Exploitation of Land*. Borah, *New Spain's Century of Depression*.

42. *Ibid.*, p. 42.

43. Chevalier, *La formation*, pp. 403–9.

44. For the economic decline of the Mexican caciques see *ibid.*, pp. 280–85. For the decline of the caciques as creative cultural intermediaries see Charles Gibson, *Tlaxcala in the Sixteenth Century*, pp. 79 ff. For a comparison of Spanish intentions and results in the socioeconomic sphere in Mexico and in the Philippines see my article in the January, 1959, issue of the new journal, *Comparative Studies in Society and in History*, "Free versus Compulsory Labor: Mexico and the Philippines, 1540 to 1648."

*Chapter IX*

1. Viana to Charles III: July 10, 1766, *BR*, L, 98.

2. *BR*, XXXIV, 283. Ordinances of Governor Corcuera (1642), Cruzat (1696), and Raón (1768), *BR*, L, 203, 254–55. Hereafter cited as Ordinances. These ordinances are a richly varied source illustrating how the Filipinos were responding to many phases of Hispanization. The version in Blair and Robertson is an abridgment and an unsatisfactory one at that. I am presently editing for publication an unabridged Spanish version of these ordinances from a manuscript which Professor Lesley B. Simpson kindly put at my disposal. Morga-Retana, *Sucesos*, pp. 207–8. Cedula of June 11, 1594, *Recopilación*, Bk. VI, tit. vii, law 16.

3. "Ordenanzas de alcaldes (Cagayan, 1739)," ms. in possession of Professor Lesley Byrd Simpson, p. 22. *BR*, X, 117; XVII, 79–81; XVIII, 316; Ordinances, L, 204–5.

4. *Ibid.*, p. 194. Plasencia, *BR*, VII, 178–79. Morga-Retana, *Sucesos*, p. 210.

5. The *fiscal*, Viana, proposed this reform to Charles III in his letter of July 10, 1766. *BR*, L, 98. Governor Raón drew up the ordinance two years later, but these ordinances were not enforced until the early nineteenth century. *Ibid.*, p. 256.

6. José Montero y Vidal, *Historia general de Filipinas desde el descubrimiento de dichas islas hasta nuestros dias* (3 vols.; Madrid: 1887–95), II, 320. Moreno y Diez, *Manual de cabezas de barangay* (Manila: 1874).

7. See Chapter IV, note 16.

8. Morga-Retana, *Sucesos*, pp. 207–8.

9. "Ordenanzas de alcaldes," p. 6.

10. *BR*, Ordinances, L, 208–9.

11. "Ordenanzas de alcaldes," p. 39.

12. *Ibid.*, pp. 4–5.

13. For an over-all evaluation of the *residencia* see Clarence H. Haring, *The Spanish Empire in America*, pp. 149–53.

14. "Ordenanzas de alcaldes," p. 39. *Cabezas de barangay* in the eighteenth century could be elected to the post of *gobernadorcillo* without ceasing to act in the former capacity. *BR*, L, 255.

15. For royal legislation dealing with the *cajas* see *Recopilación*, Bk. VI, tit. iv.

16. Colín-Pastells, *Labor evangélica*, I, 449–50.

17. Audiencia to Philip III: July 19, 1609, and July 12, 1610, *AGI/AF* 20.

18. Rios Coronel discussed the abuses in the administration of the *cajas*. *BR*, XVIII, 314–15.

19. *BR*, Ordinances, L, 195, 235–36, 244 ff.

20. See Chapter VII, note 27.

21. *BR*, XI, 31–32; XVI, 321–26. Morga-Retana, *Sucesos*, p. 208. Francisco de Santa Inés, *Crónica*, I, 456.

22. *BR*, VII, 158; IX, 239–40; XI, 49–51; Ordinances, L, 196. Morga-Retana, *Sucesos*, p. 208.

23. Ríos Coronel, *BR*, XVIII, 318, and XI, 49–51. Cunningham, *The Audiencia in the Spanish Colonies as Illustrated by the Audiencia of Manila, 1583–1800* (Berkeley: University of California Press, 1919), pp. 98–104.

24. *BR*, XVII, 95–96; XX, 86; LI, 202. Rey, *Confessonarios*, pp. 170, 208–9, 221.

25. For an example of an extremist statement of this feeling widely held by the Spanish regular clergy see my *Millennial Kingdom*, pp. 85 ff.

26. *Census of the Philippine Islands*, 1903 (3 vols.; Washington, D.C.: U. S. Government Printing Office, 1905), III, 583, 594, 595, 689. Dean Worcester, *The Philippines Past and Present* (New York: Macmillan, 1930), p. 671.

27. Juan de Solórzano Pereira, *Política indiana* (5 vols.; Madrid and Buenos Aires: Compañía Ibero-Americana de Publicaciones 1930), I, 395–404. First edition is 1648.

28. Philip II to Governor Tello: May 25, 1596, *BR*, IX, 255–56. Audiencia to Philip III: July 3, 1606, *AGI/AF* 19.

29. José Duque, O.S.A., to Charles II: March 21, 1689, *AGI/AF* 25.

30. "Ordenanzas de alcaldes," pp. 5–6. Degree of Governor Anda: November 9, 1764, "Ordenanzas para corregidores y alcaldes mayores" (Manila: 1764), p. 113 ff. See note 2 of this chapter for an explanation of this ms.

31. *BR*, XXVIII, 210–13; L, 119–24, 169–72. Also see my article "Philippine Linguistics," pp. 165 ff.

32. For Tlaxcalan responses to political Hispanization see Gibson, *Tlaxcala in the Sixteenth Century*, pp. 89 ff.

## Chapter X

1. Colín-Pastells, *Labor evangélica*, I, 213; II, 506–7. Murillo Velarde, *Historia*, pp. 33, 44, 48, 77.

2. Audiencia to Philip III: June 30, 1605, *AGI/AF* 19.

3. Francisco Combés, S.J., *Historia de las islas de Mindanao y Iolò* (Madrid: 1667), pp. 197 ff. Murillo Velarde, *Historia*, p. 77.

4. Concepción, *Historia*, VI, 89–113. Also see the account of Juan de los Angeles, O.P.: March, 1643, *BR*, XXXV, 128–62. Corcuera's administration was also notable for a series of severe jurisdictional conflicts with the mendicant orders. The Jesuits usually sided with the governor against the mendicants in these disputes, for both Corcuera and the Society shared a common objective in waging war against the Moros.

5. Concepción, *Historia*, VII, 69 ff. The standard secondary work on Mindanao in the seventeenth century is José Montero y Vidal, *Historia de la piratería malayo-mahometana en Mindanao, Joló y Borneo* (Madrid: 1888), pp. 243 ff. Uprisings in Pampanga and Pangasinan, close to the center of Spanish power, were also factors precipitating the withdrawal from Zamboanga. The Sangley revolt occurred after the Zamboanga decision had been taken.

6. According to the Jesuit report published in *ibid.*, pp. 250–52, the Society administered to 4,251 families in the *residencia* of Zamboanga and 2,750 families in the *residencia* of Iligan-Dapitan for a total figure of about 28,001 people. For the Recollect figures see Luís de Jesús, *Historia general de los religiosos descalzos del orden de los ermitaños del gran padre San Avgvstín de la congregación de España y de las Indias* (Madrid: 1681), pp. 40–44.

7. The most concise collection of sources is Lorenzo Pérez, O.F.M., "Los aetas e Ilongotes de Filipinas," *Archivo Ibero-Americano*, XIV (November–December, 1927), pp. 289–346. For a brief but authoritative account see Felix and Marie Keesing, *Taming the Philippine Headhunters* (Palo Alto: Stanford University Press, 1934), pp. 62–65.

8. *BR*, L, 212–13, 248–49. Also see Chapter IV, note 17.

9. The resistance of the mountain province to Spanish penetration contrasts in some respects with the effective opposition the Spaniards met from the Araucanian Indians in central Chile. In response to the sustained pressure exerted by the Spanish colonists, who were anxious to secure an abundant supply of cheap labor, Araucanian culture underwent some intensive changes. Spanish pressure produced a counter-pressure among the Araucanians. These transformations facilitated the task of the Araucanians to preserve their independence for two hundred years. Some features of Spanish culture were adopted in order to strengthen resistance patterns. Outstanding among these changes was the emergence of a modified form of political-military centralization. In the case of the mountain province no comparable cultural changes occurred, since Spanish military, political,

economic, and religious pressure on the area was never as sustained or as intense as Spanish pressure against the Araucanians. For an evocative analysis of how Araucanian culture changed see Robert Charles Padden, "Culture Change and Military Resistance in Araucanian Chile, 1550–1730," *Southwestern Journal of Anthropology*, XIII (Spring, 1957), 103–21.

10. My colleague in the Philippine Studies Program, Paul Lietz, is presently engaged in studying for the Mindanao area various aspects of this radical change in Spanish methods of penetration.

11. *BR*, XXV, 148–49; XXXV, 125–26.

12. The sources for the Pampangan revolt are the following. Díaz, *Conquistas*, pp. 568–90. Murillo Velarde, *Historia*, pp. 254–56. Baltasar de Santa Cruz, O.P., *Historia de la provincia de santo rosario de Filipinas, Iapón y China* (Zaragoza: 1693), pp. 331–34. Concepción, *Historia*, VII, 9–35.

13. See Chapter IV, note 10.

14. Santa Cruz, *Historia*, pp. 337–40. Murillo Velarde, *Historia*, pp. 254–57. Díaz, *Conquistas*, pp. 604–6. *BR*, XXXVIII, 161–81, 181–215.

15. Concepción, *Historia*, XI, 280; *BR*, XLVIII, 27–36.

16. Murillo Velarde, *Historia*, pp. 17–18. Concepción, *Historia*, V, 20–23. Juan de Medina, Historia, pp. 226–28. Díaz, *Conquistas*, pp. 132–36.

17. The same sources as in note 16.

18. Concepción, *Historia*, VI, 247–81. Díaz, *Conquistas*, pp. 517–23.

19. Concepción, *Historia*, XII, 40–43.

20. Bishop of Cagayan to Philip III: April 12, 1605, *AGI/AF* 76.

21. *BR*, XVIII, 318.

22. John Howland Rowe, "The Incas Under Spanish Colonial Institutions," *Hispanic American Historical Review*, XXXVII (May, 1957), 155–99.

23. Gregorio F. Zaide, *The Philippines Since Pre-Spanish Times* (Manila: R. B. García, 1949), pp. 440 ff., and his *Dagohoy, Champion of Philippine Freedom* (Manila: Enríquez, Aldaya, 1941).

*Chapter XI*

1. José Ortega y Gasset's essay "Meditation in the Escorial" in Ortega's *Invertebrate Spain*, Mildred Adams, translator (New York: W.W. Norton, 1937), p. 208.

2. As early as 1586 Bishop Salazar, who had spent many years in Mexico, warned that Mexican-inspired legislation often conflicted with Philippine conditions. Colín-Pastells, *Labor evangélica*, I, 449.

3. Clarence H. Haring, *The Spanish Empire in America*, p. 123. Underlying the "I obey but do not execute" formula is the principle of Justinian that the prince would not willfully commit an injustice. *Recopilación*, Bk. II, tit. i, law 24.

4. For some recent characterological studies of the mestizo upon which my remarks are based see Gordon W. Hewes, "Mexicans in Search of the Mexican," *The American Journal of Economics and Sociology*," XIII (January, 1954) 209–23 and my article "México y lo Mexicano," *Hispanic American Historical Review*, XXXVI (August, 1956), 309–18.

# Bibliographical Essay and
# List of Sources

## Printed Sources

Our single most voluminous kind of sources are the chronicles published periodically by the various religious orders. They also contain considerable material on missionary activity in China and Japan, since the Philippines were the Spanish missionary headquarters for all the Orient.

Juan de Grijalva's chronicle of the Augustinian province of New Spain (Mexico, 1624) is particularly useful for the early contacts between the Augustinians and the Filipinos. Gaspar de San Agustín's account (Madrid, 1698) is a richly detailed, chronological description covering events up to 1616. Casimiro Díaz's continuation of San Agustín reached the year 1694. Abundantly informative, it is also a prolific source for information on the native uprisings in the lowland provinces.

One of the principal characteristics of Juan de Medina's Augustinian chronicle is its tone of disillusion. Serving in the Philippines from 1610 to 1635, he became discouraged and was granted permission to return to Spain. He died on board a galleon en route to Acapulco. Medina suffered from a "second-generation complex." The sanguine if unrealistic hopes of the first generation were not materializing.

Marcelo de Ribadeneyra's Franciscan history (Barcelona, 1601) is a foil to Medina's. Ribadeneyra was an eloquent spokesman of the first generation of missionaries, who were inspired by a seemingly boundless optimism about the total success of the missionary enterprise. Ribadeneyra's chronicle is invaluable for its account of Franciscan methods of indoctrina-

199

tion. Actually both the optimism of Ribadeneyra and the pessimism of Medina were exaggerated manifestations. Subsequent chroniclers would take a more realistic view of missionary possibilities and accomplishments.

Francisco de Santa Inés, whose work covers the period to 1600, does not add an unusual amount of new material about Franciscan activity. Juan Francisco de San Antonio's three volumes, which bear a Manila imprint of 1738-44, are more informative. Based largely on Ribadeneyra's published account and Juan de la Llave's unpublished manuscript, San Antonio's work has much detailed material dealing with resettlement and indoctrination methods. Like Santa Inés, San Antonio did not describe the seventeenth century. The Franciscan emphasis on the sixteenth century to the exclusion of the seventeenth century can only be explained in terms of events in Japan. The martyrdom of St. Pedro Bautista in 1597 was the spectacular event that absorbed a good deal of the attention of the Franciscan chroniclers. Domingo Martínez's compendium (1756) attempted to fill this wide vacuum in Franciscan historiography by covering the whole seventeenth century. Its general superficiality and its lack of detail make it, however, one of the least interesting of the Franciscan sources.

Two extra-Philippine accounts throw considerable light on Franciscan activity in the islands. They are Marcos de Alcalá's chronicle of the Discalced province of St. Joseph in Spain and Baltasar de Medina's history of the Discalced province in Mexico. The former is useful for the Spanish background of the Philippine Franciscans. The latter also contains pertinent information, for the Discalced province in Mexico was founded and maintained as a midway station linking the Discalced provinces in Spain with the Philippine province. The vast majority of Franciscans established in Mexico belonged to the Observant branch of the Order.

Four chronicles depict the exploits of the Dominicans in the Philippines. The first chronicle was written by Friar Diego Aduarte, Bishop of Cagayan (1632-36). Published in 1640 and again in 1693, Aduarte's chronicle contains a wealth of detail about initial Dominican contacts with the recalcitrant natives of the Cagayan valley. This work is also notable for its realistic tenor, avoiding the extremes of both optimism and pessimism. Baltasar de Santa Cruz published a second volume on events from 1637 to 1688. Santa Cruz's volume is more hagiographical than Aduarte's and hence less interesting for historical purposes. Vicente de Salazar's continuation covering the period from 1669 to 1700 (Manila, 1742) is invaluable for Dominican activity among the then hostile Sambals. Domingo Collantes published a volume in 1783 covering events from 1700 to 1765.

The importance of the work of the Jesuits is reflected in the literature they published. The first account is Pedro Chirino's (Rome, 1604). Based on the Annual Letters that the Jesuit authorities dispatched to their superiors in Rome, many of which were then published, Chirino's account is a rich and varied source for all aspects of missionary activity. Published three years after Ribadeneyra's, Chirino's relation is similar in tone. Both authors were first-generation missionaries. Each one was eloquently and exuberantly optimistic, although Chirino may have been somewhat more restrained in tone than Ribadeneyra.

Francisco Colín's history (Madrid, 1663) carries the story down to 1616. What Colín did was to fill in and to expand with a prolific assortment of detail Chirino's outline. It is indeed a fine job of historical synthesis. Diego de Oña in 1706 wrote a continuation of Colín covering the period from 1611 to 1665. This innocuous chronicle fell so far short of the high standards of Jesuit historiography that the authorities had the good sense not to publish it. Of only marginal historical value, it may be consulted in manuscript form on microfilm at St. Louis University (*ARSI*, roll 167).

Pedro Murillo Velarde's account (Manila, 1749), which according to J. T. Medina is the finest example of printing done in the islands, surveys Jesuit activity from 1613 to 1749. Although it is an informative source, this work is inferior in quality to the earlier accounts of Chirino and Colín. It lacks the structural organization and the historical sense of the later books. For a Jesuit account it contains a large dose of hagiography. Juan Delgado's work, finished in 1754 but not published until 1892, is a foil to Murillo Velarde's. It is not a chronicle as such. Encyclopedic in scope, it offers a harmonious synthesis of such diverse topics as preconquest culture, missionary methods, the psychology of the Filipinos, botany, and zoology. Enlightened and urbane, Delgado belonged to that pre-expulsion generation of Jesuits who were imbued with some aspects of the spirit of the Enlightenment. Francisco Combés' history of Mindanao (Madrid, 1667) is another significant Jesuit account chronicling some dramatic chapters in that clash between the Cross and the Crescent in the southern Philippines.

For the early missions of the Augustinian Recollects the principal source is Andrés de San Nicolás' history of the Recollects (Madrid, 1664). San Nicolás chronicles the exploits of the Recollects in Spain as well as overseas for the period to 1620. The Philippine information is detailed and abundant. Luís de Jesús' continuation of the chronicle covering the decades between 1620 and 1650 is inferior in interest, since the stress is often hagiographical.

One of the classics of Philippine missionary historiography is Juan de la Concepción's fourteen volumes (Manila, 1788–92). Concepción surveyed events in the archipelago from the time of Magellan to 1759. No mere parochial account of the accomplishments of his own Recollect Order, this work synthesizes on the basis of abundant documentation and with a sophisticated historical criterion the major ecclesiastical and political events spanning a period of over two centuries. These volumes remain perhaps the outstanding example of synthetic historiography produced in the islands.

No discussion of early Philippine historiography would be complete without a reference to Antonio de Morga's account (Mexico, 1609). A conscientious and vigorous representative of the Spanish bureaucracy, he spent seven years in the islands (1595–1602), first as the principal judicial officer and later as a member of the Audiencia. His account is an invaluable source for such topics as Hispano-Dutch hostility, native self-government, the indigenous labor system, and Spanish exploitation of labor. On some controversial issues touching the clergy (episcopal visitation and clerical exploitation of labor) Morga's published account borders on the innocuous. In his private correspondence with his superiors, however, Morga made trenchant critiques of what he regarded as missionary abuses (for an example see Retana's edition of Morga, pp. 247–62).

The contrast between Morga's then unpublished correspondence and his published account of 1609 brings to light one essential characteristic of all these chronicles. They are "official" histories. Factual material was often omitted which was considered excessively controversial or which might discredit the character and the purposes of Spanish colonization. In studying the disciplinary crisis among the Augustinians, for example, information in the Augustinian chronicles turns out to be sparse and reticent. Neither do the missionary chronicles furnish much assistance in investigating ecclesiastical demands placed on native labor or the charging of sacramental fees by the regular clergy.

No objective and comprehensive picture of Philippine developments can be obtained from an exclusive reliance on the missionary chronicles. The latter must be supplemented by an examination of the voluminous correspondence between the lay and ecclesiastical figures in the islands with the authorities in Spain. A representative selection of this correspondence can be found in that monumental collection of sources compiled and edited by Emma Helen Blair and James Alexander Robertson. This collection spans the entire Spanish period from Magellan's discovery to the end of the Spanish regime. Alongside substantial selections from the ecclesiastical chronicles, there is a prolific assortment of documents from the Spanish archives. The defect of this pioneer and laborious work is not the publishing of the documents in English translation, although most scholars would feel more at ease in the original language. It is rather that the translations are usually awkward and often downright ambiguous. Nevertheless, as a collection of sources it is incomparable, especially for the sixteenth and seventeenth centuries. Forty-two of the fifty-two volumes deal with the period prior to 1700.

Some of the gaps in the Blair and Robertson series are filled by another outstanding collection of sources published by Pablo Pastells, S.J., in his edition of Colín's *Labor evangélica*. The Pastells selection is notably strong for the Sánchez mission to Spain (1586) and for its varied selection from the informative Jesuit Annual Letters. The Pastells text is still the single richest source on the question of episcopal visitation.

Perhaps the finest single collection of printed materials on the Spanish period in the Philippines is in the Edward E. Ayer collection at the Newberry Library in Chicago (see my article, "The Philippine Collection in the Newberry Library," *The Newberry Library Bulletin*, III [March, 1955], 229–36). The Newberry also has an extensive collection of Philippine linguistic items (Doris Varner Welsh, *Checklist of Philippine Lin-*

*guistics in the Newberry Library* [Chicago: The Newberry Library, 1950]).

The Library of Congress has an incomparable collection of twentieth century items. In addition, its holdings for the Spanish period are varied and extensive.

## Manuscript Sources

Although the printed sources for the early Spanish period are abundant and accessible, they must be supplemented by manuscript sources. The Newberry has a small but choice collection of Philippine manuscripts, a calendar of which was recently published (*Calendar of Philippine Documents in the Ayer Collection of the Newberry Library*, Paul Lietz, ed. [Chicago: The Newberry Library, 1956]). For the purposes of this study, however, this manuscript collection was of real but limited value. Virtually all the significant items for the early Spanish period have been published in the Blair and Robertson series. Since the Blair and Robertson texts were sometimes ambiguous in meaning or were abridgements, it was indeed useful to be able to consult the original Spanish text. Equally convenient was the possibility of consulting the Blair and Robertson transcripts from the Spanish archives in sixteen volumes and the Ventura del Arco transcripts from the *Real Academia de Historia* in five volumes, most of whose contents appeared in some form in Blair and Robertson.

The most outstanding manuscript-on-microfilm collection containing substantial information on the early history of the Philippines located in the United States is the Knights of Columbus Foundation for the Preservation of Historic Documents at the Vatican Library at St. Louis University. In the *Jesuitica* section of this collection the most interesting Philippine items are to be found in the *Archivum Romanum Societatis Iesu*, that is, documents microfilmed from the Jesuit archives in Rome. There is, for example, a rather complete series of the Annual Letters from the Philippine province during the seventeenth century. Many of these have never been published, and several of the published texts are today scarce. Of even greater interest to the historian is the series of letters addressed by the Jesuit provincial superiors in Manila to the general of the Society in Rome. In this correspondence the provincial superiors are apt to be much more candid than in the published Annual Letters, which in the nature of things were carefully edited for public consumption. Of real value also is a large assortment of letters addressed by the rectors of the local *residencias* to the provincial superior in Manila. These letters provided the raw material from which the Annual Letters for the whole province were constructed as well as furnishing the primary material upon which the Manila authorities could make their confidential reports to Rome.

Another important section at St. Louis University is a microfilm copy of the transcripts made by Father Pablo Pastells of documents from the *Archivo General de Indias*. Only a small portion of this material concerns the Philippines as such. Of this fraction the bulk has already been published by Father Pastells in his edition of Colín's *Labor evangélica*. Nevertheless, there are a few choice, unpublished, seventeenth-century items. In another section of *Jesuitica* microfilm there are a few interesting Philippine items in the *Fondo Gesuitico al Gesu di Roma*.

The microfilm holdings at St. Louis University, as the preceding outline suggests, are of solid value for Philippine studies for the period from 1581 to 1767, when the Society was expelled from the Spanish dominions.

In both Mexico and in the Philippines there are considerable archival resources of interest. According to Herbert Bolton's *Guide to the Materials for the History of the United States in the Principal Archives of Mexico* (Washington, 1913), Philippine sources in the *Archivo General de la Nacion* are plentiful for the eighteenth century, with relatively few documents relating to the period before 1700. In the Philippines, archives sustained severe and extensive damage during the last war. Their present state is revealed in an article by Edgar B.Wickberg, "Spanish Records in the Philippine National Archives," *Hispanic American Historical Review*, XXXV (February, 1955). Poorly housed and inadequately catalogued if at all, these records are apparently abundant for the eighteenth and nineteenth centuries and scant for the period before 1700. I sincerely regret not having had the opportunity to examine these archival resources in both Mexico City and in Manila.

Such an examination might have been desirable, but it was not indispensable for the completion of this study. For the Habsburg era the richest depositories of archival records are not in the Philippines or in Mexico but in Spain. Although Philippine officials often disregarded or evaded the directives of the Council of the Indies, they found it expedient to send detailed reports to Spain justifying their course of action or inaction. These voluminous records were originally deposited in the Spanish national archives at Simancas founded by the Emperor Charles V. In the eighteenth century the *Archivo General de Indias* was established in Seville by Charles III. Today this archive is the single richest depository of manuscripts relating to the history of Spain's overseas possessions.

A three-months visit to Seville during the fall of 1954 enabled me to examine some of these Philippine records. Of the approximately one thousand *legajos* of manuscripts, more than one-half belong to the period between 1700 and 1840. The records for the two earlier centuries are, nevertheless, abundant. The great collections of primary sources edited and published by Blair and Robertson and Father Pastells are in the main selections from the *Archivo General de Indias*. It would be no exaggeration to say that these editors wisely picked out some of the choicest items. Yet these published collections are selections, and they must be supplemented by further archival consultation.

For the completion of this study I examined those *legajos* which contained the correspondence of the ecclesiastical authorities with the Council of the Indies, in particular, the correspondence of the superiors of religious orders, the archbishops of Manila, the bishops of the suffragan sees and the cathedral chapter of the archdiocese of Manila. Among the secular sources consulted were the correspondence of the governors of the colony, the members of the Audiencia, and private Spanish citizens. All these *legajos* were in the *Audiencia de Filipinas* section, and those of greatest interest proved to be the following: 6, 7, 8, 18, 19, 20, 21, 34, 35, 36, 37, 38, 39, 40, 41, 42, 43, 44, 74, 75, 76, 77, 78, 79, 80, 84, 85, 302. Archival material was of outstanding interest for the following topics: missionary logistics, pre-Hispanic dependent status, the encomienda, local self-government, the disciplinary crisis in the Augustinian order, the question of ecclesiastical visitation, the Patronato, the Church's demands on native labor, and sacramental fees.

The Philippine bundles for the eighteenth century in the *Archivo* have scarcely been exploited. In fact, few of these *legajos* have been opened by investigators. Only eight volumes in the Blair and Robertson series deal with the eighteenth century. Few items in these eight volumes are Seville documents. Actually the choice eighteenth-century selections in Blair and Robertson came from the manuscript collection purchased by Edward E. Ayer from the *Compañía de Tabacos* or from the Ventura del Arco transcripts, both of which are in the Newberry. Until these voluminous eighteenth-century sources in the *Archivo* are examined, it will be virtually impossible to make any durable conclusions about that period.

There are excellent Philippine manuscript materials in Madrid. An outstanding collection can be found in the Jesuit papers located in the *Real Academia de Historia*. The Ventura del Arco transcripts in the Newberry are copies of documents from this collection. The Blair and Robertson transcripts in the Newberry also contain some further material from the *Academia*. It would seem that many of the most interesting Philippine documents in the *Academia* have already been published. The National Library and the *Archivo Histórico Nacional* also have a few Philippine holdings.

Actually the most important Philippine collection in Madrid is not yet accessible to research. The manuscripts of the *Museo y Biblioteca del Ultramar* are stored in a Madrid basement waiting for adequate housing and cataloguing. This collection is the archive of the former ministry of *Ultramar*, which in the nineteenth century had jurisdiction over Spain's remaining colonies. Although this archive is probably the most comprehensive in existence for the nineteenth century, many casual references suggest that it also contains valuable holdings on the earlier centuries.*

A most significant manuscript relating to the Philippines is the one located in the library of the *Palacio de Oriente* in Madrid. It is the survey of Bisayan society written by Francisco Ignacio Alcina, S.J., who died in 1674. An evaluation of its contents can be found in note 1, Chapter II.

Outside Madrid there are two collections of outstanding Philippine interest. One is the library of the *Colegio de Filipinas* in Valladolid. Founded

---

* Note to second printing: This collection has recently been placed in the *Archivo Histórico Nacional*, where it is available for scholarly research.

in 1732 by the Augustinian Order as a seminary for training missionaries for the Philippines, its collection of books and manuscripts is particularly strong for the eighteenth century. The archive in Pastrana has a multitude of documents relating to Franciscan activity in the archipelago. Some of these holdings have been edited in various issues of the *Archivo Ibero-Americano*, an historical journal published by the Franciscan Order in Madrid. I regret that I was unable to visit either Pastrana or Valladolid.

## List of Sources

This list of printed sources is selective rather than exhaustive. Certain items have been intentionally excluded. There is no need to include all the standard bibliographical works of reference. Works which have been cited only a few times are omitted. Particular items in the Blair and Robertson series and the Pastells edition of Colín have not been listed individually.

Acosta, José de, S.J. *De promvlgatione evangelii apud barbaros*. Salamanca: 1589.

Aduarte, Diego, O.P. *Historia de la provincia del sancto rosario de la orden de predicadores de Filipinas, Iapón y China*. Zaragoza: 1693.

Agurto, Pedro de, O.S.A. *Tractado de qve se deven administrar los sacramentos de la sancta eucharistia y extrema vnction a los Indios de esta Neuva España*. Mexico: 1573.

Alcalá, Marcos de, O.F.M. *Chrónica de la santa provincia de San Joseph de religiosos descalzos*. Madrid: 1738.

Alcina (Alzina), Francisco Ignacio, S.J. *Historia de las islas e indios de Bisayas . . . dividida en dos: la primera natural . . . la segunda eclesiástical y sobrenatural . . . .* Manuscript, library of the Palacio de Oriente, Madrid.

Astrain, Antonio, S.J. *Historia de la compañía da Jesús en la asistencia de España*. 7 vols. Madrid: Razón y Fe, 1912–25.

Blair, Emma Helen, and Robertson, James Alexander. *The Philippine Islands, 1493–1803*. 55 vols. Cleveland: A. H. Clark, 1903–9.

Borah, Woodrow W. *Early Trade and Navigation Between Mexico and Peru*. Berkeley and Los Angeles: University of California Press, *Ibero-Americana*: 38, 1954.

———. *New Spain's Century of Depression*. Berkeley and Los Angeles: University of California Press, *Ibero-Americana*: 35, 1951.

Boxer, C. R. *The Christian Century in Japan, 1549–1650*. Berkeley and Los Angeles: University of California Press, 1951.

Cano, Gaspar, O.S.A. *Catálogo de los religiosos de n.p.s. Agustín de la provincia del smo. nombre de Jesús de Filipinas*. Manila: 1864.

Chevalier, François. *La formation des grands domaines au Mexique. Terre et société aux XVIe–XVIIe siecles*. Paris: Institut d' ethnologie, 1952.

Chirino, Pedro, S.J. *Relación de las islas filipinas*. Manila: 1890. (First edition, Rome, 1604.)

Cline, Howard F. "Problems of Mexican Ethno-History; The Ancient Chinantla," *Hispanic American Historical Review*, XXXVII (August, 1957), 273–95.

*Colección de documentos inéditos relativos al descubrimiento, conquista y organización de las antiguas posesiones españolas de América y Oceanía*. 42 vols., Madrid, 1864–84.

Colín, Francisco, S.J. *Labor evangélica*, ed. Pablo Pastells, S.J. 3 vols. Barcelona: Henrich, 1900–1902.

Combés, Francisco, S.J. *Historia de las islas de Mindanao y Ioló*. Madrid: 1667.

Concepción, Juan de la, O.R.S.A. *Historia general de Philipinas*. 14 vols. Manila: 1788–92.

Cook, Sherburne F., and Simpson, Lesley Byrd. *The Population of Central Mexico in the Sixteenth Century*. Berkeley and Los Angeles: University of California Press, *Ibero-Americana: 31*, 1948.

Costa, Horacio de la. "Church and State in the Philippines during the Administration of Bishop Salazar," *Hispanic American Historical Review*, XXX (August, 1950), 314–36.

———. "The Development of a Native Clergy in the Philippines," *Theological Studies*, VIII (July, 1947), 219–50.

———. "Episcopal Jurisdiction in the Philippines in the 17th century," *Philippine Studies*, II (September, 1954), 197–217.

Cunningham, Charles Henry. *The Audiencia in the Spanish Colonies as Illustrated by the Audiencia of Manila (1583–1800)*. Berkeley: University of California Press, 1919.

Delgado, Juan, S.J. *Historia general, sacro-profana, política y natural de las islas del poniente llamadas Filipinas*. Manila: 1892.

Díaz, Casimiro, O.S.A. *Conquistas de las islas filipinas*. Manila: 1890.

*The Doctrina Christiana: The First Book Printed in the Philippines, Manila, 1593. A Facsimile of the Copy in the Lessing J. Rosenwald Collection, The Library of Congress, Washington, D.C.* With an introductory essay by Edwin Wolf. Washington, D.C.: Library of Congress, 1947.

Fernández Navarrete, Domingo, O.P. *Tratados históricos, políticos, ethicos y religiosos de la monarchía de China*. Madrid: 1676.

Foster, George M. "Cofradia and Compadrazgo in Spain and in Spanish America," *Southwestern Journal of Anthropology*, IX (Spring, 1953), 10 ff.

Gayo Aragón, Jesús, O.P. *Ideas juridico-teológicas de los religiosos de Filipinas en el siglo xvi sobre la conquista de las islas*. Manila: University of Santo Tomas Press, 1950.

Gibson, Charles. *Tlaxcala in the Sixteenth Century*. New Haven: Yale University Press, 1952.

Gómez Platero, Eusebio. O.F.M. *Catálogo biográfico de los religiosos franciscanos de la provincia de San Gregorio magno de Filipinas*. Manila: 1890.

Grau y Monfalcón, Juan. *Memorial informatorio*. Madrid: 1637.

——. *Justificación de la conservación y comercio de las islas filipinas*. Mexico: 1640.

Grijalva, Juan de, O.S.A. *Crónica de la orden de n.p.s. Augustín en las provincias de la Nueva España en quatro edades desde el año de 1533 hasta el de 1592*. Mexico: 1624.

Hanke, Lewis. *The Spanish Struggle for Justice in the Conquest of America*. Philadelphia: University of Pennsylvania Press, 1949.

——, and Millares Carlo, Augustín, editors. *Cuerpo de documentos del siglo xvi sobre los derechos de España en las Indias y las Filipinas*. Mexico City: Fondo de Cultura Económica, 1943.

Haring, Clarence H. *The Spanish Empire in America*. New York: Oxford University Press, 1947.

Hernáez, Francisco Javier. *Colección de bulas, breves y otros documentos relativos a la iglesia de América y Filipinas*. 2 vols. Brussels: 1879.

Jesús, Luís de, O.R.S.A. *Historia general de los religiosos descalzos del orden de los ermitaños del gran padre San Avgvstín de la congregación de España y de las Indias*. Madrid: 1681.

Keesing, Felix, and Keesing, Marie. *Taming the Philippine Headhunters*. Palo Alto: Stanford University Press, 1934.

Kroeber, A. L. *Peoples of the Philippines*. New York: American Museum of Natural History, 1928.

Kubler, George. *Mexican Architecture in the Sixteenth Century*. 2 vols. New Haven: Yale University Press, 1948.

Marín y Morales, Valentín, O.P. *Ensayo de una síntesis de los trabajos realizados por las corporaciones religiosas españolas de Filipinas*. 2 vols. Manila: 1901.

Martínez, Domingo, O.F.M. *Compendio histórico de la apostólica provincia de San Gregorio de Philipinas de religiosos menores descalzos de n. p. San Francisco*. Madrid: 1756.

Medina, Baltasar de, O.F.M. *Chrónica de la santa provincia de San Diego de México de religiosos descalzos de n.p. S. Francisco en la Nueva España*. Mexico: 1682.

Medina, José Toribio. *La imprenta en Manila desde sus orígenes hasta 1810*. 2 vols. Santiago de Chile: 1896 and 1904.

Medina, Juan de, O.S.A. *Historia de los sucesos de la orden de n. gran p. S. Agustín de estas islas filipinas*. Manila: 1893.

Mentrida, Alonso, O.S.A. *Ritval para administrar los santos sacramentos sacado casi todo del ritual romano y lo demás del ritual indico*. Manila: 1669.

Merrill, Elmer Drew, *The Botany of Cook's Voyages*. (*Chronica Botanica* series, XIV, numbers 5 and 6.) Waltham, Massachusetts: 1954.

Moreno y Díez, Rafael. *Manual del cabeza de barangay*. Manila: 1874.

Morga, Antonio de. *Sucesos de las islas Filipinas*, ed.W. E. Retana. Madrid: Victoriano Suárez, 1909.

Murillo Velarde, Pedro, S.J. *Historia de la provincia de Philippinas de la compañía de Jesús*. Manila: 1749.

Ocio y Viana, Hilario, O.P. *Compendio de la reseña biográfica de los religiosos de la provincia del santísimo rosario de Filipinas*. Manila: 1895.

Ortiz, Tomás, O.S.A. *Practica del ministerio.* Manila: 1731.

Padden, Robert Charles. "Culture Change and Military Resistance in Araucanian Chile, 1550–1730," *Southwestern Journal of Anthropology,* XIII (Spring, 1957), 103–21.

Pérez, Elviro, O.S.A. *Catálogo bio-bibliográfico de los religiosos agustinos de la provincia del santísimo nombre de Jesús de las islas filipinas.* Manila: College of Santo Tomas Press, 1901.

Phelan, John Leddy. "Free versus Compulsory Labor: Mexico and the Philippines, 1540 to 1648," *Comparative Studies in Society and History,* I (January, 1959).

———. *The Millennial Kingdom of the Franciscans in the New World: A Study of the Writings of Gerónimo de Mendieta (1525–1604).* Berkeley and Los Angeles: University of California Press, Publications in History, No. 52, 1956.

———. "The Philippine Collection in the Newberry Library," *The Newberry Library Bulletin,* III (March, 1955), 229–36. Spanish translation in *Coleccionismo,* XLII (October, 1955).

———. "Philippine Linguistics and Spanish Missionaries, 1565–1700," *Mid-America,* XXXVII (July, 1955), 153–70.

———. "Pre-Baptismal Instruction and the Administration of Baptism in the Philippines during the Sixteenth Century," *The Americas,* XII (July, 1955), 3–23.

———. "Some Ideological Aspects of the Conquest of the Philippines," *The Americas* XIII (January, 1957), 221–39.

Pigafetta, Antonio. *Magellan's Voyage Around the World,* ed. James Alexander Robertson. 3 vols. Cleveland: Arthur H. Clark, 1906.

*Recopilación de leyes de los reynos de las Indias.* 4 vols. Madrid: 1681.

Rey, Fernando, O.S.A. *Confessonarios.* Manila: 1792.

Ribadeneyra, Marcelo de, O.F.M. *Historia de las islas del archipielago y reynos de la gran China, Tartaria, Cuchinchina, Malaca, Sian, Camboxa, y Iappón, y de lo sucedido en ellos a los religiosos descalzos de la orden del seraphico padre San Francisco de la prouincia de San Gregorio de las Philippinas.* Barcelona: 1601.

Ricard, Robert. *La "conquête spirituelle" du Mexique.* Paris: Institut d' Ethnologie, 1933.

Rowe, John Howland. "The Incas Under Spanish Colonial Institutions," *Hispanic American Historical Review,* XXXVII (May, 1957), 155–99.

Sábada del Carmen, Francisco, O.R.S.A. *Catálogo de los religiosos agustinos recoletos de la provincia de San Nicolás de Tolentino de Filipinas.* Madrid: Asilo de Huérfanos del Sagrado Corazón de Jesús, 1906.

Salazar, Vincente de, O.P. *Historia de la provincia de el Santissimo Rosario de Philipinas,* China y Tvnking. Manila: 1742.

San Agustín, Gaspar de, O.S.A. *Conquistas de las islas Philipinas: la temporal por las armas del señor don Phelipe segundo el prudente y la espiritval por los religiosos del orden de nuestro padre San Agustín.* Madrid: 1698.

San Antonio, Juan Francisco de, O.F.M. *Chrónicas de la apostólica provincia de S. Gregorio de religiosos descalzos de n. s. p. San Francisco en las islas Philipinas, China, Japón* . . . . 3 vols. Manila: 1738–44.

San Nicolás, Andrés de, O.R.S.A. *Historia general de los religiosos descalzos del orden de los ermitaños del gran padre San Avgustín de la congregación de España y de las Indias*, Madrid: 1664.

Santa Cruz, Baltasar de, O.P. *Historia de la provincia del santo rosario de Filipinas, Iapón y China, de la sagrado orden de predicadores.* Zaragoza: 1693.

Santa Inés, Francisco de, O.F.M. *Crónica de la provincia de San Gregorio Magno de religiosos descalzos de n.s.p. San Francisco en las islas Filipinas, China, Japón, etc.* . . . . 2 vols. Manila: 1892.

Schurz, William L. *The Manila Galleon.* New York: E. P. Dutton, 1939.

Scott, James Brown. *The Spanish Origin of International Law: Francisco de Vitoria and His Law of Nations.* Oxford: Clarendon Press, 1934.

Simpson, Lesley Byrd. *The Encomienda in New Spain.* Berkeley and Los Angeles: University of California Press, 1950.

———. *Exploitation of Land in Central Mexico in the Sixteenth Century.* Berkeley and Los Angeles: University of California Press, *Ibero-Americana:* 36, 1952.

Solórzano y Pereira, Juan de. *Política indiana.* 2 vols. Madrid: 1648.

Sommervogel, Carlos, S.J. *Bibliothèque de la campagnie de Jésus.* 11 vols. Brussels and Paris: Alphonse Picard and Oscar Schepens, 1890–1932.

Spencer, J. E. *Land and People in the Philippines, Geographical Problems in a Rural Economy.* Berkeley and Los Angeles: University of California Press, 1954.

Torres Lanzas, Pedro. *Catálogo de los documentos relativos a las islas Filipinas existentes en el archivo de Indias de Sevilla.* 8 vols. Barcelona: 1925–34.

Zaide, Gregorio F. *The Philippines Since Pre-Spanish Times.* Manila: R. B. Garcia, 1949.

# Index

Acuña, Pedro Bravo de, 96
Agurto, Pedro de, 68
*Alcaldes mayores:* duties of, 100, 109, 125, 128–29; abuses of, 128, 129
Alcina, Francisco Ignacio de, 38, 59–60, 82, 179
Alexander VI, 42
Almazan, 146
Annulments of marriage, 62–63
Apocalypticalism: influence on Spanish imperialism, 4–5
Aquinas, Thomas, 9, 88
Araucanians: comparison with Moros and mountain province, 197
Architecture: domestic, vii, 48; ecclesiastical, 75–76, 188–89
Aristotle, 114
Audiencia: Chinese, 78; encomienda, 96; dependent class, 115; land tenure, 118; *cajas de comuni-* *dad*, 127; *alcaldes*, 128; administration of justice, 129–31
Augustine of Hippo, 9
Augustinian Recollects, 49–50, 167–76
Augustinians: abuses among, 35–36, 103; their missions, 36, 49–50, 167–76; catechismal instruction by, 60–61; Manila convent, 98
*Ayuey. See* Dependent class
Aztecs: comparison with Filipinos, 26–28

*Bajo de campana*, 49
Bankaw, 148
Baptism: role of encomenderos, 54; attitude of chieftains toward, 54; role of children, 55; miracles, 55; Mexican precedents, 55–56; prebaptismal instruction, 55–56; number of baptisms, 56; opposition to, 57